D0710322

SILENCE
AND
FREEDOM

SILENCE
AND
FREEDOM

Louis Michael Seidman

STANFORD LAW AND POLITICS
An Imprint of Stanford University Press
Stanford, California
2007

Stanford University Press
Stanford, California

© 2007 by the Board of Trustees of the Leland Stanford Junior
University. All rights reserved.

Printed in the United States of America on acid-free,
archival-quality paper

Library of Congress Cataloging-in-Publication Data

Seidman, Louis Michael.

Silence and freedom / Louis Michael Seidman.
    p. cm.
Includes bibliographical references and index.
ISBN 978-0-8047-5620-4 (cloth : alk. paper)
1. Right to counsel—United States. 2. United States. Constitution.
5th Amendment. 3. Self-incrimination—United States. I. Title.
KF9625.S45 2007
345.73'056—dc22   2007008533

Typeset by Thompson Type in 10/15 Sabon

For Bob, Peter, Maureen, and Julie

What we cannot speak about, we must pass over in silence.

LUDWIG WITTGENSTEIN

Tractatus Logico-Philosophicus, D. F. Pears & B. F. McGuiness, trans., 1994

Contents

Acknowledgments

FROM EARLIEST CHILDHOOD, I have enjoyed conversation, argument, and debate. I have therefore come to grips with the topic of silence in the only way I know how: by talking about it. Writing this book has proved to be the occasion for lots of stimulating conversations, and I am tremendously grateful to those who participated in and made these conversations possible.

Two deans, Judith Areen and Alexander Aleinikoff, gave me the time off from my ordinary teaching duties so that I could not only talk, but also think about this project in peace and quiet. Mark Tushnet read the entire manuscript and, as usual, provided encouragement and criticism in just the right doses. I have had six truly wonderful research assistants who not only energetically and cheerfully tracked down obscure sources, but also helped me to think through the problems that this book tackles: Lewis Brown, David Cohen, Miriam Lederer, Brian Shaughnessy, Graeme Smyth, and J. Penn Stabler. My assistant, Ralph Freeman, solved technical problems with the manuscript that briefly threatened my sanity. I will be forever grateful.

Many people read parts of the manuscript. I am especially grateful for comments and suggestions that I received from Lama Abu-Odeh, Alexander Aleinikoff, Mitchell Berman, David Bernstein, David Fontana, Steven Goldberg, Abner Greene, Vicki Jackson, Emma Jordan, Gregory Klass, David Luban, Stephen Master, Erin O'Hara, Julie O'Sullivan, Kevin Quinn, Gari Ramachandran, Kevin Reitz, Philip Schrag, Warren Schwartz, David Skeel, Marc Spindelman, William Stuntz, Robin West, and Katheryn Zeiler. I benefitted greatly from discussions of parts of the manuscript at the University of Provence Colloquium on Confessions, the Georgetown University Law Center Summer Workshop Series, the Princeton University Conference on Torture, the New York University Law School Criminal Law Discussion Group, The Constitutional Theory

Colloquium sponsored by The University of Pennsylvania Law School, and workshops at the University of Texas Law School, University of Minnesota Law School, and The University of Oregon Law School.

Much of Chapter 6 is drawn from my article, TORTURE'S TRUTH, 72 U. CHI. L. REV. 881 (2005). I am grateful to the editors of the *University of Chicago Law Review* for permission to publish it in this new form.

As important as friends and colleagues are to me, I have found that it is my family that ultimately provides the peace at the core that makes writing possible. I have dedicated previous books to my parents, my wife, and my children. This one is for my brothers and sisters-in-law.

SILENCE
AND
FREEDOM

CHAPTER 1

Introduction:
The Strangest Right

"YOU HAVE THE RIGHT TO REMAIN SILENT." One could make a pretty good argument that these words, drawn from the Supreme Court's famous decision in *Miranda v. Arizona,*[1] have had more impact on the public imagination than any other phrase in the history of constitutional adjudication. But what a strange right this is. Of all the activities that are especially worthy of protection, that define us as human beings, foster human potential, and symbolize human ambition, why privilege silence?

Even when it does not hide criminal misdeeds, silence often connotes alienation, exemplified by Bartleby's laconic and enigmatic refusal to explain his noncooperation,[2] or frustrating inarticulateness, as when Billy Budd violently lashes out because he cannot speak.[3] Silence is always defined by what is lacking. It is what we hear when nothing is spoken, what we communicate when we have nothing to say. By itself, silence is altogether meaningless, gaining significance only when supplemented by speech, as when Sherlock Holmes explains why the dog did not bark in the night,[4] or when John Irving tells us why the Alice Jamesians cut out their tongues.[5]

At least, at first, it seems that a person who remains silent is passive. He does nothing to work his will on the world, to create, or to share with others. Silence is not about the striving, aspiration, and connection that we normally associate with human fulfillment. Instead, it is often about emptiness and loneliness. It is the dead who are silent. How can this void form the core of a basic human right?

The ambition of this book is to provide a defense of, an explanation for, and limits on a right to silence. My argument is complex, and I cannot hope to capture all of it in this brief introduction. My basic claim, though, is simple enough. It has two branches. First, silence can be an expression of freedom, and when it is, it is not alienating at all.

This is so, at least in part, because sometimes language imprisons us. The limitations of human speech deny us access to important experiences

I

and thoughts. Some kinds of silence can be liberating because they are efforts to transcend these limitations. For example, a contemplative silence can produce understanding, acceptance, and wisdom. In individual relationships, silence is not only sullen. Sometimes, it is the deepest form of communication.

Similarly, a defiant silence can demonstrate determination, courage, and will. For example, a long line of martyrs from a variety of faith traditions have given up their lives rather than renounce their god. I admire the courage Dashiell Hammett, who went to jail rather than name names,[6] and of the thousands of anonymous draft resisters who refused to take a military oath that was a prelude to participation in an immoral war. These silences speak to us. They are a manifestation of connection, commitment, and meaning. When we are free in this deepest sense, we are able to communicate by how we act and by who we are. Words only get in the way.

Second, even when silence is the result of alienation, we need to protect it in order to give meaning to speech. Put slightly differently, for speech to be truly free, there must also be silence. While in some contexts, silence *is* freedom, in others, it is the necessary frame for freedom. Words have meaning only when there is space between them, and when we insist on filling in the space, we are left with nothing but babble. It is therefore important to remain silent when there is nothing to say. When one confronts an ineffable mystery, breaking a silence only brings speech into disrepute.

The linkage between silence and freedom is apparent in a variety of different contexts, and I explore many of them in the pages that follow. At first these contexts may seem disparate, but in fact they pose a common set of problems. In Chapter 2, I set out an analytic framework that helps explicate the connections and that I will use throughout the rest of the book. It turns out that problems of silence and freedom map onto common categories in political thought, including views associated with classical liberalism and classical republicanism.* For present purposes,

---

* It is important to understand that these categories, and additional categories discussed below, are meant to be analytic tools, rather than descriptions of real thinkers. They are useful for organizing the discussion, and they reflect widely shared sensibilities, but most of us have views too complicated to be captured by these fairly crude distinctions.

we can define classical liberalism as a political stance emphasizing a sharp distinction between public and private and insisting that freedom is associated with a private sphere. In contrast, classical republicanism is a stance emphasizing deliberation about the common welfare as a human good and identifying freedom with collective self-governance. Speaking very generally, classical liberalism pushes us toward a right to silence, while classical republicanism pushes us toward a duty to speak.

These two positions sometimes stalemate each other, but it may be possible to break out of the stalemate, or at least deepen the analysis, by considering two more skeptical views that are, in some sense, deformations of the liberal and republican positions. I label these views radical libertarianism and pervasive determinism. Radical libertarians hold that in a meaningless and absurd universe, nothing constrains human choice. In contrast, pervasive determinists emphasize the ubiquity of power and large-scale, impersonal forces that determine human action. In complex ways, both of these stances help us to understand a right to silence in circumstances where republican and liberal views fail to capture all of our intuitions about how things are.

With this analytic structure in place, I turn to specific contexts in which the linkage between silence and freedom is controversial. Chapter 3 concerns forced apologies. Although apology plays a crucial role in maintaining the illusion of human connection, I argue that the right to silence in the form of a right not to apologize is equally crucial.

Chapters 4 and 5 take up the issues of self-incrimination and confession. Here, my claim is that silence protects the freedom to choose between public obligation and private commitment. Surprisingly, though, in this context, silence as freedom does not necessarily translate into a legal right to remain silent. Sometimes when the law requires speech, it confronts us with the necessity of making an authentic choice for silence.

Chapter 6 turns to the problem of torture. Here, my thesis is that the torture prohibition can best be understood in terms of a right to silence. In this context, the right is essential to preserve the distinction between mind and body on which (the illusion of?) human freedom depends.

In Chapter 7, I discuss a right to silence as an adjunct to the right to speech protected by the First Amendment. On the conventional account, the First Amendment protects a right to silence in order to make speech truly free. There is something to this account, but, surprisingly, it turns out that in at least some situations, coerced verbalization is actually a form of silence, and the option of remaining silent is actually a form of coerced speech.

Chapter 8 considers suicide. At least from a secular perspective, the choice of death is a choice for endless silence. Yet I argue that some suicides can speak to us and that, in the case of all suicides, there is a necessity to remain silent about the choice for silence.

Chapter 9, a brief conclusion, focuses on the difficulty of maintaining silence about silence itself.

There are two introductory words of caution about my project: First, readers who like the hard edges of legal argument and have no taste for paradox are bound to be disappointed. I believe that silence, speech, freedom, and oppression have dialectical relationships with each other, and the form of my argument is designed to emphasize this characteristic. Silence is a right, but it also comes with an obligation: to speak quietly or not at all in the face of doubt and mystery. Hence, I have no desire to bludgeon the reader into conclusions through the force of speech. This book is intended as more of a meditation than a brief for a position. It has silences and gaps of its own, which, I hope, are sufficiently capacious and profound to allow the reader freedom to reach her own conclusions.

This leads to the second caution: I do not pretend that I have finally resolved the paradox of silence. Precisely because silence is absence, there is a certain futility that attaches to any effort to give it meaning. Nothing I say in the pages that follow, therefore, can dispel a basic contradiction at the core of my project. The problem is that this account, as tentative as it is, nonetheless, disturbs a silence. It could not be otherwise, because silence can never defend itself. Only by resort to its opposite can silence assert its importance.

CHAPTER 2

Some Useful Dichotomies

WE CAN BEGIN TO UNDERSTAND WHY the right to silence is both attractive and problematic by noticing the ways in which it intersects with some familiar arguments that have shaped American political thought.* A right to silence fits comfortably with the views of classical liberals, while it is in some tension with the views of classical republicans.

REPUBLICAN SPEECH AND LIBERAL SILENCE

Consider first the republican position. If one went searching for the most eloquent words to appear in a judicial opinion, as opposed to the words most frequently quoted, one would not find them in *Miranda v. Arizona*. Instead, one might well settle upon Justice Louis Brandeis's famous concurrence in *Whitney v. California*.[1] *Whitney* involved a First Amendment challenge to a criminal prosecution under a state statute that prohibited membership in an organization that advocated "crime, sabotage, or unlawful acts of force and violence or unlawful methods of terrorism as a means of accomplishing a change in industrial ownership or control, or effecting any political change." Justice Brandeis reluctantly concurred in the majority's judgment rejecting this challenge, but only because Ms. Whitney had not raised below factual questions that Brandeis believed dispositive. Nonetheless, he took pains to distance himself from the majority's narrow construction of the right to speak. For Brandeis,

Those who won our independence believed that the final end of the state was to make men free to develop their faculties; and that in its government the

---

* Before embarking on this discussion, I feel compelled to note that I am a law professor by trade—not a philosopher or political theorist. I have neither the expertise nor the interest to develop these theories in the detail that they might deserve in other settings. Rather than a freestanding explication, this theoretical material is meant to frame the more specific legal and doctrinal discussions in the chapters that follow.

deliberative forces should prevail over the arbitrary. They valued liberty both as an end and as means. They believed liberty to be the secret of happiness and courage to be the secret of liberty. They believed that freedom to think as you will and to speak as you think are means indispensable to the discovery and spread of political truth; that without free speech and assembly discussion would be futile; that with them, discussion affords ordinarily adequate protection against dissemination of noxious doctrine; that the greatest menace to freedom is an inert people; that public discussion is a political duty; and that this should be a fundamental principle of the American government. . . . Believing in the power of reason as applied through public discussion, they eschewed silence coerced by law—the argument of force in its worst form.[2]

This passage reflects the classical republican view of government, political rights, and human fulfillment. Thinkers in the republican tradition going back to the ancient Greeks have associated freedom with collective deliberation.[3] Notice that for Brandeis, individuals do not start in a state of freedom, as natural rights theorists like Locke and Rousseau supposed. Rather, it is "the final end of the state . . . to make men free." For republicans, the state meets this obligation when it encourages citizens to engage in public lives.

How does the republican view relate to the right to silence? As Brandeis's *Whitney* opinion demonstrates, republicans are more comfortable defending the opposite of silence—that is, speech. Republicans tend to think that speech, especially political speech, is important because it connects us to each other. Through the process of unconstrained debate, communities form their collective identities and individual community members gain a sense of solidarity that allows them to transcend the petty and selfish interests that divide them. It requires emphasis that people do not come to these debates fully formed. Rather, it is through the act of speaking that people discover who they are.[4]

In contrast, silence and isolation amount to a failure to perform one's civic duty. They reflect a stolid insistence on thwarting of one's own human potential, and produce an "inert people," which Brandeis identifies as the "greatest menace" to freedom. Freedom requires not the timidity and passivity of silence, but the courage and exuberance of full-throated expression. The problem for liberals, then, is how to respond to this republican attack on silence. A response might begin by noting that the same justice who authored the republican case for speech in *Whitney* also wrote a great liberal defense of silence. A little more than a year after his *Whitney* concurrence, Justice Brandeis wrote an equally famous dissent in *United States v. Olmstead*,[5] The issue in the case was whether Olmstead's words, captured through a warrantless wiretap, could be introduced against him in a criminal trial, The majority, relying upon its view that the Fourth Amendment protected against only physical trespass, affirmed Olmstead's conviction, but Justice Brandeis strongly disagreed.

The makers of our Constitution undertook to secure conditions favorable to the pursuit of happiness. They recognized the significance of man's spiritual nature, of his feelings and of his intellect. They knew that only a part of the pain, pleasure and satisfactions of life are to be found in material things. They sought to protect Americans in their beliefs, their thoughts, their emotions and their sensations. They conferred, as against the government, the right to be let alone, the most comprehensive of rights and the right most valued by civilized men. To protect that right, every unjustifiable intrusion by the government upon the privacy of the individual, whatever the means employed, must be deemed a violation of the Fourth Amendment.[6]

The *Whitney* concurrence and the *Olmstead* dissent form two pillars of the American civil liberties tradition. Yet the two opinions are remarkably different in tone and philosophy. Whereas the *Whitney* concurrence defended a public duty to speak, the *Olmstead* dissent championed a private right not to speak, or at least a right not to have private speech used for public purposes. The Brandeis of the *Whitney* concurrence equated happiness with public engagement, whereas the Brandeis of the *Olmstead* dissent equated it, instead, with immunity from government interference. The *Whitney* concurrence celebrated the connections that form us as human beings, while the *Olmstead* dissent seems to have assumed that humans are already formed when they defend their right "to be let alone." How could a single justice within the space of a year author two opinions so different in their philosophical commitments?

I will return to Justice Brandeis's embrace of both silence and speech later in this chapter. First, though, it will be helpful to investigate the link between the *Olmstead* dissent and classical liberalism. Whereas republicans value group solidarity and collective self-determination, liberals emphasize human diversity. The starting point for liberal political theory is that under modern conditions, people with wildly different aspirations, cultures, and beliefs often share a common territory and must find a way to form a common government.[7] Of course, a narrowly sectarian state may be able to control the populace through sheer force, but it cannot provide a just basis for uncoerced cooperation. The only sort of state that people with deeply divergent views would voluntarily support is one that is neutral between those views. This sort of neutrality, in turn, is impossible to maintain unless the government allows broad leeway for individuals to decide on important matters for themselves.[8]

The different concerns of republicans and liberals lead, in turn, to very different conceptions of rights and freedom. For republicans, autonomy is not the same thing as following individual whim. A person who "freely" embraces narrow self-interest is a slave to his passions and selfish desires. Instead, freedom means aligning one's life with the behaviors that maximize human potential. On the republican account, this means living a publicly engaged life, and it is an important function of the state to encourage its citizens to lead such lives. Hence, one has a right to free speech because the good life requires the deliberative engagement that can only be achieved through speech.

Liberals, in contrast, conceptualize freedom in terms of individual autonomy rather than collective identification. Whereas republicans tend to identify "rights" with doing the right thing, liberals object to any official, public, and collective determination of what is right. Instead, for liberals, rights provide the room for people to make these determinations for themselves.[9] Thus, a liberal might concede that silence is absence, but it is an absence that leaves empty space that individuals can fill with plans for their own lives, where, in Brandeis's words, they can develop "their beliefs, their thoughts, their emotions and their sensations." Whereas republicans believe that these attributes emerge only through public deliberation, liberals insist that government must get out of the way if they are to develop unfettered. Without such space, a totalizing and overbearing government is likely to stifle human fulfillment and impose deadening uniformity.

Although these orientations are plainly different, it would be a mistake to exaggerate the extent to which these differences lead to different outcomes when we get down to cases. Often, republicans and liberals will arrive at what John Rawls has called an "overlapping consensus."[10] In particular, it does not follow from what I have said above that republicans necessarily favor compelled speech or that liberals necessarily favor compelled silence. It does follow, however, that even when republicans and liberals reach similar conclusions, they will do so for different reasons and that these differences will at least occasionally lead to different results. Thus, a liberal defense of free speech rests less on the need for democratic deliberation and more on the connection between speech and individual self-expression and on the fear of government orthodoxy. Republican opposition to compelled speech, in turn, rests less on the desirability of maintaining a private sphere and more on the role that unfettered discussion plays in achieving public ends.

To see how these two approaches might lead to different outcomes along the dimension of speech and silence consider first a hypothetical statute, common in other political cultures[11] but unknown in ours, that makes voting mandatory. A republican might well favor such a statute, while a liberal might well oppose it. While republicans would surely oppose government coercion that dictated *how* one should vote, they are less likely to oppose coercion requiring *that* one vote. For republicans, people have a civic duty to engage in the form of speech we call voting, and the government plays an important role when it encourages fulfillment of that duty. Without such encouragement, voters face what economists call a collective action problem. It is in the public interest that each of us vote, but because each individual vote has an infinitesimal chance of affecting election results, people left to their own devices are likely to succumb to private concerns that make voting seem like a waste of time.[12] This silence is hardly an exercise of freedom; rather, it is dictated by the tyranny of alienation and separation.

Liberals, in contrast, might be worried not just about regulating the content of speech, but also about overriding a right to silence. For them, individual freedom includes the freedom to choose the private sphere as a site for human development. Perhaps you and I think there is a duty to vote, but the state has no business insisting on such a duty for everyone. The state exceeds its just jurisdiction when it dictates to individuals the contents of a good life. Such a life might include participation in democratic elections, but the right to be "let alone" also includes the right to remain silent on election day.[13]

Compare a mandatory voting statute to a statute permitting parents to educate their children in private schools or at home. Now it is liberals who are more likely to favor the measure and republicans who are more likely to oppose it. To be sure, private education poses a hard case for liberals. They generally treat individuals as capable of rational choice, but historically most liberals have made an exception for children, who, quite obviously, are not fully capable.[14] For most liberals, that exception has weight enough to justify public education. At the same time, though, they take diversity seriously and are therefore likely to worry that state coercion might disrupt the relationship between parents and children, privilege the views of some at the expense of the views of others, or impose a deadening orthodoxy. In short, they are receptive to the claim that mandatory public education might silence dissident voices by brainwashing children with state propaganda. For some liberals, the appropriate solution to this conundrum is to provide a system of public education with an opt out for parents who object.[15]

In contrast, republicans are more likely to see public education as facilitating speech and private or home education as imposing silence. For them, the state has a duty to inculcate public spiritedness.[16] The state cannot meet this obligation if parents are able to wall their children off from contact with fellow citizens.[17] Because republicans believe that people realize their potential through engagement with others, they are likely to believe that it is the isolation of home education, rather than exposure to public education, that silences speech.

UNIVERSALISTS AND PARTICULARISTS

It follows from what I have said above that there is at least a loose association between classical liberalism and a right to silence and that defenders of this right need to ward off republican criticism. We can gain a deeper understanding of these differences by linking them to two other dichotomies. The linkages here are less obvious, and the correlations less robust, but they are nonetheless revealing.

Consider first the tension between universalist and particularist values. Whereas republicans tend to celebrate universalism, liberals are more inclined toward particularism. By universalism, I mean commitments to treating all members of the community with disinterested equality and to universally accessible public reason as a means of settling differences between these individuals. In contrast, particularism insists on the value of special relationships that, by their nature, are neither disinterested nor equal and that cannot be defended by, and should not be held hostage to, public reason.

In recent years, modern scholars sympathetic to republican values have argued that universalist assumptions motivated both sides of the debates surrounding the adoption of the U.S. Constitution.[18] On this account, both federalist supporters and antifederalist opponents of the Constitution supported their positions by linking universalism to the republican ideal. Although they reached different conclusions about the merits of the proposed Constitution, both federalists and antifederalists opposed what Madison famously called "factions" or what we today might label special interest groups. Both the framers of the Constitution and their opponents feared that factions might gain control of the levers of government power and so turn public institutions into a means of gaining private advantage. Factions were dangerous both because they relied on raw power rather than publicly accessible reason to achieve their ends and because they attempted to utilize the instruments of state coercion in a fashion that favored the interests of some citizens over others. Thus, they threatened both the ideal of disinterested equality and the ideal of publicly accessible reason.

It is easy to see the association between factionalism and silence. When an "inert people" remain silent, they leave empty space for factions to flourish.[19] Narrow self-interest is most likely to prevail in the suffocating quiet of back rooms, where deals that could never withstand universalist criticism are made. Only the commitment of a publicly engaged populace ready to speak out for universalist values can avoid the corruption of public power.

Liberals, too, worry about faction, but their worry leads them in a different direction. Their concern is more grounded in modern public choice theory and antifoundationalism than in the views that republicans attribute to the framers. To understand the concern, we need to distinguish between two separate liberal arguments. First, many liberals are much less optimistic about the prospects of rescuing government from faction or about the ability to settle our differences by resorting to publicly accessible reason. If one believes that government will inevitably be infiltrated by special interest groups, then there is a strong case for limiting the reach of government power. *Just because* citizens are entitled to disinterested equality from their government, *therefore* a government that will not achieve this goal must be sharply limited. And, liberals remind us, we have several centuries of experience to demonstrate that governments will never achieve this goal. Here, liberalism is linked to public choice theory, which has modeled the ways in which political "markets" are inevitably corrupted by faction.[20]

Similarly, the liberal commitment to diversity leads to doubts that disagreements can be uncontroversially resolved through reasoned discourse. Of course, contestants in our political struggles regularly make claims that all reasonable individuals must come to a particular conclusion or support a particular policy. Once again, we have some experience with claims of this sort. At various times, it has been thought that natural reason dictated slavery, the subordination of women, and laissez-faire capitalism. Today, we can see that these claims amounted to exercises of raw power clothed in claims of uncontroversial reason.

This experience, together with the brute fact of continuing variation in moral and political views, has led liberals to be cautious about the reasons offered for government action. Just as some liberals agree with republicans about the danger of faction but conclude from this premise, contrary to republicans, that government action should be limited, so too some liberals think that matters should be left to the private sphere when public disputes cannot be resolved by universally accessible reason.* Other liberals are even more skeptical. They believe that there simply are no winning, uncontroversial arguments grounded in universally accessible reason for any particular set of government policies. Although not all people holding this position carry it to its logical conclusion, it would seem to follow that the only alternative to unprincipled public coercion is to allow individuals to lead their own lives according to their own reasons.[21] Here, liberalism is linked to the postmodern worry about how any supposedly reasoned argument can be grounded on an uncontroversial foundation.[22]

The second liberal argument turns the first on its head and emphasizes the liberal commitment to particularism. Suppose that we somehow manage to maintain a public-regarding republican state that advanced policies for reasons that all citizens agreed with. I have already discussed why liberals are very skeptical that this state of affairs will ever come about, but, ironically, even if it did, they might still insist on an expansive private sphere. Such a state would, by hypothesis, be universalist in orientation, but liberals recognize what republicans seem to ignore: the importance of countervailing particularist values. On the liberal account, people are not just public citizens. They are also friends, lovers, family members, and participants in a network of intimate associations. When they operate in this sphere, they make choices that are not "reasoned" in the republican sense and do not respect the right of all fellow citizens to equal and

---

*   Although others might read him differently, this seems to me to be the implication of John Rawls's position. Rawls argues that,

As far as possible, the knowledge and ways of reasoning that ground our affirming the principles of justice and their application to constitutional essentials, and basic justice are to rest on the plain truths now widely accepted, or available, to citizens generally. . . .

[I]t is only in this way, and by accepting that politics in a democratic society can never be guided by what we see as the whole truth, that we can realize the ideal expressed by the principle of legitimacy: to live politically with others in the light of reasons all might reasonably be expected to endorse. (JOHN RAWLS, POLITICAL LIBERALISM 224–25, 243 [1993].)

The implication of this view seems to me to be that when the "reasons all might reasonably be expected to endorse" run out, the government may not legitimately act and that the matter should therefore be left to the private sphere.

disinterested beneficence. Instead, these choices are based upon what Brandeis referred to as beliefs, thoughts, emotions, and sensations.[23]

Imagine, for example, the following pillow talk between A and A's thoroughly universalist partner, B:

A: I love you sweetie.

B: I love you too, honey.

A: (snuggling next to B) I'm so lucky!

B: (pushing A away). Not really. You should know that I don't love you any more or less than I love any other fellow human being.

A: What? What are you talking about?

B: You see, I view it as my moral obligation to treat everyone with equal and disinterested beneficence, at least when there is no publicly accessible reason to treat them differently. It's true that I'm attracted to you, but I can't come up with a reasoned argument why I should be. So I have an obligation to treat you no differently from the way I treat our next-door neighbor or someone living in Australia.

This is not a relationship that is likely to last, and I doubt that many of us would blame A for its problems. What, though, does all this have to do with a limited public sphere? If, as republicans insist, the state is to be entirely public, then, liberals claim, for just that reason, its writ must also be limited lest it hold our private particularist values hostage to public universalist justifications. Put differently, republicans argue that the coercive power of the state is justified by its commitment to universalist values. Just so, respond liberals, and therefore the power should be used sparingly.[24]

Liberal particularism is directly linked to a right of silence. When we speak, we make our thoughts and beliefs public and so subject them to public criticism. This criticism will often amount to holding those thoughts and beliefs to universalist standards. But many of our particularist commitments cannot, and should not, be made to withstand such criticism.

Consider, for example, the controversy surrounding the provisions in the Patriot Act that permit government officials to gain access to library records.[25] Viewed from one perspective, the anger that the provision has engendered is hard to explain. We are regularly held publicly accountable for our acts. Why, then, should we not be held accountable for our thoughts as well? Why should we be ashamed of the books we choose to read, and if we are ashamed, why is that not reason enough to avoid reading them?

It does not take much work to see what is wrong with this argument. All of us have thoughts, hopes, fantasies, and desires that we would not want to be forced to defend in public. Such a defense would require us to demonstrate that having these mental states is, in some sense, consistent with the public interest. But no sane person's internal mental life can withstand this sort of scrutiny. The way to avoid having to make such a defense is by protecting a right to remain silent about these internal mental states. Without such a right, the overbearing force of universalism is likely to stymie essential mental freedom.

MODERATE DETERMINISTS AND LIBERTARIANS

Still another overlapping debate that helps understand a right to silence is between ontological libertarians and determinists. There is a vast and sophisticated philosophical literature about this argument,[26] but for present purposes, it is necessary to make no more than a crude distinction. Libertarians believe that human action is caused by exercises of will that are, themselves, uncaused. Determinists, in contrast, believe that seemingly free decisions are actually determined by preexisting causes. As we shall see, radical versions of these positions are incompatible with standard liberal and republican thought. Many people, though, do not push these views all the way to their logical conclusions. Instead, they have general orientations that cause them to be more or less skeptical of arguments that human choices are free or determined. Again, speaking very roughly, we can say that there is a loose association between moderate libertarianism and liberalism on the one hand and between moderate determinism and republicanism on the other.

Liberals value the private sphere because it is the site of uncoerced human choice. This view necessarily implies that such choice exists and that it is logically and ontologically anterior to the community, which might threaten the ability to act upon the choice. Put differently, a central premise of liberal political and moral theory is the dignity to which unfettered individual will is entitled. The burden is on those who would restrict the exercise of that will, and the burden will seldom be met unless the exercise itself threatens the exercise of another's will.[27]

Republicans, in contrast, claim that these supposedly free choices are already situated within a cultural and a political matrix. Republicans, and especially their close cousins, communitarians, argue that the unattached and disembodied individual imagined by liberal political theory simply does not exist. What could it possibly mean to posit a "me" that is independent of all the socially determined values, beliefs, and commitments that make up my personality? It is simply incoherent to imagine people who somehow exist apart from the societies that form them. On this account, then, the individual choices that liberals start with are not "free," but instead reflect the community from which they emerge. Moral meaning derives not from the choices themselves, but from the necessary alignment between the lives we live and the community we belong to.[28]

How do these competing insights relate to the competing values of silence and speech? For liberals, silence is in some sense the purest manifestation of human freedom. Like Thoreau's retreat to the isolation of Walden Pond, the act of remaining silent uniquely reflects unbridled human choice. This is so precisely because silence separates us from others. Whereas speech ensnares us in a web of other people, and so threatens our freedom, silence demonstrates the ineradicable and exhilarating loneliness of pure choice.

Republicans, in contrast, are skeptical that this kind of choice is either possible or desirable. They associate moral meaning not with courageous and isolated exercises of the will, but with deep connection to a community without which we simply could not comprehend the physical world. For them, silence amounts to an ultimately futile effort to deny that connection and so to deny the very possibility of human meaning.

TWO SKEPTICAL RESPONSES

These disputes between republicans and liberals, universalists and particularists, moderate determinists and moderate libertarians help us to frame and understand the controversy about a right to silence. Standing alone, however, they do little to resolve that controversy. For example, even if we understand why liberals tend to favor a right to silence while republicans do not, this understanding does not get us very far unless we know whether we are liberals or republicans. It is at just this point that the analysis runs out of steam. Because these are debates about the very framing of human preferences, they are resistant to resolution through logical argument. The most that we can hope for is that one approach or another will appeal to us on some deeper, intuitive level. Yet it is just these intuitions that arguments on both sides destabilize. Why should I trust a "private" intuition if my true self emerges only from public engagement? Conversely, how do I know that my attraction to universalism is not gained only by suppressing particularist obligations?

To make matters worse, most of us do not have clear intuitions about these matters to begin with. Most "normal" people, to the extent that they think about these questions at all, find themselves simultaneously on both sides of the divide. Yes, our previously mentioned hypothetical B is a very strange person, but now imagine a particularist A who is ready to lie, cheat, and steal in order to make himself and his family marginally happier. Surely, we would chastise him as well for an indefensible privileging of the well-being of himself and his intimate associates over the rights of other people.

One might conclude from these examples that healthy people find themselves somewhere in the middle, avoiding the extremes on both sides. On this view, one might recognize some special obligations to intimate associates, but also recognize limits on those obligations imposed by our duty to the overall community. It is fine for me to buy presents for my own children even though children in the Sudan could better use my money, but it is not acceptable for me to bribe an admissions officer to get them into college.

My own sense, though, is that this "golden mean" approach does not always capture the way that we behave, or, for that matter, our sense of the way that we should behave. Yes, it is fine to buy presents for one's own kids, but should we not at least feel some guilt about not sending the money to the Sudan? Oddly, it is ambivalence about these decisions, an inability to come to rest or to be fully satisfied with one's behavior, that seems to mark morally whole people.

Moreover, even when we do reach a stasis of sorts, it is often not marked by a stable equilibrium in the middle. Rather, we sometimes end up in a place that is logically inconsistent yet, in some sense, morally satisfying. For example, I regularly vote for candidates who promise to raise my taxes. Votes like this make sense because when I go to the polls, I think of myself as a public citizen. When it comes to filling out my own tax returns, however, I never make a voluntary contribution to the Internal Revenue Service. In the privacy of my own study, I focus on my obligations to myself and my family. Similarly, I would vote for candidates who pledged to end "environmental racism," but I am not about to buy a house next to a toxic dump. Perhaps I am deluding myself, but I do not believe that I am alone in this sort of behavior. The behavior suggests not so much a consistently held middle position as a deeply contradictory set of responses that cannot be reconciled with any overarching theory.

If I am right about all this, then it should come as less of a surprise that Justice Brandeis authored both the *Whitney* concurrence and the *Olmstead* dissent. The tension between the two opinions reflects the human condition. As legal scholars like Duncan Kennedy[29] and David Luban[30] have taught us, human beings seem to be hardwired to be both social and independent, both attracted to others and fearful of them. The greatness of the Brandeis opinions, when taken together, stems from the very fact that they embrace this contradiction, which is rooted in our deepest instincts and in an odd sense expresses our deepest aspirations.

Unfortunately, though, contradiction is not very helpful in resolving whether or when there should be a right to silence. Much of this book will argue that we can make additional progress in thinking about such a right by breaking down some of these dichotomies. Here, I want to introduce two skeptical ideas that might help to do so by attacking, respectively, the liberal and republican positions.

The first might be called pervasive determinism. I use this term to cover a very wide variety of diverse writings in many different disciplines arguing in one way or another for the ubiquity of large scale forces and power relationships as determinates of ordinary social interactions. For example, social anthropologists purport to have demonstrated that the naturalness and seeming autonomy of individual choices are in fact constructed and sharply constrained by culture.[31] Michel Foucault and his followers are preoccupied by the way that power is constitutive of personal identity.[32] Scholars working in the Freudian and Marxist traditions have used the tools of psychoanalysis and political economy to situate and deconstruct the supposedly autonomous nature of human interactions. Sociobiologists purport to have demonstrated how naturally selected genetic predispositions cause a wide variety of human behaviors.[33] Finally, within the legal tradition, American Legal Realists argued that supposedly "free" agreements between private individuals are always molded by largely invisible background public interventions that shape markets.[34]

It would be silly to suppose that these various ideas present a unified conception of human agency. They are nonetheless linked in their skepticism toward robust conceptions of human freedom. To see how this skepticism intersects with the debates described above, we need to back up a step.

As we have already seen, republicans reject the liberal insistence on a thin state. Because the state forms citizens, it has an obligation to teach them how to live good lives. The most powerful modern proponents of this view are communitarians, who argue for government programs like President Bush's "faith-based initiative" or government-led efforts to promote worthy goals like stable marriages or abstention from substance abuse.[35]

An important part of the liberal criticism of these programs plays off the republican insistence on state universalism. Liberals will claim that they have no objection to religious faith, for example, but when the state embraces religion, it inevitably corrupts it. Because state-supported religion must be made to serve universalist purposes, it will be deprived of the very characteristics that make it valuable.[36]

Suppose, for example, there is empirical evidence that the most effective treatment for alcoholism is the encouragement of religious commitment. Because communitarians reject the liberal thin state, they will see no reason why the government should not sponsor such treatment. Sophisticated liberals have an answer to this argument. Belief in God, they will insist, is not about cost-effective government health measures. One should believe in God (if indeed, one *should* believe in God) because God exists, not because the belief helps the state achieve its secular objectives. State support for religion conditioned on its effectiveness in achieving these objectives corrupts the very thing that makes religion valuable.

Similarly, even if it is true that stable marriages lead to less poverty, and even if reducing poverty is a legitimate state objective, it does not follow that the state should achieve this objective by promoting stable marriages. Marriage, liberals might claim, is about love and human connection. Because the state cannot be about these things, when the state supports marriage to achieve utilitarian goals, it corrupts the very essence of what a marriage is. For liberals, then, maintaining an autonomous private sphere is essential because only the private sphere can nurture and preserve uncorrupted particularist values.

It is at this point that the dark shadow of pervasive determinism appears. Why should anyone believe that the private sphere, any more than the public sphere, offers a refuge for such values? Perhaps there simply is no such refuge.

Two forms of the argument merit special attention, one rooted in legal theory, the other in the biological and social sciences. The legal theory was first developed in the early part of the twentieth century by American Legal Realists and modernized at the close of the century by advocates of Critical Legal Studies.[37] Briefly stated, the argument is that there simply is no such thing as a private sphere because there are always background, discretionary public actions that form the sphere. Common law rules of contract, property, and tort do not simply exist. They are promulgated by governments to achieve government purposes. These rules constitute the private sphere, and, importantly, this sphere could be constituted differently if government officials decided to promulgate different rules. Since there is no private sphere, there is also no private realm free from government coercion. All private decisions are "coerced" in the sense that contingent government allocations of entitlements form these decisions.[38]

Whereas the legal theory operates on the macro level, the scientific theories operate on the micro level. Social psychologists who study our ordinary social interactions are adept at showing that things are seldom as they seem. Our emotions, beliefs, fears, and hopes do not come from no place. They serve complex purposes that are often shielded from consciousness. Importantly, many of these purposes concern the exercise of power. We are always enmeshed in a complex economy of power that, through various well-honed, but usually unconscious or semiconscious devices, we attempt to turn to our advantage. Thus, everyday interchanges with strangers and loved ones alike can best be understood as detailed rituals of deception, aggression, and defense.[39]

Advocates of evolutionary biology make an analogous point. They, too, argue that traits like loyalty, altruism, and love cannot be taken at face value. Like the social psychologists, they see these traits as rooted in power struggles, rather than in self-sacrifice—albeit, in the case of evolutionary biologists, struggles that occurred in the very distant past. The traits have nothing to do with human virtue and choice. Instead, they are determined on the genetic level and amount to highly evolved instinctual adaptations to the environment, based upon the unwilled, impersonal, and thoroughly unlovely processes of struggle for survival and natural selection.[40]

How does pervasive determinism relate to a right to silence? If there is no protected sphere where humans can nurture individual freedom, then the liberal argument based upon immunity from public coercion loses most of its steam. It is hard to talk about rights of any kind, much less a right to silence, if all of human conduct can be reduced to unchosen or unconscious manipulation of others.

Oddly, though, even if talk of rights and duties fits uneasily with pervasive determinism, silence might nonetheless be an appropriate response to it. In the face of overpowering nihilism, what, after all, is the point of speech? On this view, all speech is nothing but self-justificatory babble that dresses up the ultimate ugliness and meaninglessness of human behavior. As we have already seen, silence is a void, and maintaining a void uncluttered with pointless chatter is at least an honest response to the absurdity of the universe. Faced with a world without meaning, we should at least have the decency to shut up.

Of course, talk of decency and of a choice to shut up itself sits uneasily with the sort of nihilism that denies the possibility of decency and choice. One might take this contradiction to provide yet another reason why we should *not* talk. After all, even the effort to justify silence breaks a silence. Perhaps then, we should *really* be silent by maintaining a "decent" silence about our own silence.

A more hopeful response would be to treat this contradiction as an invitation to explore the limits of this variety of skepticism. It is hard, perhaps impossible, to be a truly pervasive determinist. A commitment to this position is nonetheless a commitment, and commitments entail a belief in freedom and choice, the very phenomena that skeptics of this stripe wish to dismiss. It is here that a second version of skepticism takes hold, a version I will label (once again with breathtaking oversimplification) radical libertarianism. This argument loosely associated with some existentialist writings,[41] claims that the denial of human agency amounts to what French playwright and philosopher Jean-Paul Sartre called "bad faith."[42]

The key insight that drives the radical libertarian argument is that pervasive determinism, like any other system of thought, cannot yield normative recommendations. All such systems ultimately "run out," and when they do, they leave us with nothing but the obligation of choice. In particular, pervasive determinism "runs out," because in a world that is truly meaningless and only about power, it must be meaningless as well to claim that one course of action is better than another. And yet, in the teeth of this knowledge, we must decide how to act. When the alarm clock goes off in the morning, I must either get out of bed or turn over and go back to sleep. It is a large mistake to suppose that pervasive determinism counsels going back to sleep.

For a radical libertarian skeptic, then, the silence of the universe is what allows for human freedom. If the universe is just nothingness, then it must follow that there is literally nothing that prevents us from choosing for ourselves how to live our lives. When we deny this fact, when we shield ourselves from our own freedom, we are acting in "bad faith."

On one level, a skeptic of this sort cannot argue for either silence or speech. This choice, like all choices, cannot be mediated or constrained by logical argument. We will simply do what we choose to do. Yet there is a sense in which radical libertarians, like pervasive determinists, are comfortable with silence. Precisely because choice cannot be dictated by argument, the effort to argue someone into a choice amounts to an insistence on constraints on action that do not "really" exist. Perhaps, then, it is better to remain silent than to attempt to fool others into believing that anything we say will require a particular choice.

Moreover, just as pervasive determinism is in tension with liberalism, radical libertarianism is in tension with republicanism. Republicans claim that we achieve meaning through association with a community, but radical libertarians insist that we must act in a world where there is no meaning. For a radical libertarian, then, republican insistence on the social embeddedness of human choice amounts to just another excuse for failure to confront our own freedom. It follows that to the extent that republicanism is associated with a duty to speak, radical libertarianism undermines it.

Of course, being a radical libertarian is also hard work. Some of the difficulty is captured by the difference between having an "insider" and "outsider" perspective. Radical libertarianism seems much more plausible from within our individual lived experience. It does seem to me, right now, that if I really wanted to, I could forsake everything and go off to Tahiti. Ironically, another part of my internal lived experience is that my own effort to pretend that I could not do this reflects self-obfuscatory cowardliness. But from an external perspective, things look very different. Is it really possible that everyone in the building in which I am now located would, right now, decide to go off to Tahiti? The failure of everyone to do this seems just as determined as the path traveled by heavenly bodies. When we think of large groups and of historical experience, the idea of radical freedom, dissociated from a web of social, political, and cultural forces, seems deeply implausible.

The upshot, then, is that radical libertarianism requires a version of the very willful blindness that it decries. The need for this blindness—in this context, perhaps an analogy to deafness is more appropriate—in turn also supports a right to silence. Recall that the public sphere is the natural location for universalism, embeddedness, determinism, and rationality. Radical freedom requires us to wall ourselves off from this sphere. Viewed in this light, there is really a double right to silence—a right to be silent, but also a right to have silence. To have radical freedom, we must silence the voices that remind us that we are the playthings of forces much larger than ourselves. Yet we must also have the right to be silent, for it is ultimately this deep and terrifying silence that constitutes our declaration of independence from the will of others.

THESE ARE VERY LARGE THEMES. Stated abstractly, I fear that they may seem overblown, pretentious, or simply irrelevant. In fact, though, the themes are played out in the formulation of ordinary legal doctrine that, without reference to these themes, might seem deeply mysterious. The payoff comes if these themes serve to demystify that doctrine. That is the work of the chapters that follow.

CHAPTER 3

Apology and Silence

WE LIVE IN THE REPUBLIC OF APOLOGY, and Bill Clinton is our President for Life. With chewed lip and watery eyes, Clinton has apologized for everything from American chattel slavery[1] to sexual indiscretion.[2] Although most other public figures are not serial apologists in his league, he is far from alone in using the power of apology to transmogrify anger and doubt into forgiveness and acceptance. In recent years, politicians,[3] sports figures,[4] entertainers,[5] clergymen,[6] university presidents,[7] Congress,[8] and religious denominations[9] have all issued abject apologies. Richard Clarke transformed the hearings of the commission investigating the September 11 disaster by a simple and graceful apology to its victims.[10] South Africa's Truth and Reconciliation Commission got apologies for some of the greatest crimes of our time,[11] while ordinary citizens, caught in the glare of daytime television, regularly apologize for some of the most trivial.[12] Every public scandal is accompanied by a drumbeat from the media demanding apologies, and discerning politicians have learned that heeding these calls can sometimes rescue their careers.

Although the evidence is more fragmentary, it appears that apologies also play an increasingly significant role in our private lives.[13] In the secular realm, apologies are among the most potent tools that our therapeutic culture has to offer. Learning how to apologize is said to save marriages, settle law suits, remake lives, and gain inner peace.[14] In the overlapping religious realm, the drama of sin, confession, repentance, and rebirth is central to the religious revival that has come to dominate our culture and our politics.[15]

On one level, the attraction of apologies is hardly mysterious. Apologies appeal to a uniquely American optimism about the possibility of fresh starts and to a deep desire for connection, community, and forgiveness.*

---

* I make no claims in this chapter about the functioning of apology in cultures other than our own.

Yet, despite that attraction, many of us also feel uneasy about apologies. There is a part of us that agrees with P. G. Wodehouse when he said that "It is a good rule in life never to apologize. The right sort of people do not want apologies, and the wrong sort of people take a mean advantage of them."[16] Yes, President Clinton was a tremendously popular leader, but he was also a target of derision, and even some of his supporters were relieved when he was replaced by a (more masculine?)[17] president who did not include the words *I'm sorry* in his vocabulary.

Many of us also feel a vague sense of discomfort when we watch another who is forced to apologize. There is something degrading about the ritual, and it is not only the participants who are degraded. People watching the spectacle from the outside sometimes feel like voyeurs, tarnished and somehow implicated by their guilty fascination with it. Perhaps against our better judgment, we cannot help feeling a certain contempt for the weakness of the apologist coupled with fear and envy of the power exercised by the person who extracts the apology.

The Clinton example also suggests a second source of unease: We worry about corrupt or dishonest apologies. Often—perhaps always—people who apologize want something from us in return. Why, precisely, should we, the targets of the apology, provide it? When we forgive in response to apology, we put to one side the always present possibility of being victimized a second time by cynical manipulation. At least sometimes, trust of this sort seems more foolish than generous.[18]

Moreover, even when apologies are made in good faith, it is not always obvious that we should respond favorably to them. There is surely some truth to Ambrose Bierce's cynical observation that to apologize is "to lay the foundation for a future offence."[19] Think, for example, of the role that apology sometimes plays in cases of domestic violence. Students of "battered spouse syndrome" have found that there is often a repetitive cycle of violence, apology, forgiveness, and further violence. The apology phase of this cycle may well be authentic, but that fact provides no guarantee that the pattern of violence will not continue.[20] Accepting apologies in these circumstances gives power to the abuser that he does not deserve.

LEGAL APOLOGIES

Unsurprisingly, the ubiquity of apology in the culture at large has put pressure on legal institutions. There are growing demands for a greater role for apology in both our civil and criminal jurisprudence. On the civil side, many of the demands come out of the alternative dispute resolution movement and are part of a broader trend toward less adversary procedures. It is claimed that apologies can avoid costly and contentious trials and lead to full reconciliation between the parties. Victims can be afforded a sense of closure and vindication, which is often far more valuable than mere financial compensation, while perpetrators are freed from guilt and reintegrated within the community.[21] Lawyers are now being trained in how to use apologies to achieve these goals,[22] and some state legislatures have responded by providing a "safe harbor" for apologies through laws that exclude from evidence expressions of sympathy or regret.[23]

On the criminal side, the Federal Sentencing Guidelines[24] and the informal sentencing practices of many states[25] already encourage convicted defendants to apologize. Some apology advocates would go far beyond this. The "restorative justice" movement would reorient all of criminal law toward reconciliation between perpetrator and victim.[26] The Georgia Justice Project has begun a remarkable effort to implement these ideals on the ground. The project undertakes the representation of criminal defendants, but only on the condition that they enter a contract agreeing to make a "life change." Perhaps the most significant commitment the defendant makes is to take responsibility for his crime and apologize to the victim.[27]

What are we to make of the legal encouragement of apologies? A starting point is to recognize that an apology is a speech act, and the failure to apologize is a silence. The interesting question, then, is whether a normatively attractive right to silence should include a right to withhold apology, and, if so, whether legal encouragement of apology violates this right. I think that the answer to both questions is "yes," but the argument for these propositions is hardly straightforward. The argument is best structured around the theoretical concerns discussed in Chapter 2. Before turning to these concerns, though, we need to understand something more about how apologies work, why they are attractive, and why in some circumstances the attraction should be resisted.

THE PARADOXES OF APOLOGY

In his brilliant study of apologies, the sociologist Nicholas Tavuchis distinguished between apologies and accounts.* Accounts offer an excuse, justification, or explanation for conduct and are designed to eliminate or mitigate moral fault. Apologies, in contrast, make no such offer. Sometimes people attempt to mix an account with an apology, but the effort to do so always weakens the force of the apology and often destroys it. When his sexual misdeeds finally caught up with him, Senator Bob Packwood issued a public statement that said "I'm apologizing for the conduct that it was alleged that I did."[28] The statement strikes us as ludicrous because it mixes apology and account. It purports to be an apology, but, by referring to the "alleged" nature of the conduct, it also implies that the conduct did not occur.

Similarly, many were left dissatisfied with Richard Nixon's post-Watergate pseudoapology: "I regret deeply any injuries that may have been done in the course of events that led to this decision [to resign from office]. I would say only that if some of my judgments were wrong, and some were wrong, they were made in what I believed at the time to be in the best interest of the Nation."[29] There is no logical inconsistency between a claim that Nixon "regret[ed] deeply" conduct that he knew was wrong and the claim that he believed at the time that the conduct was "in the best interest of the Nation." There are nonetheless two features of the statement that doom it as an effective apology. First, notice the odd conjunction of the subjunctive ("if some of my judgments were wrong") and the declarative ("and some were wrong"). In subtle fashion, Nixon is trying to have it both ways. He wants to get credit for a forthright apology ("some were wrong") while also introducing the possibility that no apology is necessary ("if some . . . were wrong"). Second, and relatedly, in the

---

* *See* NICHOLAS TAVUCHIS, MEA CULPA: A SOCIOLOGY OF APOLOGY AND RECONCILIATION 17 (1991). The discussion that follows is heavily influenced by Tavuchis's analysis, but I should not be understood as precisely tracking the distinctions that he draws.

very sentence where he admits error, he also offers excuse and mitigation (the wrong judgments "were made in what I believed at the time to be in the best interest of the Nation.") Because Nixon wanted to have it both ways, he ended up having it neither way. To be effective as an apology, there must be an unambiguous and unqualified admission of fault. Precisely to the extent that Nixon insisted on offering an ineffectual defense, he failed to make such an admission and, therefore, failed to apologize.

The distinction between apologies and accounts leads to the first of apology's many paradoxes. Successful apologies, like successful accounts, shift the moral balance and place pressure on their target to reintegrate the apologist or account giver into the moral community. Yet an apology, unlike an account, provides no reason why the perpetrator deserves reintegration. An account consists of a kind of brief for the position that the initial decision to exile was mistaken. But an apologist offers no such brief. On the contrary, apologies concede that the exile decision was just. One who apologizes seems to be asking for the benefit of reintegration on the ground that he does not deserve it. Why should this lack of desert shift the moral balance?

This puzzle is closely related to a second paradox. Apologies differ not only from accounts, but also from recompense. As Disraeli once remarked, apologies only take care of "that which they do not alter."[30] Of course, a person who apologizes might also take measures to make the victim whole, but such measures are not a necessary element of apology. Sometimes recompense will be impossible, yet an apology is still effective. Indeed, as Disraeli implied, in these circumstances, apologies take the place of recompense. But if apologies do not restore an individual to the position she enjoyed before the injury, why should they be accepted? And why is it that an apology without recompense is often sufficient to produce closure, while recompense without apology is often deeply unsatisfying?

One intuition about both sets of problems is that their solution has something to do with the apologist's state of mind. Although authentic apologies do not necessarily entail recompense, they do necessarily entail regret. Someone who regrets misconduct is less likely to repeat it, and, so, is a more likely candidate for safe reintegration into the community.

This is surely part of the story, but it cannot be all of it. Indeed, it leads to a third series of paradoxes. On the one hand, a person who feels regret may nonetheless repeat the misconduct,[31] while on the other hand, someone who feels no regret may be quite unlikely to do so. The difference between the two cases is not the likelihood of recurrence, but the mental pain felt by the perpetrator who regrets his prior actions. But why should the victim get solace from this pain?

Moreover, regret may be necessary to work apology's magic, but it is not sufficient. Imagine that you have wronged me in some way and that I discover (perhaps by reading your diary or through a third person) that you deeply regret your conduct. The discovery does not count as an apology if you have never personally told me of your regret. Apologies are necessarily interpersonal acts. Secret "apologies" will not do the trick even when the secret is revealed.[32] Nor can the task of apologizing be delegated. If I am to apologize, I must do it myself; it is not sufficient to have another tell the target of my regret.[33] What is it, then, about the face-to-face confrontation that makes apologies work?

In the rest of this section, I will argue that it is just these seeming paradoxes that make apologies effective. Apologies are powerful precisely because they make so little instrumental sense. Because they are in tension with self-interest and with means/ends rationality, they remind us that these are not the only forces that guide our behavior. The point holds for both the perpetrator and the victim of the initial misconduct.

Consider, first, the perpetrator. By declining to offer an account, she engages in an act of unilateral disarmament. She demands nothing and offers no defense. Instead, she freely leaves herself open to attack and, indeed, concedes the justice of the attack.[34] This point is most apparent when apologies go badly. How many of us have participated in both ends of dialogues that go something like this?

A: Honey, I'm terribly sorry for what I did. I have no excuse at all.
B: Well, you ought to be sorry, and you're certainly right that you have no excuse.

What is A supposed to say next? Perhaps she in fact had an excuse. Indeed, perhaps she is not in the wrong at all. Nonetheless, having forgone an account for the sake of an apology, it will be very difficult to back up and now withdraw the apology and offer an account. The requirement that the apology be face-to-face reinforces this defenselessness. One who apologizes risks being crushed—if not physically, then at least psychologically. She "pays" for her wrong by putting her faith in the hands of a person who has a strong motive to retaliate and with no assurance that retaliation will not be forthcoming.

It is significant, as well, that the apologist demands nothing in return. While the apologist may ask and hope for forgiveness, and while forgiveness may result from the apology, the hope of forgiveness cannot be the motive for the apology. To see the point, imagine the following dialogue:

A: Honey, I'll admit that I'm wrong and say that I'm sorry, but only if in return you will forgive me. Otherwise, it's nothing doing.
B: Go take a hike [or more likely, stronger words to this effect].

In the first dialogue, B is under some moral pressure to forgive. Of course, one cannot know whether forgiveness is warranted without knowing a great deal more about the severity of A's misdeeds, but A's apology at least puts forgiveness on the table. B is under no such pressure in the second dialogue. Apologies cannot be bargained for because bargaining is about instrumental rationality and apologies are not.

This point is only reinforced by the example of public "apologies" that are bargained for. Consider, for example, the elaborate negotiations between the United States and North Korea that eventually led to the release of the crew of the U.S. spy ship Pueblo, an intelligence vessel held for ten months by the North Koreans on the ground that the ship had violated its territorial waters. The dispute was finally settled when the North Koreans agreed to release the crew in exchange for a public "apology" by the United States.[35] American officials signed the appropriate document, but disclaimed the "apology" both before and after it was signed. Their point was that it was not a "true" apology because it had been signed only to secure the release of the crew, and they were surely correct on this score. Whatever the appropriateness of the absurd signing ritual, it did not amount to an apology in any meaningful sense precisely because it was motivated by instrumental rationality.

Similarly, instrumental rationality does not explain the victim's responsibility to forgive. Of course, there is not always such a responsibility. As Tavuchis points out, apology and forgiveness make sense for a middle band of behavior that is neither so trivial as to make apology unnecessary nor so serious as to make forgiveness inappropriate.[36] When we are in this middle band, however, the target of an apology can seem churlish or small-minded when he does not forgive.

But what is it about the apology that gives rise to a claim to forgiveness? As we have already seen, the apology provides no guarantee that the offense will not reoccur and no argument for why forgiveness is deserved. Is it not the very nonrationality of forgiveness—the very lack of desert and absence of guarantee—that makes it so attractive?

Just as the apologist insists on nothing for the apology, so, too, the apology's target is assured of nothing in exchange for forgiveness. Both acts are "free" in the sense that they are unconditional. The acts are not compelled by the usual forces of self-interest that normally dominate our behavior. What one gets from the interchange is not advantage in the usual sense, but a glimpse of what unmediated communication with another human being might be like. The perpetrator now understands that she has done the wrong thing. This understanding comes about not because the perpetrator has something to gain instrumentally by professing the understanding. Instead, the perpetrator has simply seen and come to grips with the truth. Similarly, the victim now understands how even good people can sometimes do the wrong thing. He forgives not because he gets anything in return, but because he has come to understand the connection that unites us even when we fail each other. Thus, apologies and forgiveness combat loneliness and alienation. When we apologize and forgive, we see and accept the other for what she is, with our vision and acceptance unclouded by our usual self-centered preoccupation with our own well-being.

Yet these very features that make apology and forgiveness so attractive also make them very dangerous. Two sources of danger are especially serious. The first is the flip side of apology's attraction. We yearn for unmediated communication with other human beings, but we also deeply fear it. Here, we return to the familiar point about our seemingly unresolvable desires for both connection and separation.[37] Connection is great, but it comes at a price, and separation can be lonely, but it also affords safety. Thus, we have already seen how the shared vulnerability of the partners in apology and forgiveness make each of them in their own way subject to exploitation. More broadly, the ritual of apology and forgiveness can be experienced as an invasion of privacy. Even if not exploited by our partner, we may feel unease about revealing so much of ourselves. Hence, the unease as well on the part of third party observers of apologies, who may feel too close to an inner sanctum for comfort.

Moreover, even after the perpetrator and victim have made this difficult and painful effort, it is likely to achieve only incomplete and ambiguous success. It is simply a sad fact of human existence that no matter how bravely we try, we can never achieve totally unmediated interpersonal communication. Here, the second danger takes hold. Even when the parties act in good faith, apologies can never completely avoid the corruption of self-interest. Their unconditional and, therefore, free character is so fragile that it simply cannot survive in the real world.

This problem with apologies is really just a specific example of a broader problem with the reward of any noninstrumental behavior. Whenever someone is entitled to a benefit only when she does not seek it, the very act of granting the benefit provides a motive to seek it, thereby endangering the entitlement. Thus, a person who does a good deed with no expectation of reward deserves to be rewarded. But if we respond to this claim of desert by systematically providing the reward, then good deed doers will soon have the expectation of reward and then they will no longer deserve it.[38]

The necessity defense in criminal law provides a parallel legal example of this sort of self-defeating behavior.[39] Roughly stated, the defense exculpates a defendant from criminal liability when the costs of the putatively illegal action are outweighed by the benefits.[40] Thus, an underage passenger who grabs the wheel of a car and steers it to safety when the driver faints is not guilty of driving without a license. The difficulty, though, is that the threatened criminal punishment itself is designed to force the actor to internalize the costs of the conduct so as to measure them against the benefits. Remove the threat by granting a necessity defense, and the resulting calculus will be distorted. We are therefore led to the following troubling conclusion: A defendant who acts in the teeth of the threat of punishment may well not deserve the very punishment we threaten because such a defendant has been forced to calculate both the costs and benefits of his conduct. Conversely, a defendant who acts knowing that she will be shielded by a necessity defense may well deserve the punishment that is now no longer available because existence of the defense will lead the defendant not to internalize the costs of her action.

Apologies and forgiveness yield a similar problem. The apology is unconstrained in the fashion described above only when the apologist is not motivated by the advantages that come with forgiveness. It is the very lack of expectation of forgiveness that makes the apologist entitled to it. Yet the recognition of this entitlement also weakens it because it leads to the expectation. Similarly, we cannot both say that the act of forgiveness is an unmediated demonstration of trust and understanding and that one who fails to forgive is churlish and small minded. The fear of being seen as churlish and small minded inevitably pollutes the generosity of the act of forgiveness.

How should the law respond to these attractions and dangers of apology? In the remainder of this chapter, my ambition is to build the case for a right to withhold apology by using the theoretical structure we already have in place. To make this discussion as concrete as possible, I will focus on a single case.

In *Utah v. Taylor*,[41] the defendant pled guilty to two counts of capital murder. During the sentencing phase, Taylor's lawyer, Levine, described to the jury his philosophy as requiring him to "help defendants admit their guilt and take the appropriate punishment."[42] The jury rejected (accepted?) this argument and sentenced Taylor to death. On appeal, Taylor claimed that Levine had not provided him with effective assistance of counsel because this philosophy interfered with Levine's obligation to provide a vigorous defense. The Utah Supreme Court rejected the argument, but for reasons that some may find surprising. The Court seems to have assumed that if Levine's motives were as he stated them, he might indeed have failed to provide effective assistance. However, the Court relied on the trial judge's finding that,

Levine did not actually believe a defense attorney should help his client admit his wrongdoing, but merely asserted that position in an effort to acquire credibility with the jury. . . . [Levine's] theory that the views expressed in his jury argument constituted a reasonable strategy under the circumstances is plausible; Levine wanted the jury to see him as a defense lawyer committed to truth and justice, with a client who was honest and repentant and thus not deserving of the death penalty.[43]

Should Taylor's death sentence have been reversed? Because an apology is a speech act, and the failure to apologize is a form of silence, it seems, at least at first, that republicans will tend to favor legal encouragement of apologies, while liberals will tend toward recognition of a right to withhold apology. In the next two sections, I argue that one can, indeed, find liberal support for a right to withhold apology, but that republican opposition is more muted than one might suppose. However, when put to the test of *Taylor,* both the republican and liberal positions are fatally confused. In the following sections, I argue that some of this confusion can be dissipated, and a right to withhold apology reenforced, by examining the problem from the perspectives of pervasive determinism and radical libertarianism.

THE REPUBLICAN CASE FOR APOLOGY

There is an obvious connection between republican political theory and the legal promotion of apology. First, as noted above,[44] apologies are necessarily social acts. There is a fit between their dialogic quality and the republican insistence on the essentially social nature of human beings. Just as republicans believe that people form their "true" selves through unconstrained debate about public issues, so, too, republicans might believe that the authentic connection that comes through noninstrumental apology and forgiveness helps to form identity.

Apology is also attractive to republicans because it provides an example of the possibility for transcendence of narrow self-interest. We have already seen that apologies make little sense in terms of instrumental rationality. The very fact that people apologize makes clear that we are not the selfish pleasure maximizers that some liberals imagine us to be. We apologize not because of what we get from the act, but because of what we owe to others in the community. Apologies sacrifice individual self-regard for the public good and are therefore rooted in universalist values. Republicans believe that political freedom rests on the ability of all of us to privilege the well-being of the community in just this way.

Finally, republicans are likely to be comfortable with government encouragement of apologies. Because republicans see the public as ontologically prior to the private, they are relatively unsympathetic to a private right to withhold apology. For republicans, it is entirely appropriate for the state to encourage people to lead public lives. Republicans, unlike liberals, do not believe that true freedom is synonymous with individual, autonomous choice. A person who stubbornly refuses to apologize is a slave to his ego. He gains freedom not through his isolated anger and guilt, but through the deep connection to others in the community that apologies achieve.

This much of the analysis is relatively straightforward, even if controversial. When it bumps up against the facts of *Taylor,* however, the republican case for apology begins to unravel. Suppose, first, that we assume Levine told the truth when he informed the jury that Taylor pled guilty because Levine had convinced him that apology was the morally desirable response to his crime. From a republican perspective, it would seem, Levine has acted in an admirable fashion. By not taking Taylor's selfish desire to avoid conviction at face value, Levine helped Taylor to form a set of preferences that was public regarding. Together their conduct exemplifies precisely how a republican lawyer—and, for that matter, a republican murderer—should behave.

If Levine and Taylor have acted just as we would want them to act, then it seems obvious that their conduct cannot form the grounds for reversal of the sentence. Surprisingly, though, some republican defenders of apology have made arguments that point to reversal as the right outcome. Advocates of restorative justice on the criminal side and of alternative dispute resolution on the civil side have both claimed that we need to make space for "safe apologies." They argue that both the criminal and civil justice systems as presently constituted are inhospitable to apology. If state encouragement of apology is, in fact, desirable, then the state should not punish someone who chooses to apologize by holding the apology against her. It follows, they claim, that rules of evidence should be revised so as not to give legal effect to statements of regret or apology in a way that harms the apologist.[45]

So, too, it might seem, Taylor should not be punished by holding his decision to take responsibility for his conduct against him. After all, had he not assumed responsibility for his act, he would have been afforded a jury trial at which he might have been acquitted. "Safe space" for his apology therefore might be taken to entail reversing a conviction based upon an apology. But of course, from a different republican perspective, reversal on this ground is quite bizarre. Vacating Taylor's guilty plea undoes the very act that republicans claim we should encourage. How can we possibly promote apology by prohibiting it?

Matters are further complicated by the fact that apologies push in opposite directions in the guilt and punishment phases of trial.[46] At the guilt stage, Taylor's apology made things worse for him. By pleading guilty and assuming responsibility for his conduct, he freed the prosecution from the burden of demonstrating his guilt beyond a reasonable doubt. When the punishment phase arrived, however, the apology at least potentially cut in the other direction. Levine plausibly (albeit unsuccessfully) argued to the jury that Taylor's guilty plea demonstrated contrition and that he should therefore be spared the death penalty.

Should Levine be allowed to make this argument? Republican theory again produces a contradiction. Because republicans favor apology, it would seem logical for them to favor evidentiary rules that encourage apology. A rule that permits the jury to treat apology as mitigation accomplishes this goal. The problem, though, is that precisely to the extent that the rule serves its purpose of encouraging apologies, it also undermines the very apologies it encourages. If the apology is made in order to gain the mitigation that it produces, then, for reasons we have already explored, it is not a real apology. It is instead yet another cynical, tactical ploy—the very opposite of the kind of apology for which the defendant deserves credit. Thus, there is a sense in which counting apologies as a mitigating circumstance destroys the possibility of apology.

We need look no further than the actual facts of *Taylor* to see how this destruction might come about. The trial court found that Taylor and

Levine's purported apology was in fact a sham, advanced solely for self-ish, tactical purposes. The state supreme court upheld the sentence for just this reason, while implying that an authentic apology might lead to reversal. A republican must surely be troubled by this outcome. In the first place, from a republican perspective, it seems perverse to permit phony, selfishly motivated apologies but not apologies that are authentic and publicly motivated. Perhaps more seriously, insincere apologies inevitably debase the language of contrition and, so, affect sincere apologies as well. Now that defendants know that they might avoid death by apologizing, they will have instrumental motives for their apologies that we cannot simply forget about. Real apologies can remain unpolluted only by somehow sifting out the phony ones.

Unfortunately, trying to apply these insights to the facts of *Taylor* again produces bizarre results. Should the court have held that Levine acted improperly by offering a phony apology? Reversing Taylor's conviction on this ground rewards the very behavior we want to discourage. Yet affirming the conviction, as the court in fact did, amounts to a statement that phony, tactical apologies are part of acceptable defense practice. Either way, a republican is likely to be left deeply unsatisfied.

LIBERALS AND THE RIGHT TO WITHHOLD APOLOGY

If this analysis is correct, it suggests that republican opposition to a right to withhold apology may be more muted than first supposed. Liberals, conversely, are sure to see the analysis as vindicating their doubts about public apologies in the first place. For them, republican confusion supports the argument for an unambiguous right to withhold apology.

It is not that liberals oppose apology per se any more than liberals oppose religion or healthy marriages. For liberals, though, these goods can survive only if they are insulated from the inevitable corruption produced by public settings. Apologies are valuable because they are private. The government is not, and cannot be, about deep, unconstrained communication between individuals or nonrational, particularistic altruism. Our public lives are dominated by disinterested universalism, by power, and by coercion. These are forces that destroy, rather than nurture the good of apology.

The point might be illustrated by what, at first, seems like a counter-example. Consider Richard Clarke's riveting apology to the relatives of victims of the September 11 tragedy.[47] Clarke's unadorned, elegant, and simple statement of sorrow, guilt, and regret during televised hearings won him immediate praise. Of all the witnesses before the commission, he alone seemed genuinely interested in reconciliation and healing. Simply put, his apology was the decent thing to do.

But should we put things so simply? A century ago, Oliver Wendell Holmes proposed that we could best understand law by examining the conduct of a bad man based upon his predictions of what judges would do in fact.[48] Suppose that we update the bad man theory and imagine the bad political consultant. This consultant is a kind of uber Karl Rove. He is very, very good at his job, which is to present his client in the best light, but he is also totally amoral. What advice would this consultant give to Richard Clarke? Almost certainly, our bad consultant would tell Clarke to do exactly what he did do. Clarke's stance of contrition cost him nothing, but won him praise and put his political opponents, foolish enough not to have hired an uber Rove, on the defensive.

I do not mean to suggest that these were in fact Clarke's motives. For all we know, his apology was authentic and heartfelt. The problem, though, is that we usually do not know.[49] In a public setting, there is always lurking in the background a quid pro quo for the act of contrition, and these background facts inevitably pollute the apology. It is for just this reason that so many public apologies (perhaps engineered by consultants less skilled than our imagined uber Rove) seem so contrived and unconvincing. When President Reagan apologized for Iran-Contra, or Bill Clinton for his sexual indiscretions, or, for that matter, Pete Rose for gambling on baseball, their speech acts bore little resemblance to the kind of unconstrained communication that apology's defenders admire. Former Harvard President Larry Summers's repeated expressions of contrition for his remarks about women scientists were a source of embarrassment rather than reconciliation. It could not be otherwise. Once the apology is in a public sphere, it inevitably becomes entangled with questions of power.

For liberals, the same argument cuts strongly against legal apologies. The point has been made most forcefully by Lee Taft.[50] Taft practiced law for twenty years before receiving a divinity degree and becoming a dean at the Harvard Divinity School. He is no opponent of apology. Indeed, he has "experienced and witnessed the healing mysteries of this sacred process many times in my life."[51] But Taft is skeptical of apologies in legal settings. Precisely because apologies are moral acts that have no instrumental value, they have a very limited place in law, he insists. Legal apologies inevitably degenerate into market exchanges, with the apology traded for favorable treatment of some sort. Thus, advocates of law reform that would create "safe apologies" are making a fundamental mistake. They "fail to see that what they consider systematic impediments to performance of apology are actually safeguards of the moral integrity of the act."[52]

Taft's position fits easily within a liberal framework. Like all good liberals, he associates authentic human connection with the private sphere and worries about the ways in which public power might destroy those connections. Apologies are about noninstrumental human communication and particularist values. Just because he shares the republican belief in state commitment to universalism and instrumentalism, he wants to shield apologies from public corruption. On this view, then, there ought to be a right to withhold apology. It hardly follows, though, that not apologizing is the right thing to do. On the contrary, this right, like all rights, provides no more than the space for people to choose to do the right thing. Government coerced "goodness" is not goodness at all, but simply acquiescence to power. Goodness implies choice, and choice implies individual freedom to choose the wrong course as well as the right one.

This argument makes sense as far as it goes, but it once again becomes confounded when dealing with a real case like *Taylor*. Suppose that Levine, as he claimed, convinced Taylor to plead guilty as an act of contrition and apology. Taft's position would seem to be as follows: As commendable as the apology is, Taylor should receive no reward for this act because to reward it is, effectively, to penalize the failure to apologize. This incentive structure turns apologies into just another chip to be played in the plea-bargaining process. But bargained-for apologies are not apologies at all. By using public processes to promote apology, we corrupt a practice that should be left in the private sphere. It follows that

Levine should not be permitted to argue to the jury that it should show mercy because of Taylor's contrition.

Surely, though, Dean Taft must feel some discomfort with this position. What if Taylor really is sincerely and deeply sorry? Is that not an appropriate ground for a jury to spare his life? Remember that Taft is a supporter of apologies. He thinks that people who apologize are, in some sense, more moral or deserving than people who do not. It will be a bitter pill to swallow, then, for us to fail to recognize this fact for systemic reasons when an individual life is at stake. Indeed, the failure to take it into account is in deep tension with liberalism's commitment to the primacy of individual dignity over collective concerns.

All this might nonetheless be tolerable if the hard-nosed position achieved the neutrality that liberals demand of government. But it does not. For liberals, apologies should occupy private space that is uninfluenced by government coercion. Although the government should not encourage apologies, neither should it discourage them. But the decision rule that Dean Taft would presumably favor does discourage apologies. After all, had Taylor remained unrepentant and insisted on a trial, the government might not have been able to meet its burden of proof. By instead taking responsibility for his conduct, Taylor gets the worst of both worlds: the government no longer has to make out its case, and the jury is not permitted to consider the apology in mitigation. The upshot is that Taylor must pay with his life, a result he might have avoided had he not exercised his "right" to apologize. If they do their jobs, future lawyers for future Taylors will explain this incentive structure to their clients. The result will be that some defendants who might otherwise have wished to assume responsibility for their conduct will be forced not to do so. It bears emphasis that this pressure does not come from nowhere. It results from a government decision rule that could be different and that is hardly neutral.

Suppose, instead, that, as the trial court found, Taylor's apology was a sham. If Taylor was not "really" apologizing, then the problem of infringing on a right of apology disappears, and, from this perspective, the result is less troubling. Yet, from another perspective, no liberal can be happy with the actual outcome in *Taylor*. Levine's behavior involves precisely the corruption that liberals like Taft fear, the substitution of a "bargained for" apology for actual contrition. The Court's recognition of this kind of subterfuge as an appropriate defense tactic legitimates the very behavior that Dean Taft most opposes.

DETERMINIST ESCAPES

A healthy dose of pervasive determinism helps dispel many of the confusions that confound both the republican and the liberal positions. A pervasive determinist shares liberal doubt that public apologies are the pure and liberating acts of human connection that republicans imagine. For pervasive determinists, though, this skepticism extends to private apologies as well. For them, no apology is what it seems. There is nothing sacred, magical, or uplifting about this human behavior. All acts of contrition—and, for that matter, all acts of forgiveness—are sanctimoniously disguised attempts to exercise power over others.

Recall that the determinist critique proceeds on both the legal and scientific levels. On the legal level, the argument builds on the realist insight that the private sphere is publicly constituted.[53] The notion that we can maintain a private sphere walled off from government coercion is therefore a myth. The liberal inability to make sense of *Taylor* is rooted in the failure to come to grips with this insight. Either the legal rule will permit evidence of apology or it will exclude such evidence. Either rule creates incentive structures that encourage or discourage apologies. Either rule, therefore, can be said to "coerce," "corrupt," or "pollute" the decision whether to apologize. Indeed, these pejoratives have no meaning because there simply are no apologies that are uncoerced, uncorrupted, and unpolluted.

The scientific argument is more complex. There is extensive literature on the sociology and psychology of apology. This work uses a variety of analytic tools and reaches a variety of conclusions, but all of it points in one direction: apologies serve social functions that are unrelated to the deep communication that is said to give them force.[54]

Some of the best work on the subject was done over thirty years ago by the great sociologist, Erving Goffman.[55] Goffman studied ordinary social interactions in meticulous detail and described the ways in which social scripts promote such interactions. A crucial part of this process is what Goffman called "remedial interchanges," without which "public life would become hopelessly clogged with the commission of minor territorial offenses and their adjudication."[56] Primary among these interchanges are apologies.

Apologies work, Goffman claimed, because they perform the vital task of allowing someone who has violated norms to be reintegrated into the community without bringing into question the norms themselves. This legerdemain is accomplished by the perpetrator "split[ting] himself into two parts, the part that is guilty of an offense and the part that dissociates itself from the delict and affirms a belief in the offended rule."[57] By apologizing, the perpetrator says in effect that it was not his "real" or "deep" self that committed the offense. This splitting, in turn, allows the victim to forgive the perpetrator without bringing into question the sanctity of the violated rule.

Goffman's account is ingenious, but it leaves unresolved why we are so ready to accept this idea of "splitting." Of course, the splitting serves an instrumental purpose, but it serves that purpose only if we hide from ourselves its instrumental value. But this is no easy matter. In an obvious sense, the perpetrator has indeed exhibited his "real" self—or at least some part of his real self—when he committed the offense. After all, who else committed it? In what sense is the guilty part of one's self less "real" than the apologizing part?

Other theorists have offered numerous reasons why we nonetheless accept the myth of splitting. Significantly, all of them agree that the acceptance involves an implicit exchange or bargain of some kind. For example, the philosopher Jeffrie Murphy argues that victims are burdened with resentment, which, in turn, is an aspect of self-respect. Resentment is unpleasant and is therefore a second cost, over and above the cost from the original offense, that the victim must bear. By apologizing, the perpetrator gives the victim the opportunity for justified forgiveness, thereby shedding resentment.[58] Although Murphy surely would not put it this way, there is in effect a bargained-for exchange: reintegration into the community traded for release from anger.

There are other, less rosy versions of the same story. It is claimed, for example, that apologies restore the victim's self-respect or reputation as someone who cannot be taken advantage of[59] or that they shore up a social hierarchy that benefits the victim.[60] Apologies put things "on the record" that can be cited in the event of future infractions or recognize the legitimacy of a claim that would otherwise be in doubt.[61] In exchange for these benefits, the victim agrees to acquiesce in the fiction that the bad act is somehow separable from the actor and that the actor can therefore be reintegrated without acquiescing in the act.

It should be obvious that all these exchange theories pose deep problems for a conception of apology that values it precisely because nothing is exchanged. More troubling still, each of these theories envisions apologies as located within an economy of power, rather than as a refuge from power.

A stripped-down version of the power-based view of apology might go something like this: By committing the offense in the first place, the offender exerts power over the victim. But the victim has power of his own, the force of our legal or cultural norms and perhaps of the organized violence of the law as well. The perpetrator might respond to this assault with competing norms (through an account for example) or simply by an additional exercise of force. Oddly, though, if these sources are unavailing, the perpetrator can also turn away the victim's assault by assuming an abject, defenseless stance (the apology). Now it is the victim rather than the perpetrator who can exert power. He has his rival at his mercy. But this new power imbalance imposes new obligations on the victim, thereby shifting the balance yet again. In exchange for the pleasure that comes with the uncontested right to crush his opponent, the victim comes under moral obligation not to exercise that right (that is, to forgive). The ultimate trade, then amounts to this: the victim gets to see the perpetrator squirm before him and to feel magnanimous when he exhibits mercy. The perpetrator, in turn, emerges from the encounter with his ego bruised but otherwise unscathed. Needless to say, this entire sadistic and masochistic dance has nothing to do with the unbargained-for and unmediated communication and connection that apology's advocates so admire. Instead it amounts to a complicated and brutal struggle, with each side using the tools at hand to its advantage.

A fascinating article by Erin Ann O'Hara and Douglas Yarn sets out a Darwinian account of apology and forgiveness that expands the canvass of this struggle.[62] Their argument is complex but, in simplified form, it runs as follows: In general, cooperation between species with an overlapping gene pool is adaptive and therefore naturally selected for. Even if individual members of the species do less well, the species as a whole is more likely to thrive if it can realize the gains of cooperation. But cooperation is always threatened by defectors, who are unwilling to reciprocate and instead take advantage of cooperation to seek selfish gain at the expense of a better group outcome. Predation of this sort might be deterred by what O'Hara and Yarn call "moralistic aggression,"[63] but this response is itself costly. Both transgressors and victims will be better off if they can reduce these costs through the process of apology and forgiveness.

According to O'Hara and Yarn, the apology/forgiveness process produces this result by allowing cooperators to identify each other at the expense of noncooperators. Thus, a person who apologizes signals to the victim of a prior transgression that, despite that transgression, she is a cooperator at heart. The problem, of course, is that defectors will attempt to send the same signal, but the ability to detect deception is also naturally selected for. There are therefore evolutionary pressures that push toward making it more costly for noncooperators to send false signals than for cooperators to send accurate ones.[64] Interestingly, in the legal context, O'Hara and Yarn conclude (albeit quite tentatively) that this can be made to hold true whether or not apology evidence is admissible against defendants. At first, one might suppose that the incentive provided by legal use of apologies would distort the signal they send, but O'Hara and Yarn think that this potential is overstated. Although a rule of admissibility for liability purposes deters all apologies, it deters more strategic than sincere apologies. Conversely, although a rule of admissibility for sanction purposes encourages false apologies, it will provide more benefits for people who apologize sincerely.[65]

There is a sense, then, in which O'Hara and Yarn are more optimistic than most pervasive determinists. They reject the assumption of some neoclassical economists that humans necessarily act in selfish and petty ways. Their account purports to demonstrate how self-interest, at least in the broadest sense, can include moral sentiments. Moreover, if they are right, the problem of strategic apology may be less severe than it first seems. Their theory connects the acts of apology and forgiveness to human flourishing in a way that other theories do not.

It does not follow that they tell an altogether happy story, however. On their account, it is hard to see how apology and forgiveness is the victory for human freedom and connectedness that both liberals and republicans imagine. Instead, the urge to apologize and to forgive is hardwired into our brains by an entirely mechanistic process. One wonders, then, why the supposition that apologies have a moral valence is not an instance of the naturalistic fallacy. Apologies may be adaptive, but so is the ability of the AIDS virus to mutate so as to become resistant to antiviral agents. Both phenomena are simply aspects of a struggle red in tooth and claw that has nothing to do with moral significance.

The tension in their argument comes to the surface when one asks whether there should be a right to withhold apology. At first it seems difficult to maintain that there are rights of any kind when morality itself is created by deterministic processes. Moreover, if "rights" have any meaning at all in a determinist world, they surely cannot amount to the preservation of free space within which selfless activity can flourish. For pervasive determinists, there can be no such space, and there is no such activity. I want to argue nonetheless that it is surprisingly difficult for pervasive determinists to completely extirpate the idea of rights, and that if there are to be determinist rights at all, they should include the right to withhold apology.

Consider first the stance that O'Hara and Yarn adopt with regard to this question. For them, legal treatment of apologies has nothing to do with the high sounding themes of individual dignity or community connection. Instead, the problem amounts to an ordinary policy decision, to be modeled theoretically and tested empirically. On their view, the legal apology regime should take account of the relative balance of power between defectors and cooperators produced by admitting or excluding evidence of apology. Their model yields recommendations based upon tentative predictions as to the likely outcome of various regimes. On the facts of *Taylor*, for example, O'Hara and Yarn's argument suggests that apology evidence should probably be admissible but that, in any event, the rule should be the same at the guilt and punishment phases. But although they think that this regime will promote cooperation more than others, they make no pretense that there is anything transcendental about it. On the contrary, they are commendably tentative in their conclusions and would no doubt be quick to acknowledge that if they made a mistake in their modeling, or if, for some unexplained reason, the empirics supported a different outcome, the regime should change.

The problem they face, however, is to explain why even these modest recommendations should survive the icy scalpel of pervasive determinism. If all we are ultimately talking about is an amoral struggle for survival, why should we care whether the legal regime encourages defection and discourages cooperation? Although O'Hara and Yarn do not pursue the point further, the usual counter at this stage of the argument is for the authors to adopt what might be called the "we just work here" defense. We are not defending any particular legal regime, they will claim. We are no more than hired help. If you want to achieve certain outcomes, then we can tell you which regime will best promote those outcomes, but the choice of outcomes must be made by folks above our pay grade.[66]

But this response will not do. O'Hara and Yarn have chosen to write an article instructing legal actors on how to maximize coooperation. They did not write an instruction manual for people who want to maximize defection, or, for that matter, who want to blow up bridges and tunnels or torture little babies. Are we really to believe that these choices do not reflect moral judgments on their part or that we are to withhold moral judgment on those who make different choices? Yet the status of these judgments is precarious, to say the least, in a world where all moral sentiment derives from evolutionary pressure. A thoroughgoing pervasive determinist must insist that these judgments, like all human activity, are no more than an outgrowth of the exercise of power. In what sense, then, do those who make different judgments deserve moral condemnation?

These observations illustrate the familiar point that it is very difficult to be a pervasive determinist all the way to the bottom. More on this presently. First, though, it is important to recognize that if one is willing to dilute pure determinist skepticism even slightly, then a right to withhold apology begins to seem quite attractive. We can begin with a modest point: Even if pervasive determinists cannot exactly recognize a right to withhold apology, they can hardly blame those who fail to apologize. On their view, all apologies are pompous and sanctimonious frauds, and one should not be blamed for refusing to go along with a fraud. But if one should not be blamed for this refusal, then why should one be punished for it? Pervasive determinists cannot be for punishment either, because, after all, they cannot be for anything. In this backhanded way, then, there is a kind of "right" to withhold apology in the sense that punishment of those who fail to apologize cannot be justified.

Partially fallen away determinists might go still further. Is there not some virtue in unmasking and refusing to acquiesce in a fraud? If pervasive determinists value anything at all, they must value truth. Why else bother to assert the truth of pervasive determinism? But then, what of the truth that a hypothetical Taylor bravely utters when he says that he is not sorry for anything and that all apologies are bunk? This hypothetical Taylor has absorbed the very lessons that pervasive determinists are trying to teach. Surely they must rejoice in that. If pervasive determinists cannot quite bring themselves to say that Taylor has a "right" to make this claim, then they must at least feel admiration and gratitude for his candor and insight and corresponding regret and disappointment when he fairs badly because of that candor and insight.

LIBERTARIAN RESPONSES

In the discussion so far, we have simply assumed that pervasive determinism is true. But of course many of us do not believe that it is true. Pervasive determinists insist that we overlook a large chunk of our lived experience with apology, forgiveness, and redemption. Yes, sometimes apologies are manipulative and dishonest, and sometimes they merely grease the wheels of social interaction. Most adults, though, have experienced other sorts of deeply meaningful interchanges that are not, or at least do not seem to be, reducible to the dark power struggles that pervasive determinists imagine. Pervasive determinists ask us to ignore this evidence from our own lives, but ignoring it is, itself, a choice, and determinist skepticism, which denies the very possibility of choice, has no tools to help us make it.

Or at least so radical libertarians would argue. Libertarian skeptics share determinist pessimism about finding a moral meaning to the universe, but they emphasize that it is a mistake to claim that any particular response to this emptiness is logically or normatively required. If the universe is empty, then it really is empty, and so there can be no arguments from logic, morals, or indeed from facts on the ground for one course of conduct or another. All that is left is human choice.

Apologies are attractive to radical libertarians because they illustrate the possibility of unconstrained choice. Of course, they will not join liberals and republicans in claiming that apologizing is the "right" thing to do. There can be no "right" things to do, at least in the sense of a "right ness" and "wrongness" that is built into the nature of things. Still, the noninstrumental, unbargained-for nature of pure apology does suggest that apologizing is at least a free thing to do. The very nonrationality of apology forcefully illustrates the mostly unrealized human capacity to transcend the kinds of fears, arguments, and doubts that, we tell ourselves, limit our own freedom.

The difficulty, of course, is that a refusal to apologize illustrates the same freedom. On at least one reading, this is the central point of Meursault's eloquent silences and ultimate refusal to apologize in Albert Camus's famous radical libertarian novel *The Stranger*.[67] A convicted killer who silently goes to his death, in effect thumbing his nose at authority, morality, condemnation, and hatred, is a powerful symbol of unconstrained human freedom in an absurd universe.

This ambivalence about apology suggests a central limitation on the radical libertarian world view. One can imagine an eager student turning to a libertarian master and saying, "OK, I understand that I can do whatever I want to do. Now, what is it that I should do?" Of course, the master can have no answer for this question, for to answer it is to claim that human freedom is limited in ways that radical libertarians claim it is not. The stony silence that greets the question encapsulates both the attraction and failure of radical libertarian thought.

But if radical libertarians cannot tell us whether we ought to apologize, at least, one might suppose, they can insist that we have a right to decide whether to apologize or not. And of course, this right contains within it a subsidiary right to withhold apology. Indeed, one might say that this right to decide and to act—inalienable in the truest sense of the word—goes to the heart of the radical libertarian conception of freedom.

But if one supposes that this freedom to decide and act translates into a legal right of the sort at stake in *Taylor,* one has misunderstood the central thrust of libertarian skepticism. For radical libertarians, republican complaints about the failure to provide a "safe space" for apologies and liberal worries about government coercion that corrupt apologies both amount to still more of the bellyaching that constitutes bad faith. These complaints are just additional ways to shield ourselves from our power to act. Of course, this power will always be embedded in a context where different actions lead to different consequences. How could it be otherwise? But in an absurd and purposeless universe, no consequence is transcendentally better or worse than any other. It follows that radical libertarians are likely to be profoundly indifferent to the legal regime in place to deal with cases like *Taylor.* Whatever that regime, people will do what they do and remain ultimately responsible for the choices they make.

We can nonetheless gain some traction on the normative legal question if we turn radical libertarian thought back on itself. In our discussions so far, we have generally assumed that any given apology is reducible to a single explanatory theory. Either the apology is the result of unconstrained choice and connection, or it is in one way or another located within a matrix of power. This simplifying assumption has been useful for sorting through the various theories of apology, but we should not take it too seriously. When I think about my own apologies, they are not explainable by a single, unified theory. Most obviously, different apologies are differently motivated. Apologies to my wife, my tennis partner, my students, or the person whose car I have just grazed are very different transactions motivated by very different concerns and constrained by different forces.

Perhaps less obviously, even if I concentrate on a single transaction, a unified theory of apology is quite illusive. A thick (and honest) causative description for any particular apology yields a complex mixture of motives, choices, fears, cultural conditioning, and hiredwired responses. Some of these are readily available to our conscious perceptions and some are not. Some that are not might be revealed by sociological or biological study, by psychoanalysis, or simply by deeper introspection. Some might never be revealed.

What is a radical libertarian to make of this indeterminate jumble that yields apologetic behavior? If, indeed, we have unconstrained choice, then, it would seem, we also have a choice about how we characterize and think about our apologies. Nothing in logic or experience requires us to think about them in a particular way, any more than anything in logic or experience requires us to apologize (or not) in the first place. We have the freedom to pick out from the hopelessly tangled strands of motivation and desire those that we wish to emphasize.

Presumably, a radical libertarian would want to pick those strands that emphasize unconstrained human choice. It is not, then, that pervasive determinists are in some ultimate sense wrong. It is, rather, that we have a choice whether or not to treat them as right. In this sense, the radical libertarian conception of freedom takes on a kind of "as if" quality. We can, if we choose, live our lives as if our decision whether to apologize is unconstrained. Of course, we could also choose to emphasize the constraints, but this is a choice as well and, a radical libertarian might say, a rather cowardly one.

Perhaps paradoxically, making this libertarian choice requires giving up on some of the freedom that radical libertarians themselves want to insist upon. If we are to emphasize certain strands and deemphasize others, then we need to shield ourselves from certain kinds of knowledge. It is at this point that libertarian thought backs into something like the liberal position on a right to withhold apology. In certain settings, the pervasive determinist account is simply too powerful to ignore. For reasons we have already explored, most of these settings are in a public sphere.

The point is not, as liberals suppose, that the private sphere is a place uniquely free of corrupting coercion. It is, rather, that the determinist account is closer to the surface when apologies are extracted in public settings. Republicans and liberals agree on norms of universality and disinterested reason as appropriate for this setting. These norms tend to be about means/ends rationality. Whether or not the norms are actually obeyed, the fact that we expect them to be obeyed makes this an unpromising environment for particularistic apology. Instead, it becomes embarrassingly obvious that public apologies are extracted for reasons of state and that they are provided for reasons of prudence. Just because we fear (on some level know) that all apologies are so motivated, we need to wall off this environment. The choice to wall it off amounts to an exercise of freedom on the meta level. By recognizing a right to withhold apologies in public settings, we precommit to thinking about apologies in certain ways—ways that, themselves, emphasize the possibility of human freedom.

How does this argument affect the appropriate outcome of *Taylor*? Libertarian skepticism solves none of the problems of sorting out the differences between encouragement and coercion that bedevil the liberal and republican analyses, but it does not have to solve these problems. Instead, the appropriate legal analysis turns on empirical questions about the workings of human thought. To put the matter quite concretely, we need to ask which legal regime is likely to keep Dean Taft believing that he has "experienced and witnessed the healing mysteries of [the] sacred process [of apology] many times in my life." On a libertarian account, the right to withhold apology is bounded by the answer to that question.

To implement this strategy, though, we need to perform one more act of mental legerdemain. We cannot ask the radical libertarian question directly, at least not all the time, for to ask it in this explicit fashion reminds us of the very thing that we are trying to forget.[68] Dean Taft can hardly say to himself that he needs to decide cases so as not to remember determinist truths, for to say this is, itself, to remember those truths. We therefore need to put in place a system that works more or less automatically without constantly reminding ourselves of the reason it is there in the first place.

For all its incoherence, liberal presumptions against public apologies serve this purpose tolerably well. The liberal position walls off public, government-induced apologies and treats them as different and special, thereby preserving a realm for freedom. The forgetting function is accomplished relatively easily because liberalism reflects deep strands in Western political thought that, for those raised in Western culture, are effortlessly accessible.

When viewed in this light, the confusions and contradictions we saw when we tried to apply the liberal position to *Taylor* are neither surprising nor necessarily disqualifying. They are not surprising because, on a deep level, the liberal position does not make sense. They are not disqualifying unless or until they become so obvious that we can no longer ignore the fact that it does not make sense. Despite my own best efforts in this chapter, we have not come anywhere near that point yet. So long as we do not, a liberal right to withhold apology protects our vital illusion of freedom.

CHAPTER 4

Silence and Self-Incrimination:
"Fuck This Shit"

YEARS AGO, I SERVED AS A STAFF ATTORNEY for the District of Columbia Public Defender Service. My colleagues and I worked long hours, under great pressure, often against overwhelming odds representing criminal defendants, many of whom were universally despised. An environment like this is bound to produce a fair amount of gallows humor (fortunately, not literally, since the District of Columbia has no death penalty) together with sustaining legends and myths. One story in particular has stayed with me for over thirty years.

A defendant—call him Mr. Smith—was charged with armed robbery. After one has seen enough of these cases, they begin to fall into familiar patterns. There is, for example, the standard alibi. It seems that Mr. Smith, along with countless defendants before and after him, was watching television with his mother and girlfriend at the time of the robbery. Unfortunately, there is also a standard line of cross-examination to challenge this alibi, a line that, at least in my painful experience, always worked. It goes something like this: "Now, Mr. Smith. You say that on June 3 at 3:26 P.M. you were watching television with your girlfriend and your mother. Would you be good enough to tell her Honor and the jury precisely what you were doing at 3:26 P.M. on June 4?"

And then the defendant is sunk. Either he has to claim implausibly that he can account for his whereabouts for every minute of every day, months or years ago, or he has to produce some explanation for why he happens to remember where he was and what he was doing at this particular time on this particular day. Defendants come up with a wide variety of unsuccessful if occasionally imaginative solutions to this problem. No doubt the worst that I witnessed was the defendant who said, "The reason I remember what I was doing was because that was the day I robbed the lady."

Of all the solutions, though, Mr. Smith's was the most memorable. On this particular occasion, an especially sanctimonious and overbearing prosecutor was playing out this dreary scene yet again when, suddenly, Mr. Smith rose to his full height and spoke words that will live as long as the English language is spoken: "Fuck this shit." Whereupon, he stepped down from the witness stand, returned to his seat, and refused to participate further in the proceedings.

Whenever I teach the self-incrimination clause to my students, I start by telling them this story. Of course, I tell them, Mr. Smith was convicted. Indeed, I say, if they want further details about the episode, they can still reach him care of the federal prison system. But in some deeper sense Mr. Smith's determined silence made him a free man. The government managed to get his body, but it will never have his soul.

The story is (I hope) evocative, but it is also deeply puzzling. What, exactly, is admirable about a violent and unrepentant criminal defying justly constituted authority? And what stance should the law take toward this defiance? The Fifth Amendment privilege to remain silent in the face of potential self-incrimination and the case law that has glossed it pose these questions, which I address in this and the following chapter.

In this chapter, I argue that the much maligned liberal argument for silence in the self-incrimination context makes more sense than its many critics suppose. The best version of the argument holds that a suspect's right to silence in the face of criminal accusation protects the ability to balance particularist and universalist obligations. Paradoxically, however, the "right" should not be understood in the usual sense of an immunity from government coercion. On the contrary, such coercion forces the very choice that liberals want to protect.

In the next chapter, I apply these insights to the problem of station house interrogation. I argue that interrogation in the station house should be subject to constitutional restriction, but that the restriction should be directed against intimacy and the illusion of intimacy rather than against police coercion. Once the problem with station house interrogation is properly understood, it turns out that current self-incrimination doctrine obstructs rather than facilitates needed reform.

A SHORT ASIDE CONCERNING METHODOLOGY

Before setting out the details of self-incrimination doctrine, we need to focus briefly on the connection between this material and the argument in the previous chapters. That argument has been mostly on the level of theory and public policy. Even if the argument is persuasive, it is not obvious how it helps resolve questions of constitutional interpretation. Perhaps there is a plausible case that the framers of the Constitution were republicans or liberals, but a claim that they were pervasive determinists or radical libertarians does not pass the straight face test. What relevance, then, do these theories have when our job is to interpret the words that they wrote?

A full answer to this question would require a deeper inquiry into constitutional theory than is possible here, but a briefer answer is sufficient to locate the argument that follows. My own (admittedly eccentric) view is that it is a mistake to tether constitutional law to either the words of the document or the intent of the framers. The most defensible version of constitutional law treats it as a series of rhetorical moves, obsessions, and poetic evocations that are normatively powerful precisely because they produce no determinate outcome but instead have the potential to unsettle any outcome that the political process produces. The potential for unsettlement makes constitutional law normatively attractive because it allows political losers to utilize our foundational principles in the hope of reversing their losses. That ability, in turn, provides just ground for asking these losers to remain within our political community.

My first-line defense of the constitutional arguments I make here is that they serve this purpose. I must acknowledge, however, that my views on this subject are not widely shared. I have set them out at length elsewhere[1] without noticeable impact, and there is no real point in rehearsing them. In my discussions of liberal and republican theories of the Fifth Amendment privilege, therefore, I intend to supplement my primary argument with an argument grounded in more conventional views that treat the Constitution and the doctrine that has formed around it as imposing significant constraints on judges and other political actors.

For the most part, even people who believe that constitutional law does and should constrain are prepared to concede that it also leaves judges with considerable freedom.[2] Originalists sometimes claim that we can reach definitive interpretive judgments by examining the original public meaning of the language or the original intent of the framers,[3] but often neither of these techniques will avoid interpretive choice. With regard to original meaning, phrases like "equal protection," "cruel and unusual punishment," or "compelled . . . to be a witness against himself" were hardly self-defining when the framers chose to use them. Perhaps these words cannot be stretched to mean anything at all, but people operating in good faith read them to mean different things when they were first inserted into the Constitution, and can read them to mean different things now.

Perhaps, then, we should focus on the intent of the framers. No doubt, the authors of the relevant language had some sort of intent about how the language would be interpreted, but the historical materials are frequently inadequate to determine what that intent was. Moreover, different framers may have had different intents, and, worse still, the intent they had may have only limited relevance to the interpretive problem we confront because they simply will not have imagined the legal issue that we must resolve. We might try to speculate what they would have thought about the issue had they in fact thought about it, but then we are interpreting (really guessing at) what they might have thought, rather than what they actually wrote. In any event, the answers we come up with are bound to be indeterminate, especially because the framers had no inkling of our modern situation.[4]

Given these difficulties, how should we resolve constitutional questions when the text and the intent of the framers are ambiguous? One influential view, associated with the work of law professor and legal philosopher Ronald Dworkin, is that we ought to use the wiggle room that constitutional law and doctrine provide to make the best of it that we can. Dworkin believes that a conscientious judge should respect the constraining force of text and doctrine even if these constraints sometimes yield unjust outcomes. Within the domain where text and doctrine do not constrain, however, we should fill in gaps by referring to a theory of justice that makes our legal system as fair and just as it can be made.[5]

There are many problems with Dworkin's approach,[6] some of which we will return to at the end of this chapter. For now, though, it is important to notice the obvious ways in which it is attractive. Thinking about constitutional law in this fashion reconciles the widespread intuition that judges should be constrained with the obvious reality that text and doctrine alone do not determine the outcomes of many hard cases.

It also connects constitutional law to standard legal methodology. A lawyer writing a brief or a judge deciding a case often confronts a series of data points (prior cases, statutes, legislative history, established practice, or constitutional provisions) that may support a range of different conclusions. Lawyers and judges typically see their task as telling a story that on the one hand encompasses as many of these data points as possible and, on the other, does so in as normatively attractive fashion as possible. It might just be that we can account for the most cases in a line of authority by determining which party had the most money or social power, but no competent lawyer would suggest in a brief that this should be the decision rule for the next case, even if the rule supported his side. Instead, he would choose an explanatory theory that accounted for fewer cases but did so in a more normatively attractive fashion. Conversely, if the most attractive theory would require overruling a large number of cases, competent lawyers and judges are likely to prefer a second-best theory. Dworkin, in effect, asks us to think about constitutional law in the way that lawyers and judges regularly think about legal argument more generally.

In the first part of this chapter, I will examine the self-incrimination clause in this Dworkinian spirit. The inquiry will be whether one can generate a normatively attractive version of the self-incrimination clause by using republican or liberal theory. As we will see, however, things become more complicated when we turn to pervasive determinism and radical libertarianism at the end of the chapter. These theories pose a challenge not only to existing Fifth Amendment doctrine, but also to an evaluative method that treats that doctrine as significantly constraining legal choices.

Before getting into these complexities, we need some understanding of what that doctrine is and how it purports to constrain. It is to these matters that we now turn.

The self-incrimination clause states that "No person . . . shall be compelled in any criminal case to be a witness against himself."[7] This simple sentence poses a host of interpretive puzzles. What is a "criminal case?" What does it mean for someone to be "compelled?" When is a person a "witness against himself?"

Suppose we begin by defining the words *criminal case*. Many lay people understandably assume that a case is "criminal" when the defendant risks being incarcerated when the case ends. The Supreme Court has not defined the term in this fashion, however. On the one hand, civil cases can lead to incarceration, as when the state brings civil commitment proceedings against someone because he is mentally ill and dangerous, or when the state or a private party initiates civil contempt proceedings to force obedience to an injunction.[8] On the other hand, criminal cases do not always result in incarceration, as when a defendant is fined or placed on probation.

How, then, should the words *criminal case* be defined? The Supreme Court's definition will strike many as disturbingly circular. In general, the Court has said that a case is "criminal" whenever the government takes advantage of the special condemnatory function of the criminal law by labeling an offense "criminal." If the government chooses not to attach this label, then there is at least a strong presumption that the case is merely "civil."[9]

This circularity is softened somewhat by the way in which the Court has defined what it means to be a witness against oneself in a criminal case. It turns out that in some circumstances, the privilege may be unavailable even in criminal cases and in other circumstances it may be available even in civil cases. Suppose, first, that I am an eyewitness to a murder and am subpoenaed by the prosecution to testify against the alleged murderer. Of course, this is a criminal case, but I nonetheless do not have a privilege because I have not been asked to be a witness against myself. Strikingly, I have no privilege even if the testimony I am required to give is deeply embarrassing, inconvenient, or dangerous. It is no excuse, for example, that I have received credible threats of retaliation if I testify.[10]

Now, suppose that I am not a mere witness to the murder but a participant in it. Suppose further that I have not been charged with the murder, but am asked to testify against another participant in a civil, wrongful death action. At first it may seem obvious that I have no privilege. Not only am I not being asked to be a witness against myself, but this is not even a criminal case. In fact, however, the Court has held that a witness can assert the privilege in this setting. The Court's reasoning is that even though the subpoena does not require the witness to testify against himself in this case, and even though the present case is not criminal, the testimony might later be introduced against him in a future criminal proceeding in which he would be a defendant. At this later point, introduction of the earlier testimony would make the defendant a "witness against himself," and, in order to avoid this possibility, the witness can assert the privilege at the earlier point.[11]

The same argument applies in other noncriminal settings where a witness is forced to testify. For example, a witness subpoenaed to testify before a congressional committee can claim the privilege even though the committee hearing is not, itself, a criminal proceeding and the witness is not, at that point, a defendant. If there is a significant risk that the testimony might later be introduced against the witness in a criminal case, he can avoid the risk of compelled self-incrimination by declining to testify at the hearing, at least with respect to questions that might yield incriminating answers.[12]

These examples help illustrate a fundamental analytic point about self-incrimination doctrine. In order to have a violation of the self-incrimination clause, two separate factors must coalesce: compulsion and incrimination. Thus, in our congressional hearing example, the witness has been compelled because if he refused to answer the questions, he could be held in contempt of Congress and incarcerated. The questions lead to potentially incriminating responses because they might later be introduced against him in a criminal prosecution. Notice that the privilege exists only if both of these factors are present; if either is eliminated, the constitutional problem disappears.

One way to eliminate the incrimination problem is by granting immunity. At one time, the Court suggested that so-called transactional immunity was required.[13] A witness granted transactional immunity simply cannot be prosecuted for transactions that she testifies about. If the defendant is assured that she will not be prosecuted, then there is no possibility that her statements will be incriminating and, therefore, she can be compelled to testify.

Transactional immunity is sufficient to permit compulsion, but in recent years, the Court has backed away from the position that it is necessary. For example, the Court has recently held that even if the police compel a suspect to make a statement during an investigation and even if there has been no grant of immunity, there still has been no Fifth Amendment violation so long as the statement is never admitted against the suspect in a criminal trial.[14] In contrast, the Court has continued to insist on immunity before a witness is threatened with contempt,[15] but it has taken the view that only use and derivative use immunity, rather than transactional immunity, are necessary. Use immunity guarantees that the testimony itself will not be introduced in a subsequent prosecution of the witness. Derivative use immunity guarantees that the testimony will not be used by the prosecution in order to secure additional testimony. The Court's current view is that if the government makes an enforceable promise of use and derivative use immunity, then the witness' testimony is no longer potentially incriminating and, therefore, the testimony can be compelled.[16]

If the government does not want to grant immunity, it can still attain the witness's testimony by negating the compulsion prong of the two-prong requirement. Perhaps counterintuitively, it turns out that the very existence of the privilege serves this function. What the privilege means, in effect, is that a witness who relies upon it and declines to testify cannot be made legally worse off because of this decision. It follows that so long as the privilege is available, a witness who declines to invoke it has not been compelled to testify. Since the witness has not been compelled, he can be incriminated—that is, his testimony can be introduced against him in a later criminal prosecution.[17] Strikingly, the Court has held that in most contexts this is true even if the witness does not know that the privilege is available. The existence of compulsion turns on whether the witness will in fact be sanctioned for refusing to testify, not on whether he thinks that he will be sanctioned.[18]

The legal maneuvering in the Monica Lewinsky affair illustrates how these principles work in practice. When Lewinsky was subpoenaed to appear before the grand jury investigating the matter, she threatened to assert a Fifth Amendment privilege, claiming that her testimony might be used against her in a subsequent criminal prosecution.* In theory, the prosecutor might have simply granted Lewinsky immunity and forced her testimony. In practice, the prosecutor was uninterested in granting immunity until he knew what Lewinsky would say (or, more cynical observers might claim, until he knew that Lewinsky would say what he wanted to hear). The result was months of negotiations. Eventually, the prosecution and Lewinsky reached an agreement and she was granted immunity.** Having been assured that her testimony would not be used against her, she could now be forced to testify, which she in fact did.

Lewinsky's testimony was secured by eliminating one prong of the self-incrimination requirements. Clinton's was secured by eliminating the other prong. The special prosecutor did not promise Clinton immunity. Because his testimony was therefore potentially incriminating, it could not be compelled. However, for obvious political reasons, Clinton was uninterested in asserting his self-incrimination right. Because that right was nonetheless available, his ultimate grand jury testimony was not compelled. This was so because, even though he had been subpoenaed, he could have failed to testify and avoided contempt by claiming the privilege. It follows that if he had been prosecuted, his testimony could have been introduced against him.

There are many other details of Fifth Amendment doctrine, some of which I discuss below. This primer is sufficient to raise the most basic

---

*   *See* R. W. Apple Jr., & Don Van Natta Jr., "The President Under Fire: The OverView; Talks Over Ex-Intern's Testimony on Clinton Appear to Bog Down," N.Y. TIMES, Jan. 30, 1998, at A1. Notice that Lewinsky's legal situation was dramatically different from that of her mother, who was forced to testify against her daughter. *See* Richard L. Berke, "Mother of Intern Makes Appearance before Grand Jury," N.Y. TIMES, Feb. 11, 1998, at A1. Lewinsky's mother had no privilege because there is no Fifth Amendment right not to incriminate another person.

** *See* David Stout, "Testing of a President: The Deal; As Long as She Tells the Truth, Lewinsky Will Be Off the Hook," N.Y. TIMES, July 29, 1998, at A14. As a constitutional matter, the prosecutor was obligated to grant her only use and derivative use immunity. In fact, her bargaining position was strong enough that she was able to insist on transactional immunity.

and puzzling question about the privilege, however. Why should we recognize it in the first place?

To be sure, there is a simple answer to this question. I believe that we incarcerate far too many defendants for terms of imprisonment that are far too long.[19] I therefore tend to favor any measure that makes prosecution more difficult. It is at least initially plausible that the privilege accomplishes this goal, albeit in a haphazard fashion. Even if its protection coincides only accidentally with just outcomes, at least the privilege is currently in place, and with little prospect of more targeted reform of the criminal justice system, it is understandable why critics of the brutality of the system would be reluctant to see it abolished.

For the rest of this chapter, I want to put this simple answer to one side, although I will return to it at the conclusion of the next chapter. There, I will argue that the privilege may actually make things worse, rather than better, for criminal defendants. For now, it is enough to observe that the answer will only convince those who already agree with me that our criminal justice system is much too harsh, and even people who share this judgment must be troubled by the inefficient way in which the privilege reduces prosecutorial power. Perhaps more significantly, this defense fails to connect that reduction to any plausible set of policy aims that actually stand behind the privilege. The question I want to address, then, is whether there is anything to be said for those policy aims when they are taken on their own terms.

When the question is put in this way, it is harder to mount a defense of the privilege than one might think.[20] It will not do to claim that the privilege, like, say, the right to freedom of speech or religion, is simply and definitionally a core component of liberal democracy. Although most other liberal democracies have some sort of privilege, many do not recognize it in anything like the strong form in which it is recognized in the United States.[21]

Moreover, the privilege produces results that, on their face, seem undesirable. In obvious ways, it impedes the state's ability to convict guilty defendants. Yet, as we have seen, it provides no protection at all for hapless and entirely innocent witnesses who are regularly compelled to testify in circumstances where the testimony is embarrassing, difficult, or even ruinous for them. Moreover, at least occasionally, the privilege can lead to the conviction of an innocent defendant. For example, if defense counsel has strong reason to believe that someone else has committed the crime, counsel might want to put this person on the witness stand and ask the person probing questions. But because the witness can claim a Fifth Amendment privilege, the jurors will never hear testimony that might cause them to avoid an unjust conviction.[22]

Outcomes like this demand some defense. Not surprisingly, republicans and liberals provide defenses that look in different directions.

THE REPUBLICAN FIFTH AMENDMENT PRIVILEGE

Defense of the privilege is an especially arduous uphill slog for republicans. Here, as elsewhere, a republican's initial instinct is to favor speech over silence. Republicans are therefore likely to be especially resistant to the elevation of silence to the status of a constitutional right.

Republicans are troubled by both the incrimination and the compulsion prongs of the fifth amendment privilege. Consider first incrimination. As we have seen,[23] republicans favor public-regarding, universalist values. Fulfilling the obligation to participate in the criminal justice system is a way of vindicating these values. Importantly, jury trials are collective exercises in which citizens are asked to set aside individual, private prejudices and to come together without precommitment to deliberate over the outcome. For those with republican sensibilities, it is clear that every person has a civic obligation to participate in this process, not only by serving on juries, but also by offering relevant testimony that will assist juries in doing justice.

Republicans are interested not just in the processes used in criminal trials, but also in their substantive outcomes. Criminals characteristically put private and selfish desires above the welfare of the community as a whole. It follows that bringing guilty criminals to justice is necessary to vindicate the public interest when it is attacked by persons acting for private gain, a crucial republican goal. For this reason, it is vital that juries reach factually accurate outcomes. But the Fifth Amendment privilege puts achievement of this goal at risk. A defendant who hides behind the privilege may escape punishment and so achieve private gain at the public's expense.

Republican hostility to the incrimination prong of the privilege is only reenforced by the arguments commonly advanced in its defense. Republicans favor resolution of disputes through public reason, which, for the most part, pushes them toward means/ends rationality. It is quite difficult to make an argument for the privilege that satisfies these requirements. The interests it protects seem especially hazy and ill defined, at least to many republicans, and do not seem to be in the service of any publicly defensible end. To the extent that they can be grasped at all, they relate to individual resistance to state power, resistance that republicans are likely to view skeptically.

Now consider the compulsion prong. Recall that republicans tend to see individual preferences as embedded in a socially constructed matrix.[24] These preferences are not necessarily "free" and should not be taken at face value. Instead, it is the role of the state to condition or channel preferences toward public-regarding ends. Accordingly, republicans might say, there is no reason to respect a criminal's selfish, particularist preference for avoiding self-incrimination. Instead, the state should encourage all of its citizens to transcend these narrow desires for the sake of the public good. For those who have committed a crime, that transcendence begins with cooperation with the prosecution.

These objections have caused some legal thinkers to reject the privilege altogether. Jeremy Bentham led the way almost two centuries ago when he wrote that "If all the criminals of every class had assembled, and framed a system after their own wishes, is not this rule the very first which they would have established for their security? Innocence never takes advantage of it; innocence claims the right of speaking, as guilt invokes the privilege of silence."[25]

Since Bentham, a few intrepid legal theorists have undertaken the unenviable task of defending the privilege within a republican framework. The most frequently advanced republican defense invokes the ideal of the adversary process. The fifth amendment, it is said, is part of a system that rejects inquisitorial justice and depends instead upon the clash between prosecutor and defense attorney to get at the truth.[26] But in this bare bones form, the argument is question begging. It is far from obvious that the adversary system is better at getting at the truth than possible alternatives,[27] and far from obvious that the privilege is a necessary component of the adversary system. With regard to the latter point, one could easily imagine a system in which prosecutor and defense attorney were each committed to victory, but in which the prosecutor could nonetheless call the defendant to the stand and ask her to give an account of the events in question. Indeed, this is the system we have for civil cases.

Yale law professor Akhil Amar has offered a more finely grained defense of the privilege. According to him, the privilege serves the republican end of securing the truth in criminal cases because "[c]ompelled testimony may be partly or wholly misleading and unreliable; even an innocent person may say seemingly inculpatory things under pressure and suspicion and when flustered by trained inquisitors."[28]

There is surely something to this point. It is easy to imagine how an innocent person might be made to seem guilty because of nervousness or through clever cross-examination. There are significant difficulties with the argument, however. For one thing, we seem quite content to permit the admission of other evidence far less reliable than defendants' statements. Consider, for example, informant testimony. Many defendants are convicted on the basis of evidence provided by witnesses who have something to gain by testifying in the way that prosecutors desire. The danger that juries will be misled by perjured testimony of this sort is obvious,[29] yet there is no rule excluding it.

Similarly, social scientists tell us that the ability of witnesses to identify people in high-pressure situations is extremely limited, and that the choices witnesses make in showups, lineups, and photographic identifications are often not much better than random.[30] Yet there is, again, no rule excluding this evidence, and, indeed, some jurisdictions permit trial judges to exclude expert testimony undermining its reliability.[31]

With regard to these and other classes of potentially misleading testimony, we are content to rely on the good sense of jurors in evaluating the weight that the evidence should be given. Indeed, relying on citizen deliberation, rather than on top-down decrees, reflects central republican values. Why, then, should we treat self-incriminatory testimony any differently?

A second problem is that compelled testimony may distort the truth, but it may also promote it. Yes, an innocent defendant forced to testify can be made to appear guilty, but guilty defendants can also hide their guilt by exercising the privilege, and, as we have seen, innocent defendants may be disadvantaged by the protection the privilege affords to guilty witnesses. Is it really so clear that on balance we will arrive at the truth more frequently by shielding a defendant and other witnesses from searching questions about the crime?

Finally, as Amar himself acknowledges,[32] putting in place a truth-promoting version of the Fifth Amendment privilege would require an important restructuring of current doctrine. The Supreme Court has made it crystal clear that the Fifth Amendment privilege is available even when there is strong extrinsic evidence supporting the truth of the compelled statement. Recall, for example, that defendants are now entitled to both use and derivative use immunity if they are compelled to testify. This means that a prosecutor is prevented from using physical evidence, perhaps a gun or a fingerprint, located because of what a compelled defendant has told government officials. Although there is always some risk that an unscrupulous prosecutor or police officer might plant physical evidence, it is hard to make a serious case that the exclusion of such evidence on balance enhances the reliability of criminal verdicts. Of course, we could modify existing doctrine; Amar makes a powerful case that we should do just this. Still, if we are to be constrained by the Dworkinian requirement of "fit," this mismatch between a reliability theory of the privilege and existing law must count against the reliability theory.

Other legal scholars have, in effect, reversed Amar's argument. Instead of claiming that the privilege allows innocent defendants to avoid testimony, they argue that the privilege allows innocent defendants to testify effectively. For example, Daniel J. Seidmann and Alex Stein have used game theoretic analysis to argue that the privilege makes juries more likely to credit the testimony of innocent defendants.[33] Their argument is quite complex, but it is not difficult to grasp its core. If there were no right to silence, they say, both innocent and guilty people would testify in their own defense. This is what economists call a "pooling" equilibrium. The innocent and guilty behave the same way, and, in many cases, jurors will have great difficulty sorting them out. Just as consumer inability to tell the difference between good and bad used cars drives down the price of both good and bad cars, jurors unable to tell the difference between perjured and truthful testimony will discount both. The upshot is that some innocent defendants who testify truthfully will nevertheless be convicted.[34]

In contrast, the privilege creates a "separating" equilibrium. If offered a right to remain silent, more guilty defendants will take advantage of it than innocent defendants. This is so because a guilty defendant who speaks runs a greater risk that what he says will be contradicted by other evidence held by the prosecution. If his alibi turns out to be inconsistent with known facts, he will have talked himself into still deeper trouble. In many cases, the sensible thing for him to do is to avoid this risk by taking advantage of the privilege. In contrast, innocent defendants who are telling the truth run a much lower risk that their version of events will be disproved. Even if there is a privilege, they will remain eager to tell their story. The upshot is that less perjured testimony will pollute the truthful testimony if a privilege is recognized. Innocent defendants will therefore have a greater chance that juries will believe their accounts.[35]

This is surely a clever argument, and there may even be some truth to it. There are nonetheless some serious problems with it.[36] One problem stems from existing doctrine. In *Griffin v. California*,[37] the Supreme Court held that a jury should not be allowed to consider the fact that a defendant remained silent as evidence supporting her guilt. The Court thought that this rule was necessary to protect Fifth Amendment rights, but if Seidmann and Stein are right, it actually undermines the privilege by reestablishing a pooling equilibrium. This is so because a jury that obeyed the *Griffin* rule would treat testifiers and nontestifiers alike, thereby depriving testifiers of the signaling advantage that the privilege supposedly gives them.[38]

Moreover, even if Griffin were overruled, there is a danger that the Seidmann and Stein argument is too clever by half. The authors require seventy-nine pages of the *Harvard Law Review* to set out their complex and tightly reasoned theory. How likely is it that ordinary jurors, who do not regularly read the *Harvard Law Review*, will think up or understand the theory?[39] Of course, if they do not understand it, they will not discount defendant testimony in the way that Seidmann and Stein predict. Oddly, the very brilliance of the argument strongly cuts against it.[40]

Toward the end of their article, Seidmann and Stein provide a smattering of empirical data that, they claim, support their thesis. A few studies do seem to demonstrate that when the right to silence is eliminated, guilty suspects switch from silence to exculpatory lies.[41] This is hardly a surprising outcome, but, standing alone, it does nothing to support the crucial claim that these lies lead to the conviction of more innocent defendants. On that point, Seidmann and Stein can cite only studies showing that conviction rates declined after *Miranda v. Arizona* made Fifth Amendment rights available in the station house.[42] But even if conviction rates did decline (and this point has been strongly contested),[43] there is no way to tell whether the decline resulted from more acquittals of guilty defendants, as opponents of *Miranda* claim, or more acquittals of innocent defendants, as Seidmann and Stein would like to believe.

Of course, it is not the fault of Seidmann and Stein that empirical tests for their claim are difficult to devise and have not yet been conducted. Still, in the absence of empirical validation, their abstract theorizing can hardly serve as a central justification for the Fifth Amendment privilege. Certainly, these highly technical republican arguments do not explain the emotional hold that the privilege continues to have over at least some of us. To understand that hold, we need to turn away from the republican world view and examine how the privilege appears to liberals.

THE LIBERAL FIFTH AMENDMENT PRIVILEGE

In the standard scholarly literature, the liberal defense of the Fifth Amendment privilege is widely derided as obscurantist, inconsistent with existing doctrine, incoherent, or just plain silly.[44] I believe that it is none of these things, but the objections to it are not silly either, so sorting through the arguments on both sides will require some work. In this section, I make the case for the liberal position. In the next section, I demonstrate how pervasive determinism and radical libertarianism require modification of that case.

The best defense of the liberal position begins with the liberal arguments for particularism and moderate libertarianism discussed above.[45] Recall that liberals differ from republicans by being more sympathetic to particularist obligations that cannot be justified in terms of the public good and by insisting on the freedom and dignity of choices made by individuals in a private sphere. To see how these commitments play out in the context of the self-incrimination privilege, consider the following facts from a real case.[46]

The prosecutor's evidence showed that Cynthia Johnson, a worker at the Bronx Veterans Affairs Hospital was convinced by a Cheryl Purvis, a payroll clerk, to help steal money by inflating paychecks. Purvis unilaterally manipulated the records to create a phony pay increase for Johnson and two others. Shortly thereafter, Johnson offered the same arrangement to other employees, who reciprocated by providing Johnson and Purvis with half of the amounts by which their paychecks were inflated.

After Johnson was convicted, the trial judge made the following findings of fact:

[Johnson] is a single mother. . . . Her [institutionalized] daughter, age 21, is . . . the mother of a six-year-old child who currently resides with [Johnson]. Also residing with [Johnson] in Florida is her son, Lamont, and two children aged six and five, as well has her youngest child, who is five months old. The father of this child is unemployed and resides in Queens, New York.[47]

Suppose one believed that offenses of this sort should generally lead to a prison sentence. Do the special circumstances of Johnson's family situation warrant a different conclusion?[48] This is a hard case. On the one hand, most people believe that defendants should receive punishments that comport with their moral guilt, regardless of contingent surrounding circumstances. It would be hard to explain to Johnson's codefendants why they should serve more time than she serves when all of them have committed the same offense. On the other hand, most people also believe that the government has an obligation not to victimize the innocent. It is no fault of the members of Johnson's extended family that she involved herself in criminal activity, yet they will end up paying a substantial price for her misconduct if she is incarcerated.

Republicans and liberals might disagree about how to resolve this dilemma, but they will at least agree on one thing: whatever treatment Johnson receives should also be extended to others on comparable facts. Perhaps Johnson and others similarly situated should receive probation when this is necessary to protect their families, but no one should receive probation because she happens to be a friend of the sentencing judge. The government's universalist obligations require it to treat all citizens with equal and disinterested beneficence.

But now suppose we ask a different question: Should Johnson have a right to resist punishment? At this point, republicans and liberals might well disagree. Republicans are universalists through and through. Both individuals and state officials are duty bound to put public obligation above private relationships. Thus, if it is in the public interest for the government to punish Johnson, it follows that Johnson has an obligation to accept the punishment.

The position of liberals is more complicated. They share the republican belief that the government should obey universalist norms, but they also value particularist, private relationships. It is therefore necessary for them to separate the public and private realms. It may be, then, that even though the judge should not favor Johnson over others because she is his friend, Johnson should favor her extended family over her more general civic obligations simply because it is her family. Just as I may be right to spend money on my own children rather than on starving children in Sudan, so too Johnson may have an obligation to her family to try to avoid incarceration.

Moreover, liberals will say, even if on balance, it is right for Johnson to accede to punishment, she nonetheless should have the right to decide whether it is right. Here, the liberal commitment to particularism connects to the commitment to moderate libertarianism. The task of balancing obligation to family and friends with obligation to state and community is excruciatingly difficult. If, as republicans and liberals agree, state decisions should be universalist in character, it follows that state decisions about this balance will leave out just the factors that make the decision so difficult. Johnson has a right to decide for herself what balance to establish because a universalist state cannot make people moral. Morality implies choice, and choice requires space within which individuals can work through hard moral dilemmas on their own.

If these observations are correct, they provide the beginning of an argument for the Fifth Amendment privilege. Yes, the state has the right to punish Johnson, but Johnson also has the right to resist the punishment through silence. Perhaps on balance she should not exercise this right, but in a free society that is for her to decide.

Notice that this version of the liberal argument turns on its head the familiar complaint that compelled self-incrimination confronts defendants with a "cruel trilemma" involving choice between incrimination, contempt, and perjury.[49] Defenders of the privilege who invoke this formulation have been singularly unsuccessful in explaining what, precisely, is "cruel" about forcing this choice.[50] On my version of the liberal argument, however, the privilege is important not because it allows a defendant to avoid a choice, but because it forces him to make one. Individuals ought to choose between incrimination and resistance, and the Fifth Amendment confronts them with just that choice.

Without further elaboration, however, the argument proves too much. If Johnson can resist punishment by remaining silent, why should she not be able to resist punishment by bribing witnesses? Moreover, the government regularly places people in positions where they are forced to sacrifice particularist goals for the sake of universalist obligation, yet no one supposes that these forced sacrifices are problematic. Surely, Johnson has no right to exemption from federal income taxes because she would rather spend the money on her family.

I must concede that I do not have fully satisfactory answers to these objections. What I can offer instead are reasons why answers are so elusive and why the failure to come up with them may be less damning than first appears. The problem derives from our starting hypothesis that we should, in some way, acknowledge the force of both universalist and particularist values. Any effort to implement such a program is bound to lead to trouble. Most people feel the pull of both sorts of obligations, but we cannot give full effect to both of them because they require contradictory courses of action.

This simple fact leaves us with a hard choice. On the one hand, we could join republicans and simply reject particularist values. This option is obviously unappealing for liberals, and a moment's reflection makes clear that it should also be unappealing to those of us who are not sure whether we are liberals or not. Do we really want to live in a world without special relationships and the special obligations that come with them? If not, then the only other option is a messy and inconsistent compromise between universalism and particularism. This compromise cannot be justified under some unified theory because such a theory would, itself, have to be either particularist or universalist, thereby privileging one of the poles that we wish to remain between. It follows that the conflicting demands of universalism and particularism cannot be reconciled.

Given this unavoidable fact, any defense of the Fifth Amendment privilege grounded in the conflict between particularism and universalism is certain to be less than fully satisfactory. Nonetheless, the Fifth Amendment privilege can be defended as, perhaps, the best compromise we can devise under these difficult circumstances. The outlines of the compromise are as follows: Our commitment to universalism means that the state may legitimately coerce its citizens for the good of the community as a whole. When individuals make choices to engage in conduct that the state outlaws, they may be punished for doing so. What the state may not do, however, is to coerce consent to the punishment itself. Although the individual has a duty not to act so as to obstruct the punishment, he has a concomitant right to avoid acting in a way that acquiesces in its infliction.

This compromise both supports, and is supported by, the fact that the privilege applies only in criminal cases. Recall that the government has substantial control over what is a criminal case; in many circumstances, it can avoid the strictures of the privilege and, so, give greater force to its universalist objectives by attaching the "civil" label to a given procedure. When it proceeds civilly, it imposes disabilities on individuals for the benefit of the community as a whole. However, these civil disabilities in no sense diminish the state's regard for the welfare of individuals asked to bear them. The obligations that universalism imposes on all of us mean that we will sometimes have to bear disabilities for the benefit of others. We can hardly expect others to make these sacrifices for us without being ready to accept them ourselves.

A criminal sanction signals something quite different. A criminal conviction amounts to a state judgment that an individual has violated the requirements of citizenship and is an appropriate target of officially imposed opprobrium. It is one thing for the state to demand our acquiescence in performing the duties of citizenship; it is another thing altogether to demand our acquiescence in a determination that we are morally wanting. The first demand is necessary for the state to function; the second involves ultimate moral judgments about the balance between particularist and universalist obligations that, liberals insist, the state must leave to individuals.

Critics of the liberal position often complain that it is inconsistent with actual Fifth Amendment doctrine.[51] As we have seen, criticism along these lines undercuts somewhat the republican theory of the privilege.[52] In fact, though, the liberal position fares reasonably well along the Dworkinian "fit" dimension.

Consider, first, the ability of the government to compel testimony in circumstances when it is not incriminating. The government can avoid fifth amendment difficulties by according a witness use and derivative use immunity. It does not have to do even this in circumstances where the witness is revealing embarrassing or deeply personal information that is not incriminating. Critics ask how the privilege can be said to protect individual privacy when it allows these gross invasions of privacy?[53]

The answer is that these critics misunderstand the kind of "privacy" that the privilege protects. The privilege is not about informational privacy—that is, the right to keep certain things secret. Instead, it is about the maintenance of a private sphere, in the sense of a sphere that is not subject to public authority. As explained above, the privilege shields certain kinds of decisions from public scrutiny. Those decisions relate not to the personal or private nature of the information revealed, but to the choice whether to acquiesce in punishment.

Other critics point to circumstances where Fifth Amendment doctrine seems to permit the state to force such acquiescence. The Supreme Court has held that the Fifth Amendment applies only to so-called testimonial evidence. For example, in *Schmerber v. California*,[54] the Court ruled that the state could extract blood from a drunk-driving suspect and introduce it against him at his trial. In subsequent cases, the Court has built on *Schmerber* to uphold compelled participation in lineups,[55] and voice and handwriting identification procedures.[56] More troubling still, in *Fisher v. United States*,[57] the Court implied that the state could force a suspect to obey a subpoena demanding the production of documents that incriminated him. Lower courts have interpreted *Fisher* to mean that in some circumstances the government can force a defendant to turn over even his personal diary.[58]

In fact, most of these outcomes are fully consistent with a liberal theory of the privilege. Consider first *Schmerber*. The important point about blood tests is that they can be performed without the defendant's consent. The liberal theory of the Fifth Amendment shields defendants from cooperation in their own condemnation, not from the condemnation itself. Blood tests and lineups can be accomplished against the defendant's will, rather than by commandeering her will. They are things done to a defendant, rather than by a defendant to herself.

Voice exemplars and handwriting exemplars are subtly different. A lineup or blood test is something that can be done to a defendant, but voice and handwriting tests can only be done with a defendant's cooperation. No amount of physical force can make a defendant speak, and although another person can physically guide a defendant's hand as he writes, it requires an act of will by the defendant to write in his own handwriting. The Court has nonetheless upheld these procedures on the ground that the defendant is not asked to reveal anything about his inner mental state. These are not inquiries into the defendant's thoughts, beliefs, or desires, at least in the Court's view. Rather, they are merely means of physical identification.[59]

From the liberal perspective I have argued for, these extensions of *Schmerber* to activities that require the suspect's cooperation are troubling. The Court is correct when it insists that the Fifth Amendment is about internal mental processes rather than physical objects, but it seems to miss an essential point: Even if what the government discovers is unrelated to mental activity, the required acquiescence involves an invasion of choice. Standard Fifth Amendment doctrine forbids the state from forcing a defendant to reveal where he has hidden the murder weapon, even though the murder weapon is a physical object. This is because the government discovers the object through an act of will by the defendant. But the government discovers the defendant's handwriting or voice characteristics through a similar act of will. If one believes that the government should not be allowed to coerce a choice to acquiesce in criminal punishment, then the cases are wrongly decided. It follows that these cases weaken the liberal argument from a Dworkinian "fit" perspective.

But although these cases may reflect a failure of analysis, it is significant that even the failure occurs within a liberal framework. Even in rejecting application of the privilege, the Court has acknowledged that the test for its application depends upon whether the defendant's inner mental state has somehow been invaded. For the Court at least, the difference between discovering a murder weapon through the defendant's statements and discovering his identity through his voice exemplar is that the statements, but not the exemplar reflect the defendant's inner thought processes.

In this regard, there is an important difference between the republican and liberal problems with fit. As we have seen, core Fifth Amendment principles conflict with republican commitments to speech, civic involvement, and public obligation. Republicans have responded to this difficulty with their Fifth Amendment reliability theory, but this theory is also in deep tension with other areas of the law and with the republican commitment to jury autonomy. In this context, then, the fit problem pushes us toward the conclusion that there simply should not be a Fifth Amendment privilege. In contrast, liberals are quite comfortable with the central intuitions that motivate recognition of the privilege. Their fit problems suggest not that there should be no privilege, but that the Court has not extended it quite far enough. Of course, if the liberal theory required extensions that seem absurd, if it meant, for example, that defendants had a privilege to bribe jurors or not pay their taxes, this would be grounds for rejecting the theory. In contrast, no one supposes that the pillars of justice would collapse if the government were precluded from requiring defendants to submit handwriting and voice exemplars.

Fisher illustrates a similar point. *Fisher* held that, in some circumstances, the government may subpoena incriminating documents from criminal defendants. The Court's reasoning was that the defendant had not been compelled to create the documents in the first place. Because the contents were not compelled, they could be incriminating. To be sure, turning over the documents in response to the subpoena is compelled, but the production usually does not amount to incriminating testimony. This is so because, in most cases, the government does not intend to introduce into evidence the act of production. Instead, it is interested only in the document's contents.[60]

Perhaps there is something to this argument, but for *Fisher*'s many critics, it amounts to logic chopping. The important point for our purposes, though, is that it is, once again, logic chopping within a framework that takes seriously the requirement that defendants not acquiesce in their own incrimination. Only a court that took this framework seriously would bother to argue that the act coerced was not incriminating and the incriminating act was not coerced. Moreover, to the extent that these conclusions are wrong, they once again suggest only that *Fisher* should be overruled, not that there is a basic flaw in the liberal position. Although the Court has so far declined to follow this course, it has sharply cut back on *Fisher*'s potential reach. The Court's current position seems to be that *Fisher* is sufficient to overcome the privilege only in circumstances where the government already knows that the document it is seeking exists. In these circumstances, the compelled act reveals only facts that are, in the Court's words, "a foregone conclusion," and, therefore, perhaps, poses less serious risks to Fifth Amendment values.[61]

None of this is to say that the liberal position is without problems. In fact, the problems run very deep. For the most part, though, they are not problems that are internal to liberalism. To understand what they are, we must move outside of the liberal framework to see how the privilege might appear to pervasive determinists and radical libertarians.

THE DETERMINIST CRITIQUE

The pervasive determinst's critique of the liberal position once again has a scientific and a legal component. The scientific component focuses on the implicit ontological dualism that lies behind the liberal argument. For liberals, the use of Schmerber's blood does not implicate the Fifth Amendment privilege because this is "just" about his body and, therefore, has nothing to do with his choosing capacity. In contrast, a defendant who is forced to confess has had his will and mind commandeered by the state.

To see the problem a pervasive determinist has with this distinction, consider the Court's effort to apply it in *Pennsylvania v. Muniz*.[62] After arresting Muniz for drunken driving, the police asked him the date of his sixth birthday. Muniz failed this pop quiz in two respects: He responded with slurred speech, and he admitted that he did not know the answer. The Court held that the fact of Muniz's slurred speech was admissible in his subsequent drunk-driving prosecution because it revealed only the "physical manner in which he articulates words."[63] The content of his answer was another matter. His failure to remember the date of his sixth birthday was protected by the Fifth Amendment because "the incriminating inference of mental confusion is drawn from a testimonial act [rather than] from physical evidence."[64]

The difficulty with this distinction is that, at least in this context, the physical may be the mental. After all, the reason Muniz did not know the date of his sixth birthday (a mental fact) was because of the physical fact that alcohol had affected his nervous system in a particular fashion. Indeed, his ignorance could be characterized as consisting of no more than the physical interaction of the chemicals he had injected into his body with the electrical and chemical events occurring in his brain. These interactions produced both the slurred speech and the failure of memory. What is the difference between them?

One might respond that this criticism, even if accurate on the facts of *Muniz,* can be confined to aberrational situations where there is some external, physical interference obstructing "normal" thought processes. But this limiting strategy is quite vulnerable. Suppose, for example, that Muniz's ignorance resulted from a substance "naturally" manufactured by his body, perhaps in "abnormal" quantity, rather than ingested. Surely the interaction of this substance with the brain is also a physical fact.

Indeed, to anyone versed in modern neuroscience, the entire enterprise of distinguishing between mind and body seems atavistic.[65] Modern brain science is relentlessly materialist.[66] Scientists watching a brain scan while different sections of the brain "light up" as people "will" different things are bound to believe that Cartesian dualism is laughably old-fashioned. For these scientists, a defendant's "will" when he consents to his own destruction is the product of nothing more mysterious than the chemical and electrical activity going on in his physical brain, which is not different in principle from the chemical activity going on in Schmerber's blood.

The legal argument of pervasive determinists is more complex and, in some ways, more interesting. It builds on the transformation of American law that came about with the advent of the New Deal and the regulatory state. These changes destabilized natural law baselines that the law had previously utilized to distinguish between freedom and coercion or public and private. Without these baselines, it turns out that these distinctions, upon which the Fifth Amendment privilege rests, become very difficult to maintain.

A real case again illustrates the point. In *Lefkowitz v. Turley,*[67] New York adopted a statute providing that if a contractor with the state refused to waive immunity and testify concerning state contracts, the contracts would be canceled and he would be denied the right to enter into further contracts with the state for a period of five years. When Turley refused to testify, the state tried to impose this bar. Turley sued, claiming that the contractual bar violated his Fifth Amendment privilege, and the Supreme Court agreed. The Court reasoned that without immunity, Turley's testimony would be potentially incriminating, and that the threat to his employment, like the threat of contempt, provided compulsion. In order to avoid a constitutional violation, either the incrimination or the compulsion had to be dissipated. The Court chose to dissipate the compulsion by invalidating the bar.

As a matter of formal Fifth Amendment doctrine, this outcome may seem unproblematic, but in fact it gives rise to a deep contradiction. Suppose we change the facts slightly. Imagine that New York required its employees to submit vouchers for reimbursement when they incur reasonable job-related expenses. Imagine further that Turley submitted a voucher claiming a large reimbursement. However, on the section of the form asking what he spent the money for, Turley wrote in bold letters "I hereby claim my Fifth Amendment privilege." Does New York have to provide Turley with the money?

The answer is almost certainly "no." True, our hypothetical Turley, like his real counterpart, has been denied money unless he waives his Fifth Amendment right. The Court has held, however, that the Fifth

Amendment privilege operates as a "shield," and not as a "sword."[68] Put differently, one can invoke Fifth Amendment rights to prevent the state from doing something to you, but not to get the state to do something for you. The state cannot make an individual implicate himself in crime by trying to take something away from him, but if an individual is seeking something from the state and has the burden of demonstrating that he has a right to it, he cannot meet this burden by claiming his Fifth Amendment privilege.

But what, precisely is the difference between taking something away from a person and not giving it to him in the first place? If we had unproblematic baselines to measure from, there would be no difficulty in determining the difference. Before the New Deal, the Supreme Court often operated as if these baselines existed. It was thought that existing distributions, protected by common law property and tort rules, provided the baseline. If the government threatened to take something from you that you owned according to these rules, this amounted to compulsion and had to be justified. In contrast, if the government conditioned a "mere subsidy," on the sacrifice of rights a person would otherwise have, this was treated as an offer rather than a threat. On this theory, the individual is made no worse off by the offer; after all, he could always refuse to accept it. Because the condition did not amount to compulsion, no justification was required.

Although the Court still sometimes treats cases in this fashion, the New Deal and the jurisprudential revolution that accompanied it destabilized these ways of thinking. Pervasive government regulation of the economy made it apparent that "natural" or common law entitlements did not precede government, but were, themselves, the product of government decisions. These baselines could be, and were, shifted by various redistributive programs. But once the Fifth Amendment privilege is untethered from these baselines, it becomes very difficult to make sense of the compulsion prong of the analysis.

Some examples will illustrate the point. In *United States v. Rylander*,[69] the respondent was ordered to produce certain books and records. Rather than producing them, Rylander told the Court that he did not possess them and that his Fifth Amendment privilege excused him from explaining why. The Court held that the privilege was unavailable in this situation because the baseline had shifted: when Rylander failed to produce the documents, a legal rule placed the burden on him to explain the failure, and he could not meet this burden by invoking the privilege anymore than a hypothetical Turley could claim entitlement to a large reimbursement by asserting his Fifth Amendment privilege.

Similarly, in *Selective Service Commission v. Minnesota Public Interest Research Group*,[70] the Supreme Court upheld a statute that denied federal student loan money to applicants who did not certify that they had registered for the draft. The anonymous respondents, who had not so registered, claimed that the certification requirement violated their Fifth Amendment privilege, but the Court held that students were required to establish their eligibility for the money and that they could not do so by invoking the Fifth Amendment.

These cases in effect turn a constitutional prohibition into a drafting problem. The Fifth Amendment issue can be made to go away in cases like *Lefkowitz* by adopting a legal rule that shifts the baseline. If we start with the assumption that contractors must affirmatively establish that they have not taken bribes in order to be eligible to contract, then *Rylander* and *Minnesota Public Interest Research Group* mean that the contractors cannot meet this burden by claiming their Fifth Amendment privilege. By shifting the baseline in this fashion, the threat of loss of livelihood turns out not to be a threat at all; rather, the government has simply declined to offer contractors a benefit (the right to contract) to which they have not proved entitlement.

To see how this shift works, consider the so-called business records exception to the Fifth Amendment. In *Shapiro v. United States*,[71] the Supreme Court held that the government could force a business to turn over records that the government required to be kept even though the records incriminated the proprietor. Before the New Deal revolution, courts often began with a natural law baseline establishing the right of individuals to engage in ordinary business activities.[72] New Deal thinking, and the massive regulation and licensing of businesses that went with it, made this baseline optional rather than mandatory. In a world where the government can prohibit a person from entering a business at all,[73] it follows naturally that the government can permit entry but require regulation that includes the production of required records despite self-incrimination objections. The Court has used similar logic to uphold a requirement that drivers involved in accidents stop and identify themselves despite self-incrimination objections.[74] To see just how destabilizing this move is, consider *Baltimore City Department of Social Services v. Bouknight,*[75] where the Court held that in some circumstances, child rearing was analogous to a "highly regulated industry" and that therefore Fifth Amendment rights were not available in this context.

To be sure, there are some limits to how far the government may go in using this technique. Most of the cases we have considered so far involve civil, regulatory regimes and are far removed from the paradigm self-incrimination case where a defendant is required to testify at his own criminal trial. At least, one might say, the Constitution fixes a baseline that requires the government to prove guilt for a criminal offense beyond a reasonable doubt. A pervasive determinist might deny even this. Why assume, he might ask, that man is born free but everywhere is in chains? Why not say that man is born in chains and should consider himself lucky when the government chooses to free him? If we start with a baseline where people are incarcerated, then every invocation of the Fifth Amendment privilege turns into an effort to use it as a sword rather than a shield.

Of course, the Supreme Court is not populated by pervasive determinists, yet there is some evidence that the justices are willing to move further down this path than one might have supposed. To see how the baseline might be shifted even in the context of a criminal trial, imagine first the following situation. A defendant is charged with murder. At his trial, the prosecution calls, let us say, ten eyewitnesses to the stand, each of whom makes a positive identification of the defendant. In addition, the prosecution puts on fingerprint and DNA evidence that places the defendant at the scene of the crime. At the conclusion of the government's case, the defendant's attorney leans over and whispers to his client something like this: "My friend, if you don't take the stand and give a pretty good explanation for all this, you are going to the clinker for a long time." The defendant, terrified by the prospect of prison, agrees to testify.

Is this a violation of the self-incrimination clause? Obviously not. To be sure, in a sense the defendant has been compelled to become a witness in his own case; he knows that if he does not, he is certain of conviction. But this is not the kind of compulsion that the privilege outlaws. The defendant's right to remain silent means that his failure to testify cannot help the prosecution meet its burden of proof. If the prosecution fails to present evidence sufficient to allow a reasonable jury to convict, the defendant is entitled to a directed verdict of acquittal. If the prosecution meets this burden, however, it has succeeded in shifting the baseline. Now it is the defendant's obligation to explain himself by testifying in his own defense and submitting to reasonable cross-examination. If he fails to do so, he runs the risk that the jury will convict him.[76] Indeed, to hold otherwise would be to prevent defendants from testifying, since their testimony is always in response to pressure placed upon them by the government's case.

So far, these results comport with our ordinary intuitions. Once we accept them, however, we are perilously near the complete unraveling that pervasive determinists predict. Consider, for example, the widespread use of plea bargaining. On its face, the practice might be thought to pose a serious Fifth Amendment problem. Prosecutors regularly threaten witnesses with much longer sentences if they insist on exercising their right to plead not guilty. Indeed, sometimes defendants are threatened with death. Surely, these threats are far more serious than the prospect Turley faced of a contractual bar or even than the threat of a contempt citation faced by a typical Fifth Amendment claimant.

Yet the Court has upheld this practice on the theory that proposed plea bargains constitute offers rather than threats.[77] A defendant feels pressure to accept the plea, but the pressure comes from the threat of conviction—the very sort of pressure felt by our hypothetical defendant at the conclusion of the government's case. Because the pressure comes from the perceived ability of the government to shift the baseline through the force of its evidence, the defendant is made better off by an offer of a lesser sentence, which he is in any event free to refuse, rather than worse off by the threat of a greater sentence. On this view, plea bargaining is like any other bargaining—it can only make both parties better off because, if it did not, the parties would not accept the bargain.

The problem with this theory, however, is that it leaves the government free to manipulate the defendant's decision by shifting baselines formed not just by its evidence, but also by the substantive criminal law. Consider this simple numerical example. Suppose that the defendant is charged with second degree murder, which carries a sentence of ten years. Suppose further that the prosecution informs the defendant that if he pleads not guilty to this offense, it will charge him with first degree murder, which carries a sentence of thirty years. If the defendant thinks that there is a twenty percent chance that he will be convicted of first degree murder, and if he is risk neutral, the threat will be ineffective. The certain cost of a guilty plea is ten years, while the expected cost of a not guilty plea is only six years. But now assume that the legislature shifts the baseline by increasing the punishment for first degree murder to sixty years. Even though the chance of conviction remains the same, the expected cost of a not guilty plea now rises to twelve years. The prosecutor's threat now puts considerable pressure on the defendant, at least if we assume no decline in the marginal cost to the defendant of additional years of punishment.

This example demonstrates that without constitutional constraints on the substantive criminal law, the Fifth Amendment fails to control the level of compulsion that the government can marshal to force self-incrimination.[78] True, the Eighth Amendment's cruel and unusual punishment clause means that there are some outside limits on the government's power to force plea bargains in this fashion, but, at least as currently interpreted by the Supreme Court, these limits are quite insignificant.[79]

Nor is this the only way in which the substantive criminal law can be manipulated so as to shift the baseline. We have already seen that the government can avoid the reasonable doubt requirement by recharacterizing criminal cases as civil.[80] Moreover, even if the procedures remain criminal, the reasonable doubt standard applies only to elements of the government's case. The Court has allowed the legislature considerable flexibility in recharacterizing these elements as "affirmative defenses."[81] If something is an affirmative defense, then the defendant has the burden of raising and proving it. It follows that with respect to this element, a defendant can no longer simply rely upon the government's inability to make its case, but must speak in order to avoid conviction.

All of these effects are further aggravated if we assume that most defendants have what economists call ambiguity aversion. In the real world, defendants often have so little information that they are unable to calculate probabilities at all. It is plausible that defendants in this situation will be more inclined to accept the certainty of a plea than undergo a risk of completely unknown size.* This problem may not be severe when defendants choose whether to take the witness stand after hearing the government's case. Even then, defendants may doubt their ability to predict how a jury will react, but at least the government's cards are on the table. Plea bargaining is more problematic because, in the absence of full discovery (rarely available in criminal cases), the defendant simply will not know what the chances of conviction are at the early stages of a case when most plea bargaining occurs.

The problem is further compounded by other techniques the prosecution has at its disposal to force early defense decisions. Consider, for example, a rule requiring the defendant to inform the prosecution prior to trial of any alibi witnesses he intends to call. Again, one might suppose that such a rule would violate the Fifth Amendment privilege because it compels the defendant to provide information that the prosecution can use to generate incriminating evidence. In *Williams v. Florida,*[82] the Supreme Court held otherwise on the theory that the defendant is "compelled" to put on an alibi defense in the first place only by the force of the government's evidence. If

---

* Although ambiguity aversion is probably descriptively accurate, it generates an interesting paradox. Suppose that one is presented with two urns. It is stipulated that urn A has 50 red balls and 50 black balls. Urn B has 100 balls, but the subject has no information about how many are black and white. Suppose that there is a payoff of $100 for picking a red ball. A person with ambiguity aversion would rather draw from urn A than urn B. My own intuition is that many people would behave this way, but the behavior does produce a puzzling outcome. Suppose that we change the payoffs so that the subject gets $100 for picking a black ball. Someone with ambiguity aversion would again choose to draw from urn A, but the subject is now behaving as if it is more probable that he would draw a black ball from urn A than urn B and that it is more probable that he would draw a red ball from urn A than urn B. Yet it would seem that both statements cannot be true.

I am grateful to Katheryn Zeiler for educating me on this subject. For an introduction to the problem, which includes a discussion of this example, see Daniel Ellsberg, *Risk, Ambiguity, and the Savage Axioms,* 75 QUART. J. ECON. 643 (1961).

this sort of compulsion does not violate the privilege at the trial itself, the Court reasoned, then it does not violate the privilege when the defendant is "compelled" to reveal the defense prior to trial.[83] Unfortunately, the Court ignored the difference between making this decision with full information (after the government puts on its case) and making it with little or no information (before the government reveals what its case will be).

How far does the Court's logic go? It is well established that when a defendant takes the stand, he can be compelled to submit to cross-examination. A defendant has the right to remain silent, and he has the right to speak, but he cannot claim both rights at once. If he "chooses" to speak (that is, if he is "compelled" by the force of the government's evidence to speak), then he must speak fully and cannot refuse to participate in reasonable cross-examination.[84]

Suppose, though, we combine this rule with the *Williams* holding. If a defendant can be compelled by the force of the government's evidence to speak at trial, then *Williams* suggests that he can also be compelled before trial. Perhaps, then, the government could force a defendant to provide a complete deposition prior to trial with the understanding that the government could introduce it only if the defendant took the stand. The Court has never gone this far, but in a series of cases, it has certainly moved in this direction. For example, in *United States v. Harris*,[85] the Court held that a defendant's pretrial statements that are considered compelled because of the failure to provide *Miranda* warnings can nonetheless be introduced for purposes of cross-examination at the defendant's trial.

To be sure, as we will see in the next chapter,[86] *Miranda* rules are different from standard Fifth Amendment requirements in important respects, but the Court has used similar analysis outside the *Miranda* setting. For example, as we have already seen, *Griffin v. California*[87] establishes a rule that the prosecution may not bring to the jury's attention the defendant's failure to testify. Allowing the jury to consider this factor would effectively compel the defendant to speak in violation of the privilege. Suppose, though, that a defendant does not testify at his first trial and a mistrial is declared for some unrelated reason. If the defendant testifies at his second trial, can the prosecution impeach him with his failure to testify at his first trial? The Supreme Court has allowed this tactic.[88] Yes, impeaching the defendant through use of his silence tends to compel speech, but a defendant who chooses to testify can be compelled to participate in reasonable cross-examination, and if this compulsion is constitutionally permissible at the trial itself, then it is also permissible prior to trial. It follows, at least for the Court, that the compulsion to speak at the first trial is retroactively justified by the defendant's decision to testify at the second.

Perhaps it bears repeating that the Supreme Court is not populated by pervasive determinists. For this reason, the Court has never carried the logic of its decisions all the way to the bottom. When a complete free fall threatens, it steps back from the precipice. Thus, the Court has at least implied that there are limits on the extent to which the legislature may shift elements of an offense from the government's case to the defendant's[89] and the extent to which a defendant can be forced to reveal his case before the government presents its evidence.[90]

Nonetheless, the examples discussed above are sufficient to demonstrate the naivete of the liberal vision. In the real world, criminal defendants are hardly isolated in a pristine private sphere where they wrestle in untrammeled freedom with hard moral problems. The criminal justice system is shot through with compulsion. How could it be otherwise? If, as the last chapter suggests, ordinary human interactions between friends, families, and lovers are best characterized as complex power struggles, then it would be surprising indeed if our system for punishing criminals created a realm of perfect freedom. On this view, then, the self-incrimination clause papers over a harsh and brutal reality that requires our understanding, but hardly merits our celebration.

Is there anything to be said for a privilege against self-incrimination in the world of pervasive determinism? For pervasive determinists the very fact that self-incriminatory speech is compelled means that the liberal concern about such speech is misplaced. Consider, for example, the Supreme Court's decision in *Doe v. United States*.[91] The case arose out of the government's efforts to secure Doe's bank records. Initially, the grand jury subpoenaed from Doe the records of transactions with three named banks in the Cayman Islands and Bermuda. Although Doe produced some of the records, he testified that none of the additional records were in his possession. The government thereupon subpoenaed the foreign banks for the records, but the banks refused to comply, citing bank secrecy laws in Bermuda and the Cayman Islands that prohibited disclosure of account records without the customer's consent.

Undeterred by these setbacks, the government then petitioned the district court for an order directing Doe to sign a "consent directive" instructing the banks to disclose the documents. Doe resisted, citing his Fifth Amendment privilege. At first it might seem that Doe should prevail. The court order, backed by the threat of contempt, is clearly compulsion, and a direct fruit of Doe's compelled response to the order would be bank records that, Doe claimed, might well be introduced in a subsequent criminal prosecution in which he would be the defendant.

The Supreme Court nonetheless rejected his claim for reasons that a pervasive determinist would understand. According to the Court, even if Doe's execution of the consent form was both compelled and incriminating, it was not testimonial for Fifth Amendment purposes. True, his signature required an exercise of will in a way that the extraction of Schmerber's blood did not. Nonetheless, the very fact that the signature was compelled meant that it revealed nothing about Doe's internal mental state. Precisely because the document "explicitly indicat[ed] that it was signed pursuant to a court order," it could "[shed] no light on [Doe's] actual intent or state of mind."[92] In this sense, the form impeached itself. It could not constitute true consent because the form itself indicated that the "consent" was provided nonconsensually.

Although the Court appeared oblivious to the fact, this reasoning once again risks a total unraveling of Fifth Amendment doctrine. After all, it will always be true that a defendant compelled to "consent" does not really consent. There is a sense, then, in which defendants are never implicated in their own punishment. When viewed from this perspective, the very effort to compel statements means that those statements no longer "belong" to the defendant and, therefore, no longer confront him with the moral choice that, liberals say, he must face.

In the case of apologies, we saw that pervasive determinists might nonetheless be sympathetic to persons who resisted participation in what pervasive determinists consider a pointless charade.[93] Self-incrimination is subtly different from apology, however. Pervasive determinists are deeply skeptical of the notion that people engage in free acts of apology, and it is hard to see how apologies have much value if they are forced and therefore inauthentic. Of course, some acts of self-incrimination are also motivated by contrition, but not all are. Moreover, whereas apologies lose their meaning when they are forced, confessions do not. Whether or not self-incrimination is motivated by contrition, and whether or not it is compelled, it can have social value because it provides information that might not otherwise be available. If one believes that all of our interactions are shot through with compulsion, then it is hard to see why we should deprive ourselves of this information just because the act of self-incrimination, like everything else that humans do, is compelled.

SELF-INCRIMINATION AND RADICAL FREEDOM

How might a radical libertarian respond to the challenge of pervasive determinism? For a radical libertarian, our friend Mr. Smith, with whom we began this chapter, is all the response that is necessary. Of course, there is power and compulsion everywhere, but none of that prevented Mr. Smith from insisting on the only kind of freedom that really matters. With a short, three-word sentence followed by an eloquent and prolonged silence, he promulgated his personal declaration of independence. His story is important because it demonstrates the possibility—indeed, the unavoidability—of human autonomy.

In this sense, radical libertarians are aligned with liberals. Like liberals, and unlike pervasive determinists, radical libertarians think that criminal suspects are confronted with hard and authentic moral choices. It does not follow, however, that radical libertarians are supporters of a privilege against self-incrimination. In Chapter 3, I argued that the radical libertarian perspective pushes us toward a legal regime that preserves the illusion of human freedom. In the context of apologies, this will often (although not always) track liberal opposition to compelled public contrition. The self-incrimination context is subtly different and may lead to somewhat different conclusions.

Before spelling out these conclusions, I want to suggest why the radical libertarian view does not translate seamlessly into a self-incrimination privilege. Consider again *Doe v. United States*. For a radical libertarian, the clear lesson from Mr. Smith's defiance is that, the *Doe* opinion to the contrary notwithstanding, Doe does in fact own his decision to sign the consent form. No matter what the government threatened him with, a radical libertarian will argue, Doe could have just said "no." When he instead said "yes," his acquiescence is his decision, for which he bears responsibility. A claim that he could not have done otherwise only alienates him from his own freedom.

A radical libertarian, then, thinks that individuals are implicated even in "compelled" acts. This hardly means that radical libertarians are defenders of the privilege, however. On the contrary, the crucial point is that individuals are so implicated whether or not there is a legal right to avoid self-incrimination. In this sense, the privilege is based upon an inherent contradiction. On the one hand, the self-incrimination clause only has meaning if individuals are responsible for surrendering to coercion. If the coercion relieved individuals of ownership over the decisions, then, as the *Doe* Court argued, they would not have consented to their own punishments, and the liberal concern about such consent disappears. It is only because compulsion does not negate individual responsibility that a problem arises. On the other hand, this individual responsibility in the face of coercion also deprives the privilege of its chief rationale. If radical libertarians are right, then freedom has nothing to do with legal rights. On the contrary, the only freedom that matters is the unavoidable responsibility to make decisions no matter what the law says.

Mr. Smith again illustrates the point. Readers may have noticed an irony in his story, which I have not yet mentioned. His case is an odd one to illustrate the Fifth Amendment privilege because, in fact Mr. Smith had no legal right to the silence that he insisted upon. As we have already seen,[94] a defendant who chooses to testify on direct examination (as Mr. Smith did) is legally obligated to submit to cross-examination. Had the prosecution so chosen, it could have secured a contempt citation against Mr. Smith and insisted on his incarceration until he resumed his testimony. His powerful silence was therefore a challenge to the law rather than an attempt to rely upon it.

Now, to be sure, something like the same point might be made about public apologies. As Camus's *The Stranger* illustrates, a person can also demonstrate radical freedom by resisting pressure to say "I'm sorry." Why, then, should there be a privilege against coerced apologies but not against coerced incrimination? Perhaps there is, in fact, no difference between the two cases. Recall that my argument for a privilege against apologies rested on contingent empirical facts, not on theoretical truths. The apology privilege is necessary because, and to the extent that, without it, in our time and place, we risk the realization that all apologies are coerced or determined and that radical libertarianism is based on an illusion.[95]

If we run the same risk in the self-incrimination context, then perhaps there should be a self-incrimination privilege as well. But there are reasons to think that the two contexts are different in ways that may lead to different outcomes. We have already discussed one difference. Apologies are effective only to the extent that they are authentic, and they can only be authentic if the apologist actually feels regret. Because these feelings cannot be coerced, the realization that coercion is everywhere risks undermining our sense of human connection that comes with apology.

There are occasions when self-incrimination also connotes regret, and, when it does, the same argument applies. Consider, for example, self-incrimination challenges to the provision in the Federal Sentencing Guideline that provides for a reduction in sentence for defendants who demonstrate remorse.[96] More often, though, self-incrimination is about surrender rather than acquiescence and about external facts in the world rather than internal mental states. A person cannot be forced to be sorry, but a person can be forced to tell us where he has hidden the murder weapon. Consequently, a broad self-incrimination privilege is unnecessary to serve the libertarian ends that a ban on public apologies accomplishes.

There is a also a second difference. Apologies are typically (although of course not always) directed at private individuals. When the government coerces these apologies to private individuals, it therefore reminds us of the pervasive determinist possibility that all apologies are similarly coerced. In contrast, there is no widespread private analogue to compelled self-incrimination. When a person testifies against herself under threat of contempt, the transaction grows out of a dyatic relationship between individual and government. The relationship is located within the public domain, associated in liberal theory with coercion and, therefore, does not implicate the private realm of freedom. In contrast, coerced apologies are typically triatic: the government attempts to compel a transaction between two individuals. Publicly coerced apologies therefore breach the public/private divide in ways that coerced incriminatory testimony does not.

Indeed, one might even argue that the illusion of radical freedom is best preserved in just those cases when self-incrimination is compelled. Suppose that at the beginning of Mr. Smith's cross-examination, the judge had informed him that he was free not to answer questions he did not want to respond to and that the jury would not hold this failure against him. On these facts, his failure to respond would surely not provide the same object lesson in the possibility of human freedom. Mr. Smith's story resonates because he defied government compulsion, but, in order to have this resonance, there must be government compulsion to defy.

Arrayed against these possibilities are the cases where individuals give in to coercion rather than defy it. If Doe signs the consent form under the threat of contempt, perhaps he will lose his innocent belief in his own agency. And perhaps others, who see the document and know the circumstances under which it is signed, will become confused more generally about when there is consent and when there is "consent." To the extent that we fear these possibilities, there is a case to be made for a Fifth Amendment privilege. To the extent that they seem far fetched, it may just be that the moral right to avoid self-incrimination that liberals value is best protected by abolishing the legal right that they defend.

THE "FIT" PROBLEM REVISITED

Liberals and republicans alike might respond that we have unfairly tilted the playing field by holding them to criteria that radical libertarians and pervasive determinists are permitted to evade. When we considered the liberal and republican arguments, we insisted on making the best possible case for existing text and doctrine. We saw as well that the arguments fit the doctrine tolerably well, albeit with some pulling and hauling.[97] But the radical libertarian and pervasive determinist positions can only be characterized as miserable failures along the Dworkinian "fit" dimension. To be either a radical libertarian or a pervasive determinist is to insist on the wholesale demolition of Fifth Amendment text and doctrine. Why don't these failures of fit defeat the arguments?

There are three possible responses to this problem. First, if we take the fit requirement seriously but nonetheless believe that libertarian and determinist arguments against the privilege are powerful, we might make marginal adjustments limiting the scope of the privilege while still giving effect to enough existing doctrine and text to satisfy the demands of fidelity. We have already seen how some branches of the Court's self-incrimination doctrine can be reconciled with pervasive determinism.[98] Perhaps these branches should be marginally expanded, while others are allowed to whither. Similarly, a radical libertarian who is also concerned about fit might adjust current doctrine somewhat so as to give more scope to the privilege when a self-incriminatory statement connotes contrition and less when it merely provides information.

The difficulty with this approach is that radical libertarianism and pervasive determinism undermine not just a few data points in our set, but the very enterprise we are engaged in. If these views are correct, then the core insights that motivate the privilege are mistaken. How can we possibly erect a coherent body of law on these rotten foundations?

The second possibility, then, is to give up on the libertarian and determinist positions. If we are indeed stuck with the fifth amendment privilege, and if it cannot be coherently reconciled with these philosophical positions, then so much the worse for the philosophical positions. Perhaps in a different country, with different traditions and a different founding document, these views deserve to prevail. In our country, they do not, at least if we are to remain faithful to law in the Dworkinian sense.

However, putting the second option in this way naturally raises an important question, which, in turn, leads to the third possibility. First the question: Suppose it is indeed true that a just conception of the privilege cannot be reconciled with fidelity to law in the Dworkinian sense. Why exactly, should we be faithful to law? In the discussion so far, we have been subjecting various philosophical positions to Dworkinian criteria. But why not reverse the procedure and subject the criteria to the philosophical positions? If we start with libertarian or determinist positions and examine the fit requirement from these perspectives, fit itself turns out not to fit very well. The third possibility, then, is to jettison the fit requirement rather than the philosophical positions that conflict with it. This possibility, in turn, circles back to an "unsettlement" version of constitutional law that treats it as a means of opening up options and destabilizing resolutions rather than as a means of constraining choice.

Both pervasive determinists and radical libertarians are likely to be unsympathetic to claims that Dworkinian law binds us. For a pervasive determinist, decisions made by the framers and by subsequent courts interpreting their work are just more examples of power exercised by some over others. Exercises of power and submission to such exercises may be pervasive and inevitable, but that is very different from saying that there is a moral obligation to submit.

Radical libertarians are likely to be more hostile still to Dworkinian analysis. For them, the fit requirement is still another way to avoid the hard fact of human choice. Dworkinians sometimes tell themselves (and us) that as much as they would like to act differently, on occasion they simply cannot do what is right, for to do the "right" thing is to violate their deep commitment to the rule of law.[99] The first reaction of radical libertarians to these pleas may be to wonder what exactly it means to do the "right" thing in a random and purposeless universe. Nonetheless, they will surely also want to insist that Dworkinian complaints about impotence are a self-inflicted delusion. In fact, there is precisely nothing preventing us from doing the "right" thing—nothing, that is, aside from the cowardly denial of our own responsibility—a denial that pompously masquerades as "the rule of law." As we have already seen, for radical libertarians law and rules have nothing to do with freedom. Freedom is about opening up possibilities, not shutting them down, about destabilizing existing structures, not exaggerating their hold on us.

It is just these terrifying realizations that explode both a Fifth Amendment privilege and a Dworkinian fit requirement. If there ultimately remains a reason to reject the radical libertarian argument, perhaps it is that this is simply more terror than many of us can reasonably be expected to live with. If this proves true, then I suppose we are stuck with the privilege after all. At least, though, we should stop pretending that its recognition marks a triumph for human freedom.

CHAPTER 5

Silence and Intimacy in the Station House

ON JANUARY 22, 1957, VINCENT JOSEPH SPANO, a twenty-five-year-old Italian immigrant with a record of mental illness, was drinking at a bar.[1] Also at the bar was Frankie Palermo, a former professional boxer who had fought in Madison Square Garden. Palermo took some of Spano's money. Spano followed him out of the bar to get it back, whereupon Palermo knocked Spano down and kicked him in the head three or four times. Dazed from the blows, Spano vomited. After the bartender applied some ice to his head, Spano walked to his apartment, got a gun, and walked back to a candy store where he thought he would find Palermo. Palermo was indeed there in the company of three friends, at least two of whom were ex-convicts. Spano fired five shots, two of which struck and killed Palermo.

On February 1, a grand jury indicted Spano for first degree murder, and a warrant was issued for his arrest. Two days later, Spano called Gaspar Bruno, a close friend, who was then a rookie police officer. Spano told him that he was planning to get a lawyer and turn himself in, facts that Bruno duly reported to his superiors.

The following day, Spano secured counsel, who advised him to answer no questions and then surrendered him to police custody. Police began questioning him at 7:15 P.M. Spano steadfastly followed his attorney's advice for six hours as waves of officers questioned him about the offense. At one point, he asked to speak to his lawyer, but the request was refused. Eventually, at about 12:40 A.M., the police hit on the idea of using Bruno to extract a confession. Bruno falsely told Spano that their earlier conversation had gotten him "in a lot of trouble," and reminded his friend that he had a pregnant wife and three children who would be at risk if Bruno lost his job. Spano refused to talk and again asked to see an attorney. Instead of complying with this request, the police twice more

95

directed Bruno to play on Spano's sympathies. Finally, on the fourth try, Spano broke and agreed to make a statement.

The statement began at 3:25 A.M. and was completed at 4:05 A.M. When they were done, the police took Spano on a search for the bridge from which he had thrown the gun. At 6:00 A.M., some eleven hours after his arrest, Spano made additional incriminating statements. These statements, as well as the statements he had made earlier, were introduced at Spano's trial, and based upon this evidence, Spano was convicted of first degree murder.

Spano's schooling had ended after junior high school. Since then, he had maintained a regular record of employment. He had no criminal record. The jury failed to recommend mercy. The judge sentenced him to die.

Spano's case is quite dramatic, and arose a half century ago. As we shall see, however, versions of these events continue to play out in hundreds of police stations and courtrooms across the country. How should we react to cases like this?

In this chapter, I argue that we ought to be deeply troubled, but that the trouble does not stem from the source on which the law has focused. I make two large and interrelated assertions that run counter to the conventional wisdom. First, the courts have traditionally treated the kind of self-incrimination claim discussed in the last chapter as central to the Fifth Amendment and the kind of station house interrogation to which Spano was subjected as peripheral. I argue that this hierarchy is upside down. As we saw in the last chapter, "core" self-incrimination claims, where the government utilizes formal processes to threaten a recalcitrant witness with contempt if he does not speak, rest on a shaky normative foundation. In contrast, I argue, the claims of suspects questioned in the station house merit our urgent attention.

Second, when the courts have in fact turned their attention to these station house interrogations, they have focused on questions of individual choice. For years, the Court resolved these cases by asking whether the statements were "voluntary" or whether the suspect's will had been "overborne."[2] Since 1966, the Court has shifted focus and inquired whether the police complied with the requirements of *Miranda v. Arizona*.[3] The *Miranda* requirements themselves, however, are based upon the self-incrimination clause. Thus, the ultimate focus remains on whether the statements were "compelled" in the constitutional sense. In this chapter, I argue that this voluntariness/compulsion focus is misguided. Instead, the question we should ask is whether police interrogation techniques invade a protected private sphere by abusing intimacy and illusions of intimacy and, if so, whether that invasion and abuse are justifiable.

Before turning to these arguments, we need to situate the problem of station house confessions in its legal setting.

A BRIEF JURISPRUDENTIAL HISTORY OF STATION HOUSE CONFESSIONS

For the first half of the twentieth century, the self-incrimination privilege played little role in regulation of station house confessions. The privilege was thought completely inapplicable to the states until 1964, when the Court reversed earlier precedent[4] and held that the self-incrimination right was "incorporated" within the due process clause of the Fourteenth Amendment.[5] Of course, most station house interrogations occur on the state level. Moreover, even with respect to federal investigations, efforts to apply the privilege to police interrogation foundered on the compulsion requirement. Police officers usually do not have the power to threaten a suspect with contempt if he does not talk, and the kind of informal pressure that officers regularly applied was thought not to amount to compulsion in the constitutional sense.[6]

Starting in the 1930s, the Court nonetheless attempted to regulate tactics in the station house by resorting to the Fourteenth Amendment's due process clause. Although the self-incrimination clause was not directly applicable to the states, the Court held that the more general guarantee of due process included a right to the exclusion of statements secured by police tactics that caused the suspect's will to be overborne.[7] In the beginning the Court restricted its oversight to cases involving physical violence,[8] but it gradually expanded the scope of its protection to include some forms of psychological pressure as well.[9] By the 1960s, it had decided some thirty-five cases on this ground. Among them was the case of Vincent Joseph Spano, whose conviction was reversed in 1959.[10]

Throughout this period, the Court attempted to make distinctions based upon factors like the length of the interrogation, the suspect's access to legal counsel or to family and friends, the suspect's sophistication and mental state, and whether there were various forms of mistreatment. It emphasized, however, that there was no single "litmus-paper test"[11] for whether a violation had occurred and that each case had to be considered based upon all of the facts and circumstances.

There were numerous problems with this approach that became increasingly apparent as the Court gained more experience with it. One difficulty was doctrinal. The Court never made clear whether the violation of due process occurred at the moment when the statement was extracted or whether it occurred when the defendant was convicted on the basis of the statement.[12] There were difficulties with both theories. Under the first approach, the application of the pressure was, itself, a deprivation of liberty without due process of law. The subsequent suppression of the statement was required not because its introduction was an independent constitutional violation, but because this was necessary to deter or punish the violation that occurred in the station house. This deterrence theory does not fit well with the Court's contemporary view that the Constitution did not mandate an exclusionary rule to deter Fourth Amendment violations.[13] Moreover, even if this approach made some sense in the early cases dealing with physical violence, it was hard to see why the use of more subtle forms of psychological coercion violated the Constitution. Recall that the Court's position during this period was that the self-incrimination clause had no applicability to these cases. Given that fact, it had to be the coercion itself, and not the self-incrimination it produced, that was the problem. But the government regularly uses the threat of long jail terms to coerce its citizens. The Court never explained why mere psychological coercion was worse than this.

Hence, the second approach. On this theory, the problem was not with the coercion per se, but with the use of coerced testimony to convict the defendant. Unfortunately, however, the Court again failed to articulate clearly just why such use deprived the defendant of due process. Granted, use of patently unreliable statements gained through torture or the threat of torture might turn the formal trial into a mockery. Such a trial is, literally, not the process that is due before a defendant is convicted of a criminal offense. The problem was that the Court applied the same rule to cases like *Spano* where no physical coercion was used and where there was little doubt as to the truthfulness of the statements. Use of statements like this did not corrupt the basic truth-finding function of the trial. Why were convictions gained through this use unconstitutional?

Beyond these theoretical problems, the Court's approach posed severe practical difficulties. Because each case turned on its own facts and circumstances, the Court's decisions had very limited precedential value. The result was that neither the lower courts nor the police themselves had a clear picture of what was permitted or forbidden. With the Supreme Court able to hear only a few confession cases each year, outcomes in the thousands of cases that never reached the High Court took on an unsettling, random quality.[14]

Beginning in the late 1950s, the Court began to experiment with some different approaches. Some of its cases hinted that it might set a time limit between arrest and arraignment, the period during which most interrogation occurred.[15] Others suggested that the problem might be solved by making the Sixth Amendment right to counsel available during the interrogation period.[16]

Ultimately, in *Miranda v. Arizona*, the Court settled on a Fifth Amendment self-incrimination approach. Two doctrinal moves paved the way for this shift. First, two years before *Miranda*, the Court finally held that the self-incrimination clause was applicable to the states.[17] Second, in *Miranda* itself, the Court seemed to hold that the confluence of custody of a suspect and interrogation by the police automatically constituted "compulsion" within the meaning of the clause.[18] Recall from the last chapter that the clause is violated whenever there is both compulsion and incrimination. Since custodial interrogation definitionally amounted to compulsion, it followed that statements gained through such interrogation had to be excluded in order to avoid incrimination.

If the *Miranda* Court had stopped there, it would have solved the station house interrogation problem by pretty much ending the practice. However, the Court went on to provide a road map to police officers if they wanted to dissipate the compulsion, thereby permitting incrimination.

Before questioning the suspect, police were directed to warn the defendant that he had a right to remain silent, that anything he said might be used against him in a criminal proceeding, that he had a right to a lawyer, and that if he could not afford to hire one, a lawyer would be appointed to represent him.[19] Contrary to popular misconceptions, the Court did not hold that the Constitution mandated these warnings or required the police to provide them. The warnings are significant only because they form part of a process whereby the police could dissipate the compulsion that otherwise existed. Recall, compulsion standing alone is not unconstitutional under the self-incrimination clause. So long as police do not wish to produce incriminating statements, they remain free to compel and, hence, not to warn.[20] If they want to incriminate, however, they must not compel, and the warnings helped to dissipate compulsion.

The rest of the process that eliminated the compulsion consisted of the suspect's waiver of his rights. Once warned, a defendant could, if he wished, indicate that he did not want a lawyer present and that he wanted to answer questions. Through the magic of this warning and waiver procedure, these answers were now no longer compelled, and, of course, because they were not compelled, they could be incriminating. The resulting statements were therefore admissible in the suspect's trial.[21]

Miranda produced a huge uproar. Shortly after the decision, Congress passed legislation purporting to undo the holding,[22] and generations of (mostly Republican) administrations have promised to appoint Justices who would overrule it. Yet, miraculously, the decision remains on the books. Indeed, in 2000, in *Dickerson v. United States,*[23] the Supreme Court, in an opinion written by Chief Justice William Rehnquist, reaffirmed the decision and held unconstitutional the statute that purported to overrule it.

Meanwhile, a large body of complex law has grown up around the basic *Miranda* doctrine. In some respects, the ruling has been cut back. For example, the court has fashioned an "emergency exception" that permits the prosecution to introduce statements secured in the absence of *Miranda* warnings if interrogation is necessary to protect the public safety.[24]

In other ways, though, the Court has actually extended *Miranda,* holding for example that once a suspect asks for counsel, any subsequent statement is automatically inadmissible even if the defendant is fully warned and waives his rights.[25] As critics of this holding have pointed out, this requirement amounts to a second per se rule on top of the basic *Miranda* rule.[26] The only exception to it arises when the defendant himself initiates subsequent conversations after claiming his counsel right.[27]

These developments have, in turn, generated both a doctrinal and an empirical controversy. The doctrinal argument starts with the familiar point that self-incrimination protection takes hold only if there is compulsion. This requirement explains why the *Miranda* Court felt bound to insist that the confluence of custody and interrogation created compulsion as a matter of law. But to say that something is true "as a matter of law" is tantamount to saying that the Court will treat it as true even if it is not. Critics of *Miranda* argue that it is surely possible to imagine cases where an unwarned suspect is questioned after arrest, but the resulting statement is nonetheless not compelled. Suppose, for example, that the suspect is already aware of his rights, that the police do no more than pose a single straightforward question, and the suspect responds simply because he deeply regrets his conduct and thinks that a confession is the right course of action. *Miranda*'s opponents complain that the Court has never explained the legal basis for ordering the suppression of such a statement.[28]

Oddly, friends of the initial *Miranda* decision have also become troubled by the equation of custody and interrogation with compulsion, albeit for different reasons. They have criticized the Court for allowing statements to be admitted in circumstances where ordinary self-incrimination principles would require exclusion. For example, there is no "emergency exception" in ordinary self-incrimination jurisprudence. If the products of custodial interrogation are really "compelled," as the *Miranda* Court insisted, then why can such statements be incriminating just because there is an emergency?[29]

This criticism from both sides, in turn, led to speculation, some of which was encouraged by the Justices themselves,[30] that somehow *Miranda* rights were not "real" Fifth Amendment rights at all.[31] Instead, the Court seemed to be asserting a vaguely grounded authority to create extraconstitutional doctrine for the enforcement of constitutional rights—doctrine that, perhaps, could be modified by Congress. In *Dickerson,* the Court ended this speculation by holding that *Miranda* was a constitutionally required rule. Unfortunately, however, the opinion did little to explain why, if this were true, *Miranda* doctrine differed from standard Fifth Amendment doctrine.

The empirical controversy concerns the actual effect of the *Miranda* decision. Opponents and proponents of the *Miranda* rule have repeatedly clashed over whether in fact it has obstructed law enforcement. There is some evidence that criminal clearance rates declined in the wake of *Miranda,* but these studies have been sharply contested, and it is virtually impossible to determine whether there is a causal connection between the case and changes in conviction rates.[32]

Interestingly, *Miranda* has also been criticized on the ground that it has actually loosened constraints on police interrogation. *Miranda* seems to have had the ironic effect of sharply limiting judicial supervision over police tactics that arguably lead to involuntary confessions in the traditional sense. For example, it is at best doubtful if Spano's conviction would be reversed today if the police comported with the technical *Miranda* requirements. As a formal matter, a defendant is still free to challenge a confession on the ground that it was involuntary even if she received *Miranda* warnings. As a practical matter, very few of these challenges succeed. Physical violence is still out of bounds, but the courts today regularly permit the kind of police threats, fabrication, and manipulation that might well have led to suppression of statements in the pre-*Miranda* era—so long, that is, as *Miranda*'s warning and waiving ritual is duly observed.[33]

Although these doctrinal and empirical issues are interesting, they also tend to distract us from what should be the central questions. As legal scholars like David Strauss,[34] Richard Fallon,[35] and Mitchell Berman[36] have pointed out, it is hardly unusual for the Court to supplement constitutional language with legal doctrine designed to implement that language. Nothing in the constitutional text provides for different standards of review in different categories of equal protection cases, for elaborate rules under the first amendment for different sorts of speech using public property, or for the complex standards the Court has devised to deal with regulation of private property. Indeed, there is nothing in the constitutional text stating that the remedy for use of a defendant's compelled statement against him is reversal of his conviction. Like all of this doctrine, *Miranda* is not "constitutional" in the sense that it is not directly commanded by the constitutional text, but it is at least plausibly necessary to enforce that text and apply it to the real world.

Participants in the doctrinal dispute also tend to ignore the inherent ambiguity and flexibility of constitutional language. We have already seen that the words of the self-incrimination clause, like many other constitutional provisions, are quite open ended. As discussed in greater detail below, in a document filled with broad and allusive language "compulsion" stands out as an especially slippery term. It does not refer to things that exist in the world like, say, the "persons, houses, papers, and effects" protected by the Fourth Amendment. Rather, it makes reference to a psychological state that is, as we shall see, more than a little difficult to define precisely. Given this imprecision, it is at least plausible that the kind of pressure that inevitably accompanies custodial interrogation always amounts to compulsion. Of course, it is also plausible that at least some custodial interrogation does not amount to compulsion. The question we ought to ask, then, is not whether custodial interrogation *is* compulsion, but whether it *ought to be treated as* compulsion. Answering this question, in turn, requires some sort of normative theory about what is wrong and right about such interrogation.

Similarly, the bare empirics of station house confessions do not resolve the crucial normative question. Suppose it were indeed true that *Miranda* warnings caused many suspects who might have otherwise confessed to remain silent. Simply looking at the numbers tells us nothing about whether this outcome is good or bad. The *Miranda* Court presumably thought its efforts were going to accomplish something. If, as *Miranda*'s defenders sometimes claim, the decision had virtually no effect on the behavior of suspects,[37] this might actually demonstrate that the decision is misguided rather than sensible.[38] Conversely, if as *Miranda*'s critics sometimes claim, the Court's ruling has led to a sharp decline in confessions,[39] this fact might be cause for celebration if these confessions were secured in violation of fundamental constitutional rights.

The crucial questions, then, are what can we say normatively about station house confessions and about the effort to control the police tactics that elicit them? It is to these questions that we now turn.

COMPULSION'S DEAD END

The standard liberal response to this normative puzzle is the claim that compelled incrimination violates human and constitutional rights. This is so, it is thought, because a core privacy right is invaded when people are forced to implicate themselves in their own punishment. We have seen that the best version of this argument is related in interesting ways to intuitions about the ability of individuals to balance their public and private obligations in a free society.[40] Nonetheless, for reasons that I have already set out at length in Chapter 4, I find this argument ultimately unpersuasive. Either such statements "belong" to the suspect or they do not. One might say that a suspect's compelled statements are not really "his," precisely because they have been forced out of him. But if this is true, then the suspect has not been implicated in his own punishment in the way that liberals claim. Conversely, perhaps, as radical libertarians insist, the suspect has moral responsibility for the statements even though they are "compelled." Despite the compulsion, the suspect could simply refuse to cooperate. But if this is true, then the suspect has been afforded the choice between cooperation and resistance. That is, after all, why the suspect is morally responsible for making the statement. Since it is precisely this choice that liberals demand, their objection to "compelled" statements evaporates.

Thus, the first problem with compulsion-based regulation of station house confessions is that it lands us back in the morass of Fifth Amendment theory. At least for present purposes, though, I am prepared to concede that this complex and controversial argument will not persuade everyone. Even if one is unpersuaded I want to insist that there is a second more straightforward reason why the concept of compulsion cannot ground the regulation of station house interrogation. The reason is simple: The concept has no analytic content.

Before setting out this argument, I want to bracket two groups of cases that need not concern us here. First, we should put to one side instances of physical coercion or the threat of physical coercion. We shall see in the next chapter that the normative argument against even these practices is weaker than is commonly supposed, but that argument requires separate treatment. Even if we ultimately conclude that physical cocrcion should be out of bounds, we would still need to confront cases like *Spano* where no such coercion was applied.

Second, we can eliminate cases where government officials utilize formal contempt as a means of securing statements. However mysterious our inhibitions against the use of this technique, there is at least no mystery about what the technique consists of. Unfortunately, though, the same cannot be said about the use of informal "compulsion."

What, precisely, do we mean when we say that a suspect like Spano has been "compelled" in circumstances where government agents have used neither physical force nor the threat of contempt to secure statements? One need only hold oneself open to the mildest and least controversial version of pervasive determinism or radical libertarianism to see the problem. At the moment before Spano made his decision to confess, there were numerous factors that weighed in favor of and against his taking this step. In favor: the prospect of relieving his guilt; the fear of harm to his friend Bruno; the desire for sleep; the knowledge that the psychologically painful and exhausting interrogation might go on indefinitely if he did not confess; perhaps the fear of police violence; the hope for better treatment if he did confess. Against: his lawyer's advice; the fear of conviction; the shame of acknowledging his wrongful act; perhaps sheer stubbornness. Spano balanced these factors and came to a judgment.

Like all judgments, this one did not occur in a vacuum. His decision was the product of interaction with other human beings and embedded in predictions about how he would be treated by those other human beings if he made one choice rather than the other. Of course, one could, if one wished, label these surrounding circumstances as "compulsion," but this label merely states a conclusion, rather than providing a reason for the conclusion. *All* decisions made by human beings are embedded in a network of human interaction and predictions about how others will react to the decisions. To claim that all these decisions are compelled simply for this reason goes far beyond moderate determinist or libertarian insights. It is to accept the most extreme version of pervasive determinism and to deny the very possibility of human freedom and responsibility.

Consider, for example, a college graduate choosing between law school and medical school. Just as Spano was confronted with reasons why one choice was better than another, so too a young person deciding on a career confronts a variety of predicted consequences that flow from one alternative or the other. Like Spano, a young person may confront subtle or overt pressure, albeit more likely from parents and loved ones than from the police. In obvious ways, the decision may be sharply constrained by financial factors. Just as Spano worried about a seemingly endless interrogation, a prospective student may consider the comparative physical exhaustion produced by medical school and law school. She may have deep worries about her future if she chooses one course of conduct rather than another. Normally, though, we do not say that the person who ends up choosing, say, law school over medical school, was "compelled" to do so. On the contrary, decisions of this kind are usually taken to be examples of free and rational decision making. To treat all such decisions as "compelled," and, therefore, not worthy of respect is to lay the groundwork for totalitarian intervention.

It is important to emphasize that the argument I have made so far does not demonstrate that all decisions are free or that they all are coerced and that these concepts therefore have no meaning. All I have shown is that the concepts are not self-defining, and that the Court was obligated to develop some mediating principles that differentiated between decisions that are not attributable to individual choice and decisions that are. This is precisely the task that the Court failed to accomplish in the pre-*Miranda* period. It never managed to explain when factors influencing a decision were "pressure" that amounted to "coercion," and when they were simply "considerations" that contributed to "choice."

The Court's failure stemmed from a fundamental problem with the task it set for itself. It attempted to treat "voluntariness" as if it were an external, analytic category, when in fact it describes a subjective mental state. As an analytic category, "voluntariness" is easy to deconstruct. As we have just seen, all decisions are made under constraint, and it is always possible to characterize the constraint as making the choice involuntary. But this analytic problem does nothing to alter the subjective sense we all have that sometimes we act because we "want" to and sometimes we act because we are "forced" to.

The problem the Court faced was that it proved impossible to translate these subjective states into categories that the law could use. A working police officer needs to know which tactics are permissible and which are not. Mysterious, nonlogical and nonmaterial states of mind are of little help in guiding this inquiry. The problem is made still worse by the fact that these states of mind, even if they were externally accessible, are quite unstable. It is not unusual, for example, for people to feel at one time that their own choices are voluntary, while thinking at another time that they are really coerced. Imagine, for example, an unhappy, middle-aged lawyer who, perhaps through therapy, "realizes" in retrospect that his parents forced him to go to law school.

In order to differentiate between these ephemeral and ill-defined mental states, the Court desperately needed a "test," some sort of standard that existed in the world and that police and lower courts could understand and apply. This imperative is what produced *Miranda*. Instead of regularly confronting police officers with an unanswerable metaphysical question, *Miranda* allowed them to rely on a bureaucratic ritual. Whereas the existence of "compulsion" is the stuff of interminable and unreadable philosophy dissertations, the *Miranda* warnings fit on the back of an index card. It is hardly surprising, then, that even some of the conservative jurists on the Supreme Court, whose allies spent years carping about *Miranda*, backed away from overruling it when the opportunity arose. As Chief Justice Rehnquist wrote with characteristic understatement, "experience suggests that the [pre-*Miranda*] totality of circumstances test . . . is more difficult than *Miranda* for law enforcement officers to conform to, and for courts to apply in a consistent manner."[41]

True enough, but the ease of application derived from the fact that the Court had given up on defining the subjective mental state that we care about. *Miranda* is easy to conform to precisely because it has so little to do with the kind of compulsion that worries liberals. The real problem with *Miranda* is not that interrogation and custody do not automatically amount to compulsion, but that warnings and waiver do not automatically amount to freedom. It is deeply implausible that all, or even most, suspects feel that they are making free choices to confess just because the warning and waiver ritual is observed. When deciding whether to waive their rights, these suspects are subject to the same coercive influences that troubled the Court in the pre-*Miranda* period. The only difference is that now the coercion comes at both the waiver stage and the confession stage, whereas before it came only at the confession stage.

If this argument is correct, then it follows that the station house confession problem simply cannot be addressed by focusing on issues of coercion and compulsion. Perhaps we should be concerned about the subjective, psychological sense that suspects often have that they are not acting freely. Unfortunately, however, as the pre-*Miranda* cases demonstrated, there is no plausible way for the law to capture or respond to these concerns. What the law can do is to control external behavior. It can impose bureaucratic procedures on the police and force suspects to execute forms. But no one should confuse this external behavior with the subjective reality that was the source of our concern in the first place.

This dilemma, in turn, suggests a deep irony. *Miranda* was the work of criminal justice liberals and, two generations after it was decided, liberals remain its staunchest defenders. Yet liberals, of all people, should understand why *Miranda* had to fail. Recall the republican and communitarian demand for state institutions and practices that are less formal and more in accord with our values.[42] The liberal response to this demand has been an insistence that when the state embraces these values, it invariably distorts them. So, liberals insist, public apologies are not real apologies, and public support for private institutions like marriage and religion inevitably water down these deeply particularist institutions with an impersonal universalism.

Liberals should understand that precisely the same problem arises when the state purports to foster a subjective sense of freedom. Bureaucratically defined "freedom" is not and can never be real freedom, and to confuse the two is to pervert the kind of freedom that we ought to care about. Because *Miranda* does just that, it leaves us with the worst of both worlds. We end up with neither real freedom in the station house nor with the appropriate suspicion and unease that might come with the realization that government coercion is invading a private sphere. Although *Miranda* does little to dissipate the psychological reality of coercion that many suspects experience, it has done a great deal to legitimate the use of tactics that, prior to *Miranda,* were thought to be deeply problematic. Liberals should understand this problem. If they did, they might happily join the ranks of *Miranda*'s opponents.

INTIMACY IN THE STATION HOUSE

It does not follow, however, that there is no good liberal critique of station house interrogation. There is plenty to criticize once one focuses on the real problem. The proper concern about station house interrogation is not that the state has failed to respect private values like psychological freedom. Instead, we ought to worry about the opposite problem. Station house interrogation is troubling because the interrogators often embrace private values themselves or use those values for government ends, thereby distorting them in just the way that liberals decry.

Spano's interrogation illustrates the risks. Two aspects of the interrogation merit special attention. First, notice the informal nature of the coercion that police applied. The officers were in face-to-face contact with Spano. So far as the record reveals, they were not following any preestablished rules or protocol. There was no time limit set on the questioning. The interrogation occurred in the middle of the night rather than during normal business hours. It could not be observed by the public, and no public record was kept of the events that transpired.

This sort of coercion stands in sharp contrast with the formal and ritualized coercion that is the more normal stuff of Fifth Amendment claims. The prototypical Fifth Amendment case involves a government subpoena that, if disobeyed, is followed by a contempt citation. When a suspect responds to the subpoena, he reports to a court house during daylight hours. He can consult with counsel, and he is asked questions in a public or quasi-public setting where a record is kept of the proceedings. If he refuses to answer questions, he is not usually hectored. Instead, the questioning stops and he is brought before a judge who typically has not been involved in the questioning. If he persists in his refusal, the judge follows established procedures to incarcerate the witness in a facility designed for this purpose.

The second aspect of Spano's interrogation that merits attention is the attempt by the police to use Spano's particularist relationships in order to secure a statement. This use was most obvious when the police brought Spano's friend, Bruno, into the picture. Apparently, Spano ultimately talked because he was unwilling to put his own legal interests ahead of the welfare of his friend.

There are also other, much more subtle ways in which Spano's interrogation and others like it depend on interpersonal relationships. In his brilliant interdisciplinary study of confessions, humanities professor Peter Brooks discusses at length the ways in which skillful interrogation depends upon the tie that the interrogating officer establishes with the suspect.[43] It is crucial to this process that the suspect be cut off from the outside world. This isolation creates a strong bond of dependency between the interrogator and the suspect in much the way that hostages sometimes grow dependent upon their captors.

In the closed room, suspects "transfer" onto interrogators relationships with intimates and authority figures just as transference occurs in classical psychoanalysis. To be sure, the interrogator (or at least one of the interrogators when the police use the "Mutt and Jeff" technique) may be a frightening figure who subtly or not so subtly hints at violence. The suspect's dependence on the interrogator for his personal safety causes a kind of regression to his earliest relationship with his parents. This threat of violence is coupled with a promise of help that encourages similar regression. The interrogator (or perhaps a different interrogator) also presents himself as the suspect's friend, who minimizes his guilt, sympathizes with him because of his predicament, and wants to help him out of his difficulties. Brooks quotes from David Simon's classic firsthand study of the Baltimore, Maryland, detective squad:

The effect of the illusion is profound, distorting as it does the natural hostility between hunter and hunted, transforming it until it resembles a relationship more symbiotic than adversarial. That is the lie, and when the roles are perfectly performed, deceit surpasses itself, becoming manipulation on a grand scale and ultimately an act of betrayal. Because what occurs in an interrogation room is indeed little more than a carefully staged drama, a choreographed performance that allows a detective and his suspect to find common ground where none exists. There, in a carefully controlled purgatory, the guilty proclaim their malefactions, though rarely in any form that allows for contrition or resembles an unequivocal admission.[44]

Both the informal character of station house interrogation and its dependence upon the illusion of intimacy threaten liberal values. The informality is troubling because it leaves the process vulnerable to the particularist reactions of police officers. An officer confronting a suspect in isolation and at close range is bound to develop personal feelings toward the suspect. Conceivably the officer might empathize with him, but more likely he will feel anger, disgust, or impatience. Indeed, an officer who felt none of these emotions, or no emotions at all, would be a very strange person. It is deeply unnatural to engage in close contact with another human being in isolation and over an extended period of time without developing some feelings about that human being.

Yet it is just these feelings that threaten universalist values. Liberals, like republicans, believe that government officials should be governed by disinterested impartiality, rather than personal connection. We do not want these officials giving criminal suspects a "break" because they like them. Nor do we want what is more likely to happen, government officials abusing suspects because they hate them or are angered by them. The formal contempt process is designed to enforce the requirement of impersonal equality when the government acts. Of course, it works imperfectly. There is no process that can altogether eliminate human reaction to other humans. Still, the starkly formal and impersonal character of judicial proceedings provides a break against particularism. It is important that in most cases the judge who imposes the penalty has not been involved in the questioning, that the coercion is applied according to preestablished rules and with preestablished limits, and that the entire procedure is ritualized and public.[45]

Suppose, though, that the officer resists the pull of particularism. Oddly, the second problem, false intimacy, arises not because the interrogating officer forms a particularist bond with the suspect, but because he creates the illusion of such a relationship without actually forming it. The problem here is not that suspects are "compelled" at least in the sense that we usually think of compulsion. It is rather that they consent and then are betrayed. The betrayal comes about because the illusion of particularist relationship is utilized for universalist ends. On this version, a thoroughly professional and universalist interrogating officer creates the impression that he cares about the suspect as an individual when nothing could be further from the truth. The officer is not the suspect's friend, advisor, and helper. The officer's job is to advance the public welfare by solving crimes and punishing the guilty. It would be a violation of his duty to deviate from this task because of actual friendship or special empathy. But one way to accomplish his goal is to create the illusion of friendship and empathy so as to exploit the suspect's desperate need for connection and for help in a moment of crisis.

For liberals, these tactics are deeply immoral because they debase the kind of interconnection and communication that is central to our humanity. Interestingly, this concern, rather than the concern about compulsion, provides a plausible grounding for the *Miranda* doctrine. This is true from the points of view of both the interrogating officer and the suspect. *Miranda*'s requirements are usually thought of as providing a warning for defendants, but their role in warning the police themselves is often overlooked. Even if the warnings accomplished nothing else, they remind police officers that they are not operating in a law-free zone. There are rules and rituals that must be observed, and there are sanctions that will be meted out if they are ignored. The very fact that these rules and rituals apply bureaucratically, automatically, and to everyone emphasizes to the police that we are in the realm of universalism.

From the suspect's point of view, the warnings provide a reminder that the interrogating officer is not his friend. If the suspect wants a true supporter, then one will be provided for him, at no cost if he cannot afford to pay.[46] But if he chooses instead to talk, what he says can and will be used against him, rather than for his own benefit.

Thus, if our concern is with false and real particularism in the station house, *Miranda* is a step in the right direction. It is only a step, however, and not a large one. Although *Miranda* warnings remind officers that they are subject to law, they do little to ensure the enforcement of law. Officers remain free to provide the warnings and then proceed as they would otherwise. Even when they violate the law, it is often their word against the suspect's in a swearing contest that they are likely to win.

Similarly, the reminder that the officer is not the suspect's friend is marginally useful, but it hardly prevents the officer from creating a false sense of intimacy. The officer as friend will convey to the suspect in one way or another that the *Miranda* warnings are a mere formality, so much paper work that the folks upstairs make us fill out before we get down to the business of getting the suspect out of this mess. Once these bureaucratic details are taken care of, officers remain free to exploit the suspect with all the subtle and not so subtle psychological tricks that they have used for years.

If we really wanted to do something about real and false intimacy in the station house, how would we take care of the problem? The solution is one that most liberals will not like but that, I think, they ought to embrace. We ought to import the formality of the court room into the station house. If police want to coerce suspects into talking, they should do so in the way that prosecutors apply coercion. They should be given the power to apply to a judge for a formal order requiring the suspect's cooperation. If the cooperation is not forthcoming, the suspect should be held in contempt and jailed for a reasonable period or until he agrees to submit to interrogation. If it is forthcoming, the questioning should be done in a public setting according to preestablished rules and in the presence of counsel.[47]

Subjecting criminal suspects to the threat of contempt may seem harsh, but is it really worse than the current regime where the police exploit a suspect's fear, loneliness, and vulnerability in order to destroy him? Yes, a contempt citation pressures the defendant to talk, but he is pressured in the way that the state should apply pressure, through disinterested, cold, and unemotional workings of the legal process. As heartless as it sometimes seems, that process discourages fatal confusion between the world of connection and special caring and the world of public values, means/ends rationality, and equal treatment. At least for liberals, it is vital that we keep this distinction straight, for to give up on it is to violate the essential integrity of the person.

Moreover, it is worth emphasizing that the fact that a suspect is held in contempt does not mean that he will or should speak. Here, as elsewhere, there should be limits on the extent of the coercion the government is allowed to apply. We do not insist on life sentences for pick pockets, and neither should we demand such sentences for people who insist on remaining silent.

Depending on the seriousness of the underlying offense, this means that some suspects will simply serve out their contempt sentences and never talk. There is no reason, though, why this result should especially trouble us. After all, under our current system, some suspects do not talk at the station house. This refusal to cooperate is the inevitable byproduct of our commitment to the individual right to balance for oneself the duties of citizenship against the pull of particularist obligation. At least part of me admires Susan McDougall who was held in contempt and spent months in prison rather than implicate Bill and Hillary Clinton, although of course part of me also objects to her refusal to perform her public duty. For reasons explored in the last chapter, no one has the moral authority to decide for her how she should strike the exquisitely difficult balance between personal loyalty and public obligation. Still, *just because* this balancing is the individual's responsibility, we should not excuse individuals from the requirement that they make this hard choice. It is right, then, that Susan McDougall, and, by extension criminal suspects, be incarcerated for contempt, but also right that at least some of these suspects resist the pressure and insist on remaining silent.

There remains, of course, the pervasive determinist critique of the liberal position and the radical libertarian response. Since we have rehearsed these arguments several times already, there is no need for more than a brief description of how they work in this context. For pervasive determinists, we live our entire lives in a metaphorical station house. The notion that there is a private sphere where people are authentically connected is an illusion no more plausible than the illusion that an interrogating officer is the suspect's friend. All private relationships are dominated by coercion, transference, and exploitation. There is no danger of confusion between what goes on in the station house and what goes on in the private sphere because there is no difference between the two.

But although pervasive determinists are likely to view liberal worries as so much sentimental claptrap, that same skepticism leaves them unable to advance an argument for why we should care about catching and convicting criminals in the first place. After all, from a perspective of pervasive determinism, criminal violence is only one more example of the violence, deceit, and betrayal that is everywhere. Although pervasive determinists are unlikely to share liberal concerns about police overreaching, neither do they have ground to complain about procedural requirements that "handcuff" the police.

Skepticism that runs this deep is profoundly unattractive, and the radical libertarian move saves us from it. On this view, skepticism provides no refuge from the necessity of choice. One choice we might make that is compatible with radical libertarianism is to structure criminal investigations so as to maintain the illusion of freedom. It is at least plausible that such a structure involves the walling off of the public sphere of power from the private sphere of intimacy. Formalizing police procedures so as to make clear that they are not intimate is a step in this direction. In this way, radical libertarians once again back into something close to the liberal position.

SILENCE, SELF-INCRIMINATION, AND SPANO'S FATE

After the Supreme Court reversed his conviction, Vincent Spano was charged for a second time with first degree murder and entered a not guilty plea. Midway through his trial, however, the prosecution permitted him to plead guilty to manslaughter in the first degree. The judge thereupon sentenced him to ten to twenty years in prison.[48] He was released in 1968, and successfully completed parole in 1975.[49]

Stepping back from all the complex theoretical argumentation, I cannot say that this is an unjust outcome. On the contrary, I would be uncomfortable to say the least with a legal regime that sent Vincent Joseph Spano to his death. To the extent that the Supreme Court's regulation of station house confessions prevented that death, it surely contributed to the cause of justice. These observations, in turn, lead back to the concern that a wholesale rethinking of the self-incrimination privilege might have the unintended consequence of making our criminal justice system even harsher than it presently is.

There was a time when I thought that this concern was dispositive,[50] but I have changed my mind. Trading formal, carefully regulated contempt proceedings for largely unregulated, treacherous, and abusive station house interrogation is not an obvious loss for civil liberties. True, the Court used its station house interrogation doctrine to reverse Spano's conviction, but it is striking that the grounds for reversal have little to do with the fundamental injustice of executing a young, first offender for a killing that, while surely blameworthy, was also partially caused by a host of mitigating circumstances.

Moreover, if Spano had been subject to formal contempt proceedings, it is not at all clear that he would have confessed in the first place. As I have already argued, there are (and should be) limits on the sanctions that the state can impose on people who refuse to testify. Faced with the possibility of capital punishment if he told the truth, Spano likely would have remained silent. And if he did speak, it would have been because the state applied legitimate pressure to achieve its public ends, rather than because the state corrupted and exploited his private friendship with Bruno.

It follows, I think, that criminal defendants would be no worse off and might be better off if police were forced to substitute formal contempt proceedings for station house interrogation. What stands in the way of this shift is precisely the self-incrimination doctrine that supposedly tempers the violence of our criminal justice system. As things currently stand, it would be unconstitutional for the government to make this trade because the contempt procedures are said to violate the self-incrimination clause. Bizarrely, the very formality of the sanction that serves to mark it as public and, so, protects the private sphere from public exploitation also makes the sanction unconstitutional under current doctrine. Whereas the police are perfectly free to use a wide variety of informal techniques that effectively force speech through the manipulation of the private for public ends, the straightforward, carefully regulated use of the contempt sanction is prohibited.

Obviously, the shape of current doctrine means that my proposal faces very substantial obstacles along the Dworkinian "fit" dimension. I have already indicated why this difficulty need not much worry radical libertarians,[51] but for the rest of us, there is a partial solution to the problem. In his provocative study of the Fifth Amendment privilege, Akhil Amar has argued that there is no constitutional basis for the derivative use immunity that the Court has insisted upon before a potential defendant can be compelled. It follows for Amar that suspects can be compelled to answer questions so long as the answers themselves are not introduced in a subsequent trial. Thus, police would remain free to use the suspect's answers to develop other evidence that could be introduced.[52]

I have previously criticized Amar's proposal,[53] and I am still troubled by some aspects of it. Moreover, there is no question that adopting his proposals would mark an important break with current law. I must confess, though, that I have rethought my position. Amar's doctrinal argument reconciles desirable reform with at least some strands of existing self-incrimination doctrine. Indeed, the argument might even be extended. It is, after all, something of a stretch to say that a suspect is compelled to be a "witness" against himself when words he has spoken in an entirely separate proceeding are subsequently introduced against him in a criminal trial. Perhaps, then, the government should be allowed to use contempt sanctions to elicit statements that, themselves, would be admissible against the defendant.

It should be emphasized that these changes are part of a package, and that the package must include measures to get at the real danger posed by station house interrogation. We have mostly failed to address that danger because we have made a mistake about what it consists of. This mistake, in turn, is the product of a fundamental misunderstanding of why silence is worth protecting. Silence has value not because it is free, as current self-incrimination doctrine would have it. Rather, silence is valuable because it bounds a separate, private sphere. Determined silence in the face of public pressure is the way that we declare our independence from the state and assert our status as private individuals. Thus, Vincent Joseph Spano should indeed have been afforded a right to remain silent, but the right, at its core, was a just claim not to have his private relationships exploited for public purposes.

As I have already argued, silence can perform this function even in the teeth of government coercion. The coercion itself is public, and its application in no way corrupts or debases particularist relationships. But silence cannot possibly perform this function when the very private sentiments we wish to protect are publicly marshaled to compel speech. That is the ultimate lesson of Spano's case. Until self-incrimination doctrine is reformulated so as to take the lesson into account, that doctrine will serve as an obstacle to, rather than a facilitator of, the human dignity it is meant to protect.

CHAPTER 6

Torture's Truth

WHAT IS IT LIKE TO BE TORTURED?

Here is how it begins. Early one morning in April 1977, some twenty people arrived unannounced at the Buenos Aires home of Jacobo Timerman, an Argentine journalist.[1] The men grabbed his car keys, handcuffed him, and threw him to the floor of the backseat of his own car. They blindfolded him, covered him with a blanket, stuck their feet on top of him, and held what felt like the butt of a gun against his body as they drove off. When they arrived at an unknown location, Timerman was taken inside a building and thrown to the floor. Someone placed the barrel of a revolver against his head and began to count. At the count of ten, the man laughed and removed the blindfold. Timerman was in the presence of Colonel Ramon J. Camps, chief of police for Buenos Aires. "Timerman," he said, "your life depends on how you answer my questions."[2]

And here is how Timerman describes his existence in the months that followed.

A man is shunted so quickly from one world to another that he's unable to tap a reserve of energy so as to confront this unbridled violence. That is the first phase of torture: to take a man by surprise, without allowing him any reflex defense, even psychological. A man's hands are shackled behind him, his eyes blindfolded. No one says a word. Blows are showered upon a man. . . . A man is then led to what may be a canvas bed, or a table, hands and legs outstretched. And the application of electric shocks begins. The amount of electricity transmitted by the electrodes, or whatever they're called, is regulated so that it merely hurts, or burns, or destroys. It's impossible to shout, you howl. At the onset of this long human howl, someone with soft hands supervises your heart, someone sticks his hand into your mouth and pulls your tongue out of it in order to prevent this man from choking. Someone places a piece of rubber in the man's mouth to prevent him from biting his tongue or destroying his lips.

A brief pause. And then it starts all over again. With insults this time. A brief pause. And then questions. A brief pause. And then words of hope. A brief pause. And then insults. A brief pause. And then questions. . . .

When electric shocks are applied, all that a man feels is that they're ripping apart his flesh. And he howls. Afterwards, he doesn't feel the blows. Nor does he feel them the next day, when there's no electricity but only blows. The man spends days confined in a cell without windows, without light, either seated or lying down. He also spends days tied to the foot of a ladder so that he's unable to stand up and can only kneel, sit, or stretch out. The man spends a month not being allowed to wash himself, transported on the floor of an automobile to various places for interrogation, fed badly, smelling bad. The man is left enclosed in a small cell for forty-eight hours, his eyes blindfolded, his hands tied behind him, hearing no voice, seeing no sign of life, having to perform his bodily functions upon himself.[3]

So that is what it is like to be tortured, at least for one person, at least to the extent that language can convey what it is like.

But what does all this have to do with a right to silence? Perhaps there should be a right to silence *about* torture. The tortured should be able to remain silent precisely because the limits of language inevitably result in misrepresenting and trivializing the experience.* But does it not also misrepresent and trivialize the experience to suggest that torture itself is about a right to silence? Timerman was the victim of obscene cruelty. He was made to feel great pain, all-encompassing, dehumanizing, unimaginable pain. Surely, one might say, this is an independent evil that stands on its own. As Elaine Scarry argues in her eloquent book about pain, if torture and silence are linked at all, it is because the excruciating pain of torture silences rather than because it forces speech.[4]

In this chapter, I nonetheless argue that torture does indeed implicate the right to silence, or, more precisely, the right to what silence represents. At least in this context, what it represents is radical libertarianism, in-

---

* Timerman begins his account with the following observations: "In the long months of confinement, I often thought of how to transmit the pain that a tortured person undergoes. And always I concluded that it was impossible. It is a pain without points of reference, revelatory symbols, or clues to serve as indicators." (JACOBO TIMERMAN, PRISONER WITHOUT A NAME, CELL WITHOUT A NUMBER 32 [TOBY TALBOT, TRANS., (1981)]).

dependence, defiance, and a disembodied will. In previous chapters, we have seen how this kind of freedom can be achieved and celebrated even in the face of government coercion. But because virtually everyone gives in to it, torture stands on a different footing. The fact that everyone gives in weakens the belief that defiant silence is central to who we are. One problem with torture, then, is that it reminds us of both the importance and impossibility of silence.

But that is not the only problem. Torture also reminds us of the nightmare to which pervasive determinism and radical libertarianism can lead. Even as they were depriving him of his right to silence, Timerman's torturer's were demonstrating their own independence, defiance, and will. If we ourselves are silent before this outrage, if we fail to condemn them and allow them to get away with it, then, it seems, everything is permissible and there simply are no absolute moral truths, just as pervasive determinists and radical libertarians claim.

One would hardly expect a staid, moralistic country like the United States to be flirting with such skepticism. Our political and religious leaders regularly attack the evils of relativism and moral equivocation. Yet in the wake of the September 11 attack, serious and well respected academics have defended torture.[5] Bush administration officials have argued for its legality,[6] and many press reports indicate that administration officials have approved interrogation techniques like "waterboarding" that causes the victim to feel like he is drowning, sleep deprivation, and keeping prisoners in stress positions for long periods of time.[7] We have apparently deported prisoners to countries where we know they will be subjected to even worse practices.[8] Scores of prisoners have been beaten, humiliated, and abused while in American custody, and at least 26 have died.[9]

Thus, our present circumstances force upon us an urgent question: Despite everything that we say, are we pervasive determinists or radical libertarians after all? One might suppose that unambiguous condemnation of torture is a way of responding to that question with an emphatic "no." However, in this chapter, I argue that even condemnation is actually a technique for insisting on silence when the question is pressed—a very deep, perhaps impenetrable silence that is essential to maintain the illusion and hypocrisy upon which our self-conceptions depend.

THE STANDARD ACCOUNT AND ITS PROBLEMS

Getting to the bottom of torture requires answering three interrelated questions: what is it, what's wrong with it, and is it ever morally permissible? In this section, I start by providing some standard answers to these questions and then attempt to problematize those answers. In the next section, I provide a different account of torture that resolves some of the problems.

Let's start, then, with what torture is. According to a standard definition, contained in Article One of the Convention against Torture, torture consists of

any act by which severe pain or suffering, whether physical or mental, is intentionally inflicted on a person for such purposes as obtaining from him or a third person information or a confession, punishing him for an act he or a third person has committed or is suspected of having committed, or intimidating or coercing him or a third person, or for any reason based on discrimination of any kind, when such pain or suffering is inflicted by or at the instigation of or with the consent or acquiescence of a public official or other person acting in an official capacity. It does not include pain or suffering arising only from, inherent in or incidental to lawful sanctions.*

---

* Convention against Torture and Other Cruel, Inhuman or Degrading Treatment or Punishment, G.A. Res. 39/46, U.N. GAUR, 39th Sess, Supp. No. 51, at 197, U.N. Doc A/39/51 (1984) (entered into force June 26, 1987).

    The Convention binds each party to "take effective legislative, judicial or other measures to prevent acts of torture in any territory under its jurisdiction" and provides that "[n]o exceptional circumstances whatsoever, whether a state of war or a threat of war, internal political instability or any other public emergency, may be invoked as a justification of torture." Id. The United States ratified the Convention in 1994, but it did so with some limiting understandings. In particular, the U.S. ratification was conditioned on the view that in order to constitute torture, an act must be specifically intended to inflict severe physical or mental pain or suffering and that mental pain or suffering refers to prolonged mental harmed caused by or resulting from (1) the intentional infliction or threatened infliction of severe physical pain or suffering; (2) the administration of application or threatened administration or application of mind altering substances or other procedures calculated to disrupt profoundly the senses or personality; (3) the threat of imminent death; or (4) the threat that another person will imminently be subject to death, severe physical pain or suffering, or the administration or application of mind altering substances or other procedures calculated to disrupt profoundly the senses or personality. *See* 18 U.S.C. 2340.

What is wrong with torture as so defined? Some people think that the only proper response to this question is silence.[10] This is so because even to ask it is to miss the point. On this view, anyone who reads the accounts by Timerman and other torture survivors and needs an explanation for why torture is evil is not in touch with the simplest human truths. No explanation will be possible for such a person, and for the rest of us, no explanation will be necessary.

Still, if some explanation for torture's evil must be provided, then the standard response begins with the fact that torture inflicts severe pain and that severe pain is an evil. This is so not just because pain is discomforting. The kind of pain that Jacobo Timerman suffered is literally dehumanizing. When the pain gets bad enough, we lose the capacity to function. We cannot think, choose, or connect to others. We are completely dominated by our torment. As Timerman himself describes the experience, "I felt I was becoming a vegetable, casting aside all logical emotions and sensations—fear, hatred, vengeance—for any emotion or sensation meant wasting useless energy."[11]

It is or will be the fate of many of us to endure this sort of pain, but there is a special problem when the pain is inflicted by government agents. At this point, the argument against torture connects in obvious ways with liberal political theory. Liberals worry about protecting individual choice from collective power. Given that worry, state-inflicted torture is the worst case scenario. Because severe pain blots out everything else, when the state tortures an individual, it entirely subsumes him. The distinction between individual will and state commands simply collapses. The individual is reduced to the plaything of state officials. No longer able to choose his own purposes, a torture victim can be used for any purpose the state desires.

It follows that if there are to be any liberal rights at all, there must at least be a right not to be tortured. There can be no individuals separate from the state and capable of asserting rights against it if the state retains the power to torture. This observation, in turn, leads to a standard answer to our third question about whether torture is ever morally permissible. The Torture Convention provides that "[n]o exceptional circumstances whatsoever, whether a state of war or a threat of war, internal political instability or any other public emergency, may be invoked as a justification of torture."[12] Given the liberal account of torture's evil, it is easy to see why an absolute prohibition is necessary. If the right not to be tortured is, indeed, a master right, then making the right contingent on circumstances denies the possibility that there can be any limits at all on state power. To say that the state may sometimes torture is to say that the state may sometimes do anything at all for collective ends regardless of the costs to particular individuals. But this view is incompatible with a political theory that begins with individuals acceding to state authority only to protect individual rights.

Thus, the standard argument provides a definition of torture that fits seamlessly with the liberal account of torture's evil and an explanation for why the torture prohibition must be absolute. The argument is quite powerful, and, as we shall see, there are elements of it that survive critical appraisal. There are also serious problems with it, however.

Consider, first, the definition. The Torture Convention definition contains some puzzling limitations. Why must torture involve an act, when a failure to act (not amounting to consent or acquiescence) can also result in "severe pain or suffering?"* Why is severe pain inflicted to achieve the ends of punishment, information gathering, or intimidation especially troublesome when some other, unspecified purposes (and one specified purpose, the infliction of a lawful sanction) are apparently outside the reach of the prohibition?

These gaps in coverage, in turn, illustrate a hidden cost of the absolute prohibition on torture: One can afford to be an absolutist only if one is very careful concerning what one is an absolutist about. In a subtle, perhaps even unconscious, way, absolutism pushes us toward a narrowing of the prohibition's coverage. This is one way in which even condemnation of torture is inevitably coupled with a disturbing silence. (At the end of this chapter, I discuss another related way in which this is true.)

---

* The Convention does bind parties to take affirmative measures to prevent torture. However, the "torture" that parties are obligated to prevent is defined so as to necessitate an act, consent, or acquiescence. Hence, a party is under no obligation to prevent failures to act even when they cause severe pain or suffering.

The clearest and most troubling silence that accompanies condemnation concerns the distinction between acts and omissions. It is not mere happenstance that most torture absolutists limit their absolutism to affirmative acts. "Agent relativity" is built into the absolutist position. A right is agent relative when a person can respect the right simply by restraining one's own conduct.[13] Put differently, agent relativity places a duty on those who want to inflict the proscribed harm themselves, but no duty on those content to let others do the dirty work without being stopped.

Agent relativity is linked to absolutism because if rights were not agent relative, a consequence of respecting the right of one person might be the violation of the right of another person. The result is a conflict of rights, so that one rights violation must be weighed against another. But absolutists also want to deny the propriety of weighing.[14]

Consider in this regard a situation invented by Joel Feinberg:[15] A dictator from country X captures citizens of country Y and threatens to torture the citizens to death unless country Y captures and tortures the dictator's opponents. If the torture right were not agent relative, it would be violated regardless of whether the leaders of country Y capitulated to this blackmail. One would then be left with the unhappy task of balancing the severity of one rights violation against another. Moreover, once it is conceded that weighing is required when torture is on both sides of the scale, it becomes evident that balancing in other situations is required as well. Torture may be a grave evil, but it is not the only evil. A sensible balancing might lead to the conclusion that torture is permitted, even mandatory, when necessary to prevent a greater evil.

These problems with an absolute prohibition raise doubts, in turn, about the standard account of why torture is an evil in the first place. Here, as elsewhere, liberal arguments are vulnerable to pervasive determinist critique that emphasizes the ubiquity of power relationships. Yes, the state is powerful and might use that power to dominate individuals, but state power might also be used to counteract the power of others.

As soon as one notices this problem, the liberal claim that torture's evil is rooted in the evil of all human suffering collapses. As we have seen, torture absolutists are quite content to tolerate suffering that might be eliminated through the use of torture. Moreover, even if we limit the universe of our concern to our own conduct and ignore the conduct we allow to happen, it turns out that most absolutists are also ready to inflict pain, even severe pain, when necessary to serve their purposes.

Some additional hypotheticals illustrate this point. First, consider a variant of the widely discussed "ticking bomb" hypothetical. The hypothetical itself has now become standard in the literature: The police know that a nuclear device is hidden somewhere in a large city, but they do not know where. They have captured the terrorist who has planted the bomb. Is it permissible for them to torture him in order to save hundreds of thousands of lives?[16]

The hypothetical was designed by torture pragmatists to make torture absolutists uncomfortable by emphasizing absolutist agent relativity in an extreme (perhaps, very unlikely) situation. Suppose, though, that we focus on a variant of the hypothetical that is discussed much less frequently. Imagine that the terrorist is actually in the process of setting off the bomb. Imagine that a police officer comes upon him while he is engaged in this activity and that the only way to stop him is, say, to shoot him in the knee cap. Imagine, finally, that the pain from being shot in the knee cap is roughly comparable to the pain that would have to be inflicted in our first hypothetical to get the terrorist to reveal the location of the bomb.* On these facts, I am confident that even the most ardent torture opponents would concede that officer is justified—indeed, required—to shoot the terrorist. If I am right about this, then it cannot be that torture opponents object to the infliction of severe pain when necessary to serve their purposes.

Now consider a second hypothetical. Suppose that we have captured a suspected terrorist who has some information about the plans and operations of the group to which he belongs. Should low level or moderate pain—something much less awful than being shot in the knee—count as forbidden torture that may not be used to extract this information? For

---

* I concede that this hypothetical is quite unrealistic. I have created it in this way so as to play off the similarity to the standard ticking bomb scenario. It is easy enough, however, to imagine much more realistic hypotheticals that raise the same problem. We might imagine, for example, a police officer who comes upon an ongoing, deadly assault and can stop the perpetrator only by shooting him in the knee cap.

example, Harvard Law Professor Alan Dershowitz has raised the possibility of sticking pins under a captive's finger nails to force him to speak.[17] Is this the kind of "torture" that should be forbidden?

The Bush administration, at least initially, claimed that it was not. The Justice Department's Office of Legal Counsel ruled that torture included only the infliction of pain "equivalent in intensity to the pain accompanying serious physical injury, such as organ failure, impairment of bodily function, or even death."[18] When the ruling was made public, it excited widespread condemnation, but even the United Nations Convention against Torture, relied upon by many of the Administration's critics, counts only the infliction of "severe pain and suffering" as torture.[19] Perhaps the Dershowitz technique involves something less than "severe" pain. And yet, I suspect, many people, and certainly most torture absolutists, would be at the very least uncomfortable with use of the technique, even though virtually all of these people would have no qualms about the officer who shoots the terrorist in the knee.

These hypotheticals illustrate a disturbing gap in the conventional account of what is wrong with torture. While it is true that torture has something to do with the deliberate infliction of pain, the evil of torture is not reducible to the evil of deliberately inflicted pain. To be sure, infliction of pain is itself an evil. Even if it turns out for some reason that what was done to Jacobo Timerman was not torture, it was still terribly wrong. Nonetheless, as our hypotheticals illustrate, sometimes the infliction of very severe pain is not torture, and sometimes (perhaps) the infliction of much less severe pain is torture.

Once it becomes clear that the evil of torture is not reducible to the evil of severe pain, we are faced with the task of distinguishing between cases where the evil of pain can legitimately be balanced against other evils and cases where it cannot. The authors of the Convention against Torture implicitly acknowledge as much. Importantly, the Convention does not outlaw all infliction of severe pain by government officials. For example, the Convention seems to authorize the use of pain as a component of lawful sanctions. Even when unrelated to lawful sanctions, severe pain is proscribed only when it is inflicted for a particular set of purposes. To be sure, these purposes (securing information or confession, intimidation, coercion, punishment, or as an act of discrimination) are apparently only illustrative, but it seems clear that they are meant to illustrate something and that this something limits the domain of the prohibition. Were this not so, the framers presumably would simply have outlawed the infliction of severe pain.

Unfortunately, however, the authors of the Convention offer no explanation for why pain inflicted for these particular purposes, as opposed to pain inflicted for other possible purposes, must be outlawed. For example, when a nation wages war, it regularly inflicts severe pain on enemy soldiers and, more often than we would like to admit, on civilian populations as well. The Convention's torture definition leaves entirely unclear why pain inflicted for the listed purposes is worse than pain inflicted for the purpose of waging a war.* The anomalies run even deeper. If one takes the definition at face value, it appears to outlaw the infliction of pain in circumstances where it might actually do some good (because, for example, it punishes or deters wrongful conduct or is useful in securing important information) while leaving completely unregulated the gratuitous, indiscriminate, and sadistic infliction of pain under circumstances where the infliction is an end in itself.

The linkage of pain to these purposes becomes still more mysterious when we consider the purposes individually. Take first the prohibition of severe pain as a means of punishment. Given the explicit exception for

---

*   *See* Alan Dershowitz, Why Terrorism Works: Understanding the Threat, Responding to the Challenge 148 (2002) ("The case against torture, if made by a Quaker who opposes the death penalty, war, self-defense, and the use of lethal force against fleeing felons, is understandable. But for anyone who justifies killing on the basis of a cost-benefit analysis, the case against the use of nonlethal torture to save multiple lives is more difficult to make."). Henry Shue has attempted to distinguish torture from death in combat on the theory that combat death, unlike torture, does not involve an assault on the defenseless, but, instead, a "fair fight." Henry Shue, *Torture,* 7 Phil. & Pub. Aff. *124,* 127–30 (1978). The argument is unpersuasive. First, it is far from clear how "fair" the fight really is when, for example, the military might of the United States is brought to bear on the army of Iraq. Second, and more significantly, opponents of torture would surely not be satisfied if torture's victims were given ineffectual weapons that permitted them to engage in futile attempts to harm their tormentors. *See also* Christopher Tindale, *The Logic of Torture: A Critical Examination,* 22 Soc. Theory & Prac. 349, 358–59 (1996) (arguing that a torture victim, like a soldier, may be a continuing threat).

pain that is incidental to or inherent in a lawful sanction, it is not clear how much bite this prohibition really has. In any event, in evaluating the prohibition, one must ask the "compared to what" question. To be sure, severe pain is an evil, but it is not the only evil. Is it really so obvious that corporal punishment, even corporal punishment inflicting severe pain, is worse than the available alternatives?[20] The exception for lawful sanctions comes close to conceding that we may be doing criminals no favor when we outlaw torture as an alternative.

This problem has particular resonance in the United States, where capital punishment is still common. Capital punishment, itself, can be physically painful.[21] Moreover, even when it is not, it seems quite likely that many prisoners on death row would gladly trade a time-bound torture session for their lives. Of course, death penalty opponents will respond that, in part for this reason, capital punishment should also be outlawed. Still, it seems plausible that at least some prisoners would be willing to undergo torture to avoid lengthy periods of incarceration. Who precisely, are we protecting by not offering prisoners this choice?

There is a similar set of problems when pain is used as a means of intimidation. A less freighted synonym for "intimidation" is deterrence, and deterrence theorists have something important to teach torture opponents.[22] These opponents tend to ignore the difference between a threat to engage in a practice and the actual use of the practice. To be sure, if the threat is to achieve its purpose, we must be ready to make good on it if called upon to do so. If we say that we are going to torture murderers, then, at least occasionally, we will have to torture some of them. However, a truly effective deterrent will not be used very often precisely because it is effective. If torture works, there will be very little torture. Depending on the shape of the "demand curve" for the conduct we wish to deter, the threat of an extremely painful punishment may end up causing less total pain than the threat of a more "humane" punishment.[23]

Of course, it is also possible that torture will be ineffective.[24] If this is the case, the practice should be avoided not because it is inhumane, but because it is ineffective. The prohibition is thus reduced to a temporally and culturally contingent judgment about efficacy—surely not what torture opponents have in mind.[25]

What, then, of the use of pain to force speech? For reasons I spell out below, thinking about this purpose gets us closer to figuring out what is really wrong with torture. For now, though, it is important to see that the most common objections to the practice are unsatisfactory. Perhaps the most obvious objection to pain as a means of extracting information or confession is that it can be, and often has been, used to obtain untrue information and false confessions. It is surely the case that most people subjected to torture will say virtually anything to stop the pain. How, then, can we be sure that they are telling the truth?

It is an important fact that almost everyone will eventually "give in" to torture, a fact that I will return to in the next section. It does not follow, however, that this fact makes torture inefficacious if we are interested in accurate information and true confessions. If we were really ready to discount information people give when confronted with powerful threats, we would be concerned about far more than torture. Consider, for example, the practice of plea bargaining.[26] As we have seen, prosecutors regularly threaten defendants with lengthy jail sentences or even death unless they plead guilty, which is, after all, a kind of confession.[27] If a defendant knows information that the prosecutor wants, there may also be a trade of a shorter sentence for testimony implicating another suspect. Often this trade is phrased as if it were an offer. The defendant is said to get a "break" in exchange for the testimony. But of course offers of this kind conceal an implicit threat. The defendant is likely to be incarcerated for many extra years unless he provides the testimony.

To be sure, we may be suspicious of confessions and information extracted under these circumstances. Thus, before a judge accepts a guilty plea, she must assure herself that there is a "factual basis" for it.[28] If the defendant chooses to go to trial, prosecutors must reveal to defense attorneys the details of any bargain they have struck in exchange for testimony,[29] and often prosecution witnesses are subjected to rigorous cross-examination about the bargain. But these protections might be put in place for torture as well.

Perhaps torture places more pressure on a defendant or a witness than other sorts of threats, although the discussion above of the death penalty and lengthy incarceration throws some doubt on this claim. Even if the threat of torture is more efficacious, it does not follow that greater pressure will lead to more truth distortion. Indeed, when the torturer is interested in truthful information, the greater pressure may lead to more truth telling precisely because the torturer is likely to threaten further excruciating pain if the information turns out to be false.

Of course, in the case of confessions, the torturer may be interested in extracting an untrue statement. But this problem does not explain why the fruits of torture cannot be used when the torture victim reveals information the truth of which is later confirmed.[30] Moreover, jurors themselves are hardly unaware of torture's potential for truth distortion. So long as the torture is made publicly known, is it really very likely that jurors will be persuaded by its fruits when there is no confirmatory evidence?

TORTURE'S TRUTH

Thus, the standard linkage between pain and the purposes outlawed by the Convention's definition of torture is problematic. There is another story about torture, information, and silence, however, that gets closer to what is really at stake. Ironically, this claim rests not upon torture's truth distorting capacity, but instead upon its ability to teach us a certain kind of truth.

The argument for this claim begins with the linkage between compelled abandonment of silence on the one hand and the values associated with liberal individualism on the other. As we have already seen,[31] the best defense of a Fifth Amendment privilege, which not coincidentally has its roots in opposition to torture, rests on the special dangers of compelled universalism when the state forces self-condemnatory speech. A person made to confess is required to privilege universalist over particularist obligation, but the freedom to balance these obligations for oneself is at the core of individual liberty. On this view, state punishment is justified only so long as the criminal is not made to consent to his own punishment. To be sure, the state is entitled to control a criminal's physical conduct and his body. It can incarcerate him and, perhaps, even whip him or kill him. The state has no business, however, controlling the criminal's mind. It can act against a criminal's will, but it cannot enlist his will for its own purposes. Because silence can be broken only by an act of will, compelled speech violates liberal values.

This line of argument helps explain why it is that silence, information, and confession have something to do with torture. On this account, torture is bad because the extraction of information and professions of guilt can come about only by the exercise of will. A tortured subject is dehumanized in the sense that she turns her will over to an alien force. The intuition standing alone does not provide a full account of the torture prohibition, however. There are two interrelated difficulties. First, as we saw in the context of the self-incrimination privilege, even persons subject to government coercion retain the capacity to assert a right to silence. Indeed, it is just this capacity that gives the coerced individual ownership over the statement. The second difficulty is that the relevance of information is established only by bringing into question the relevance of pain. A pair of self-incrimination cases, both of which we have discussed above in a different context,[32] usefully illustrates both problems.

In *United States v. Hubbell*,[33] a prosecutor served a subpoena on Hubbell requiring him to produce some 13,120 pages of personal documents and records. The prosecutor then used these documents to indict Hubbell for various crimes related to tax, mail, and wire fraud. (Hubbell had been Hillary Rodham Clinton's friend and law partner, and the prosecutor was interested in what Hubbell could tell him about the Clintons.) When the case came before the United States Supreme Court, the Court held that the subpoena violated Hubbell's self-incrimination right and dismissed the indictment. In contrast, in *Schmerber v. California*,[34] a police officer, who suspected Schmerber of drunken driving, ordered that blood be extracted from his arm. A blood test, demonstrating that Schmerber had alcohol in his body, was introduced against him at his trial, and he was convicted. Schmerber claimed that the use of his own blood against him in a criminal prosecution violated his privilege against self-incrimination, but this time, the Supreme Court rejected the claim and affirmed the conviction.

From the standpoint of a liberal defender of the self-incrimination privilege, the different treatment of Hubbell's and Schmerber's claims makes sense. Hubbell was forced to do something. The subpoena required an exercise of his will. He was the one who had to "consent" by turning over his papers, thereby in effect cooperating in his own destruction. In contrast, Schmerber was not forced to do anything. To be sure, something was done to him—his body was subjected to an invasive procedure—but the procedure was completed *against* his will, rather than by *utilizing* his will.* He was therefore not made to subordinate his particularist to his universalist obligations in the way that Hubbell was. If one believes that the government should not be permitted to require individuals to will their own destruction, both *Schmerber* and *Hubbell* seem rightly decided.

We have already seen, however, the way in which the liberal account rests on a contradiction. After all, Hubbell *could have* resisted. He retained the option of going to prison rather than turning over the papers. The possibility of exercising this option meant that he remained "free," at least in a certain sense, to balance for himself his universalist and particularist obligations. The very fact that he had this choice is what distinguishes his case from Schmerber's. Why, then, should the self-incrimination privilege shield him from making the very choice that liberals demand he be allowed?

There is a second difficulty when we think about two cases through the prism of torture. The cases are hard to reconcile with the standard linkage that torture opponents make between forced speech on the one hand and pain on the other. After all, what happened to Hubbell was unconstitutional even though he suffered no physical pain and was not threatened with physical pain. In contrast, Schmerber was forced to undergo an invasive procedure that inflicted pain upon him. On the facts of

---

* It does not follow that whenever incriminating evidence is gained through use of the defendant's will, the Fifth Amendment privilege is implicated. The exercise of will is a necessary, but not sufficient, condition for the privilege to attach. As explained in Chapter 4, it must also be shown that the exercise of will reveals something about the defendant's internal mental state and not just "physical" or "nontestimonial" evidence. *See*, e.g. , *United States v. Doe*, 487 U.S. 201 (1988) (court order requiring defendant to sign form directing foreign banks to release records not covered by Fifth Amendment privilege); *United States v. Dionisio*, 410 U.S. 1, 5–7 (1973) (voice identification not covered by Fifth Amendment privilege); *Gilbert v. California*, 388 U.S. 263 (1967) (handwriting exemplars not covered by Fifth Amendment privilege). *Cf. Pennsylvania v. Muniz*, 496 U.S. 582 (1990) (privilege protects against use of defendant's inability to give date of sixth birthday, but not his slurred speech to establish his intoxication).

the *Schmerber* case, the pain was quite minor, but the logic of *Schmerber* applies to much more serious pain. For example, on the Court's theory, a major operation designed to extract a bullet from a suspect's body would not raise self-incrimination problems.*

Even though opposition to torture and the self-incrimination privilege are historically linked, these examples suggest that there is actually a serious tension between the two. This is so because opposition to torture is focused on the body, whereas opposition to self-incrimination is focused on the mind. Although both torture and the self-incrimination privilege concern information and confession, the evil they address seems different. Torture is about physical pain, while the privilege is about disembodied will. The challenge, then, is whether we can give an account of torture that captures its physicality and embodiment.

We can begin to meet the challenge by focusing on the fragility of the distinction between *Hubbell* and *Schmerber*. As we have already seen, pervasive determinists have a critique of this distinction. To a pervasive determinist, there simply is no such thing as disembodied will. This perspective finds powerful support in modern neuroscience. For serious students of the brain, Hubbell's "will" is as much the manifestation of wholly determined physical processes as Schmerber's drunkenness.[35]

This is not to say that what happened to Schmerber and Hubbell is a source of no concern. Instead, the point is that from a "scientific" perspective, the locus of the concern in both cases is the Fourth Amendment protection against unreasonable searches and seizures, rather than the Fifth Amendment privilege against self-incrimination. Whereas the Fifth Amendment is about the realm of metaphysics, where mysterious, nonmaterial entities like will and choice float around in the ether, the Fourth Amendment protects real things that one can get one's hands on. It is about "persons, houses, papers, and effects."[36] For hard-nosed materialists, the brain is, after all, just another "effect." Hence, both Schmerber and Hubbell have potentially valid claims under the Fourth Amendment,

---

* It does not follow that such an operation would be constitutional. The Supreme Court has held that it would violate the Fourth Amendment protection against unreasonable searches and seizures. *See Winston v. Lee*, 470 U.S. 753, 766 (1985).

but only because a material thing (Hubbell's brain or Schmerber's blood) has been interfered with.* Put differently, materialists return our focus to embodied pain, but this refocusing only reintroduces the puzzle about the relevance of forced speech.

So far, I have focused on the fragility of the *Schmerber/Hubbell* distinction when viewed against the backdrop of scientific materialism. It turns out, though, that the plausibility of scientific materialism is also fragile. Here, radical libertarian insights take hold. Whatever scientists say, surely few of us actually live our lives as if reductive materialism were true.[37] Such a belief would require us to treat our own goals, beliefs, feelings, and emotions as no more than the byproduct of entirely determined, physical processes. It is doubtful that even scientific materialists can really believe this. I am told that neurologists, too, fall in love, join political movements, get angry and sad and overjoyed and fearful.[38] Can they really believe that all these experiences are no more than the outputs of a complex machine?[39] Neurologists study the physical brain when it is subject to all sorts of stimuli, but do they ever study the brain of neurologists who are studying the brain? Even neurologists treat their own theories as somehow outside the determined, physical processes that they are studying.

None of this is to deny that scientific materialism is "true," if, indeed, truth has any meaning when it departs from ways that we are destined to see the world and live our lives.[40] On the contrary, my central claim is that our repugnance to torture is rooted in our fear that it is true. On some level we know that materialism is true. How could a mind possibly

---

* I do not mean to say that the claim would prevail. In fact, the Court rejected Schmerber's Fourth Amendment claim. But whereas it held that the Fifth Amendment was simply inapplicable to the drawing of blood, it found that the Fourth Amendment applied, but was satisfied. *Compare* 384 U.S., at 767 ("if compulsory administration of a blood test does not implicate the Fifth Amendment, it plainly involves the broadly conceived reach of a search and seizure under the Fourth Amendment") *with* id., at 771 ("The officer in the present case, however, might reasonably have believed that he was confronted with an emergency, in which the delay necessary to obtain a warrant, under the circumstances, threatened 'the destruction of evidence.'"). On the limited Fourth Amendment protection afforded against subpoenas, see *Oklahoma Press Publishing Co. v. Walling*, 327 U.S. 186 (1946).

exist without a material substrate? But on a different level, we also know that dualism is true. How could my deepest beliefs and desires amount to no more than chemical reactions?

It is this insight that links embodied pain with speech and silence. The severe pain that torture entails puts special pressure on radical libertarian notions of freedom. Whereas individuals threatened with contempt citations or lengthy interrogations can always demonstrate independence and defiance, this is not a real option for torture victims. What is wrong with torture, then, is that it reminds us of something that we do not want to know: that our belief in materialism and our belief in the existence of human will cannot be reconciled. Moreover, torture forces us to resolve the conflict by admitting, against our "will" (if you will) that we have no will. When the pain is intense enough, we must concede that we are no more than our bodies.

Elaine Scarry has made the point as eloquently as anyone. For her, "[i]ntense pain is world-destroying. In compelling confession, the torturers compel the prisoner to record and objectify the fact that intense pain is world-destroying." This is so because "physical pain always mimes death and the infliction of physical pain is always a mock execution." Torture reminds us of death in a concrete way, and when we are so reminded, we "[begin] to experience that body that will end . . . life, the body that can be killed, and which when killed will carry away the conditions that allow [a person] to exist."[41]

Of course, Scarry is not claiming that we do not die. It is not, then, that torture convinces us of something that is not true. Quite the contrary, torture convinces us of a truth that we literally cannot live with. The torture victim learns that he is the slave to his body, that all that he believes, values, and loves is, in the end, hostage to his physical well-being, that he is willing to give up everything to bring about the cessation of physical pain. For many torture victims, this lesson is reenforced by the sense of betrayal—of self and others—that torture produces. When the torture victim speaks, revealing the location of a comrade in arms, for example, or verbally repudiating the cause he has fought for, the victim is often implicated in the destruction of relationships and commitments that, he had previously thought, defined his essence. It turns out, the victim learns, his essence lies elsewhere. It consists of something much more base, of the flesh and sensations he shares with animals rather than the ideas and ideals that, he had thought, linked him to something higher. How can we expect a person who has learned this lesson to continue his life? How is he again to make sense of his plans, hopes, and attachments? Even when the victim's body survives, torture is a kind of death precisely because it reduces the victim to his body.

Anyone who doubts any of this need only listen to the voice of the tortured. Consider the words of Jean Amery:

Whoever is overcome by pain through torture experiences his body as never before. In self-negation, his flesh becomes a total reality. . . . [O]nly in torture does the transformation of the person into flesh become complete. Frail in the face of violence, yelling out in pain, awaiting no help, capable of no resistance, the tortured person is only a body, and nothing else beside that. . . .

Whoever has succumbed to torture can no longer feel at home in the world. The shame of destruction cannot be erased. Trust in the world, which already collapsed in part at the first blow, but in the end, under torture, fully, will not be regained. [42]

We do not want to know what Jean Amery knows, and our fear of this knowledge is what explains torture's linkage between pain on the one hand and forced speech on the other. Information and confession are important components of torture because they can be extracted only by the exercise of will. They are not the only components of torture, however. After all, the state regularly uses various forms of coercion to commandeer the will so as to extract information and confession in circumstances that do not remotely resemble torture. I do not file my tax returns because of a perfectly free and uncoerced impulse to tell the government about my sources of income.[43]

The problem with torture is not just that the victim's will is commandeered but that it is commandeered by the dehumanizing realization that all that we associate with being human is an illusion. Threats to the body uniquely carry this consequence because they alone lead us to forsake the version of ourselves that makes us something other than a corporeal machine. It follows that although torture's detractors are right to focus on pain, many of them are mistaken about the role that pain plays. It is not the pain itself that is the essence of torture's evil. It is rather what the pain produces, the terrible betrayal of our self-understanding of human life.

This conception of torture helps explain the insistence of torture's opponents on nonconsequentialism. Because torture's truth dispels the illusion upon which human freedom depends, torture is difficult to justify as a means to advance human ends. To justify torture because of its consequences is to engage in a rational investigation of means and ends. But torture denies the possibility of rationality and choice. If we are to learn torture's truth, there literally cannot be humans, and without humans, moral inquiry into means and ends loses its meaning.*

I believe that an argument along these lines provides the best account of what is so bad about torture, but it requires a redefinition of what ought to count as torture. How would the Convention definition have to be changed to fit this account? First, this understanding of torture changes the purposes that should be prohibited. On this account, the prohibited purposes include those ends, but only those ends, that require an exercise of the victim's will in order to be achieved. Usually, these ends require the overcoming of silence, although they may, or may not, involve the acquisition of information. Consider, for example, the use of physical pain to force a victim to profess a religious belief. This purpose is not among those specifically listed in the Convention definition (although it may well fall under the "coercion" rubric), yet it is surely a form of torture. This is so because such a profession can come about only through an exercise of the victim's will. Compare this case to the case of

---

*   I do not mean to suggest here that this argument defeats the consequentialist position on torture. "Acoustic separation," (a process whereby we send messages to some people, but the messages are not heard by others) or psychological denial might permit us to use torture against some without allowing torture's truth to defeat the projects of the rest of us. This is not merely a theoretical possibility. Torture exists, yet most of us seem to have little difficulty hanging onto the "illusion" of human freedom. So long as the illusion can be maintained, consequentialists might insist that the cost of torture to some is sometimes worth the benefit achieved for others. On "acoustic separation," see Meir Dan-Cohen, *Decision Rules and Conduct Rules: On Acoustic Separation in Criminal Law*, 97 HARV. L. REV. 625 (1984). On the desirability, vel non, of hanging onto this illusion, see pp. 140–142, *infra*.

a victim forced to undergo extremely painful surgery to extract a bullet to be used as evidence against him. Although this practice is covered by the Convention definition (because it involves severe pain inflicted for the purpose of gaining information), I would not count it as torture. The surgery can be performed on the victim; she need not—indeed, typically cannot—perform it on herself. It therefore avoids the special paradoxical mental element that is torture's hallmark.*

I think that it also follows from my argument that, contrary to the Convention definition, torture usually has nothing to do with punishment or intimidation, at least if we take intimidation to mean general deterrence. Punishment and intimidation do not require the overcoming of silence so long as the target need not acquiesce in it. Of course, there may be other objections to severe pain when it is imposed for these purposes. It is worth emphasizing again that torture is not the only evil in the world. But neither retributive punishment nor disabilities imposed so as to discourage misbehavior by others have the special characteristics that make torture an evil. They are things that are done to people, not things that people do to themselves. They therefore do not produce the degradation that comes with the sacrifice of will for the sake of body.

Finally, I think that it is a category mistake to define torture as involving severe *mental* pain.** The infliction of mental pain has its own problems as a means of advancing the state's ends, but it will not do to assert that the state may never use this technique. Witnesses and suspects are regularly subjected to severe mental pain to extract information. A person who is worried about spending months incarcerated for contempt if she does not testify surely suffers severe mental pain, sometimes even

---

* It is worth emphasizing that the fact that it is not torture does not mean that it should be permissible. It may, for example, constitute an unreasonable search or seizure. *See Rochin v. California,* 342 U.S. 165, 172–74 (1952) (holding that stomach pumping to secure evidence violates the due process clause); *Winston v. Lee,* 470 U.S. 753, 766 (1985) (holding that compelled surgery to secure evidence is "unreasonable search" within the meaning of the Fourth Amendment).

** I put to one side, here, the severe mental pain that may occur because of the very threat of torture to oneself or to another. Moreover, it is easy to imagine cases where the boundary between mental and physical pain is indistinct. Indeed, the difficulty of drawing this line is central to my argument.

resulting in breakdown or suicide, but this is hardly torture. Torture is about the body, not the mind, or, more precisely, it is about what happens to the mind when we realize that we are only body.

SOME TROUBLING SECOND THOUGHTS

So that is what is so bad about torture. Or, at least, that is the best I can do to explain what is bad about torture. Still, I must confess that I remain troubled about whether the explanation makes torture bad enough. The problem with torture's truth is that, just maybe, it really is true.

We can see torture's truth through the eyes of both the torturer and his victim. Consider first the torturer, or rather, consider two types of torturers. The first is what might be called the republican torturer. He is cool, unemotional, bureaucratic, and controlled. He acts pursuant to carefully drafted legal regulation that emerges from democratic deliberation and that permits the practice only when a cost/benefit analysis supports it. He gets no personal pleasure from his job, but he feels bound to do his public duty, which necessitates subordinating private concerns for the benefit of the public good. For this torturer, it is quite unfortunate that the torture victim must suffer excruciating pain, but that is what is necessary to achieve the just aims of the community as a whole. Through heroic mental control, the republican torturer overcomes his natural revulsion and forces his body to behave.

This is the sort of torture that apologists for the practice want to defend, yet, in my judgment at least, it demonstrates the nightmare that republicanism can lead to. Oddly, it is the very rationality of the republican torturer that is so terrifying. It is the total victory of mind over body, the uncompromising insistence on privileging universalist obligation over particularist empathy, that makes his cold cruelty seem less than human.

Compare the republican torturer to his radical libertarian colleague. This is the crazed, sadistic torturer whose prerational rage comes from the knowledge that everything is permissible. He is controlled by no statutes, no superiors, and no moral code. He acts because, he realizes, there is nothing that prevents him from acting. No one defends the radical libertarian torturer; yet, if I had to choose, I suppose I would prefer him to his republican colleague. At least his freedom and his rage puts him in touch with something that (for me at least) is recognizably human and not merely mechanical. Ivan Karamazov may, indeed, have had it right when he says that "[i]n every man . . . a demon lies hidden—the demon of rage, the demon of lustful heat at the screams of the tortured victim, the demon of lawlessness let off the chain."[44]

But although the republican torturer is creepier (by my lights), the radical libertarian torturer is more troubling. The problem is that this kind of torturer has been shielded from torture's truth in just the way that, I have claimed, we ought to be shielded. No one who has absorbed that truth can believe in unmediated freedom. Torture's truth is that our will is an illusion and that we are all captives of forces beyond our control. Precisely because he has not absorbed this truth, the radical libertarian torturer can experience the ecstasy that comes from defiance, independence, and liberation from morality and common decency. In this odd way, might not opposition to torture morph into a kind of defense of the practice? Or, to put the matter the other way around (and perhaps more plausibly), might not the celebration of individual freedom that lies at the heart of opposition to torture actually promote a culture of torture?

We face similar difficulties when we focus on the torture victim. Jean Amery did not want to know what he learned as the blows fell, but that does not make what he learned any less true. Indeed, it is horrible precisely because it is true. Maintaining a silence about that truth is a luxury that the overprivileged can afford to indulge. For us, the truth that torture teaches—that in the end it is only our bodies that count—flits only briefly across our consciousness and is easily repressed most of the time. But it is not just torture's victims who lack this luxury. Consider, for example, people without enough food to eat, without shelter or sustenance, much less books and intellectual pursuits. The dispossessed must expend all of their energy meeting their physical needs. For them, the preeminent place of physicality is a daily fact they cannot escape. Indeed, it defines their lives. And when we think about the reality that there are millions and millions of these people, one has to wonder: what is so bad about torture then?

It is not just that the ability to silence torture's truth is unequally distributed. That ability might also actually make the poor worse off. One might, of course, take an optimistic view. Perhaps the fight against torture is the first installment in a general campaign in favor of mind over body, a struggle that would ultimately provide relief for the dispossessed as well. It seems more likely, though, that the same culture that produces opposition to torture also provides the middle class with a kind of insulation from the dispossessed. Is it not, after all, our squeamishness about our own bodies—our disgust with and disappointment in our embodiment—that both makes torture horrible and helps distance us from the underprivileged?[45]

Torture dehumanizes because it turns us into our bodies, but torture victims are not the only people who endure this unhappy fate. Precisely because the poor seem to be within the grip of overwhelming physical need, they strike the rich as less human and, so, less worthy of concern.[46] More subtly, we may push them aside because their physicality reminds us of our own, the very fact about our existence that we wish to deny. And it takes little imagination to see the way in which the same sort of denial is at work in discrimination against other vulnerable groups like the disabled and the elderly.

Of course, it would be bizarre to suggest that the endorsement of torture is a first step in a program of moral inclusiveness. Still, if the impulses I describe are indeed at work, it is far from clear that condemnation of torture is a step toward universal empathy. The condemnation rests on a deep desire to escape our bodies, and it is just this desire that causes us to attempt to escape those who demonstrate what our bodies might yet become.

Moreover, even the condemnation, in a backward sort of way, admits the terrible force of torture's truth. The condemnation is necessary only because we in some sense know and cannot fully avoid that truth. The strongest condemnation suggests the greatest need for repression and so provides the most powerful affirmation of that truth. In this way, even torture's most dedicated opponents are implicated in the practice. Perhaps, then, we need to end our silence about torture's terrifying truth. We need to understand torture and all that it tells us about ourselves, rather than simply outlaw it. We need, in short, to talk about torture. Whether we can have this conversation while also hanging on to our humanity remains to be seen.

CHAPTER 7

Free Speech and Free Silence

AS THE PRECEDING CHAPTERS ILLUSTRATE, sometimes compelled speech risks a special kind of corruption and self-betrayal. Compelled apologies and confessions threaten our norms of authenticity and particularist engagement. Even when we are dealing with words that are neither apologetic nor confessional, speech that results from certain forms of extreme coercion distances us from self-conceptions about agency and will. Suppose, though, that compelled speech is neither confessional nor apologetic and is not elicited by torture. Should there be a broader, more generalized right to silence to guard against betrayal and corruption?

In one of the most famous episodes in American constitutional history, the Supreme Court answered this question with a resounding "yes." In *West Virginia State Board of Education v. Barnette,*[1] a case decided amid war and patriotic fervor and in the shadow of recent precedent to the contrary,[2] the Court stood resolutely with members of a small minority religion who were unwilling to allow their children to salute the flag and recite the Pledge of Allegiance. Speaking for a majority of his colleagues, Justice Robert Jackson wrote that, "If there is any fixed star in our constitutional constellation, it is that no official, high or petty, can prescribe what shall be orthodox in politics, nationalism, religion, or other matters of opinion or force citizens to confess by word or act their faith therein. If there are any circumstances which permit an exception, they do not now occur to us."[3]

These are powerful words, expressing a noble sentiment. As we shall see, however, the star is not quite as fixed as Justice Jackson supposed. It turns out that Jackson's eloquence covered over a host of complexities and contradictions. Over the long term, powerful rhetoric alone cannot maintain coherence when the conceptions underlying it are this confused. Once one understands how confused they are, it should come as no surprise that the subsequent history of *Barnette* has not been altogether happy. Doctrinal elaboration on Justice Jackson's soaring sentiments has ranged from the trivial, to the puzzling, to the malign.

Some later cases are merely embarrassing. Within a period of seven years, the Court has upheld against a compelled speech attack a government program requiring fruit growers to contribute to a fund supporting generic advertising,[4] then struck down a virtually identical program for mushroom growers,[5] and then upheld an actually identical program for beef producers.[6]

Other decisions are more consequential and problematic. The Supreme Court has relied on the compelled speech doctrine to invalidate a law requiring professional fund-raisers to disclose to prospective donors the percentage of their donations actually turned over to charities,[7] a regulatory decision requiring a public utility to include information written by a public interest group in its billing envelopes,[8] a statute requiring newspapers to afford candidates space to reply to editorial attacks,[9] and an antidiscrimination law construed to prohibit the Boy Scouts from dismissing a gay scoutmaster.[10]

Many other decisions are best characterized as confusing. Although fund-raisers may not be compelled to tell potential donors the percentage of their contributions that actually go to the charity, lawyers may be compelled to tell clients the costs they will have to pay.[11] The owner of a car may not be compelled to use a license plate containing a slogan with which he disagrees, but the owner of a shopping center may be forced to open her property to persons distributing leaflets supporting a cause that she opposes.[12] Workers in a union shop have a right to withhold contributions that the union will use for political purposes that the workers oppose, but students at a university have no right to withhold fees funneled to student organizations that they oppose.[13]

Barnette also leaves some very significant problems unresolved. For example, if students have a right not to participate in the Pledge, do teachers have a similar right? If they do, do they also have a right not to teach Darwinian theory? What should we make of a student who demands a passing grade on a biology exam on which he refuses to apply that theory?[14]

Perhaps the most contentious unresolved issue involves the intersection between *Barnette* and the Supreme Court's prohibition of state-sponsored prayers in public schools. *Barnette* did not invalidate the Pledge; it merely created a constitutional right to opt out. More recently, however, in the school prayer context the Court has held that an opt out is insufficient to dispel the informal coercion pushing students toward participation.[15] As we shall see, *Barnette* was decided under a free speech theory, while state-sponsored school prayer was said to violate the establishment clause. Still, unless the constitutional definition of coercion is somehow different in the speech and establishment contexts, the two lines of cases read together suggest that even "voluntary" recitation of the Pledge is unconstitutional in the context of public education.*

It is something of a puzzle why the *Barnette* principle, which seemed so clear and right when Justice Jackson enunciated it, has led to so many problems. In this chapter, I argue that many of these difficulties result from not thinking hard enough about the relationship between silence and speech on the one hand and government coercion on the other. Here as elsewhere, the relationship can be illuminated by bringing republican, liberal, radical libertarian, and pervasive determinist theories to bear on the problem

A REPUBLICAN APPROACH

The Supreme Court's encounter with the Pledge of Allegiance began not with its *Barnette* decision in 1943, but three years earlier with its decision *Minersville School District v. Gobitis.*[16] The controversy arose out of a concerted lobbying effort by the American Legion to pass statutes that required teachers to spend at least ten minutes each day on patriotic exercises fostering "one hundred percent Americanism." According to

---

* Most recent controversy about the Pledge has centered around the words "under God,"inserted by Congress long after the *Barnette* decision. Note, however, that when *Barnette* is read together with the school prayer cases, it suggests that reciting the Pledge in a school setting may be unconstitutional even if the words "under God"were removed. In *Newdow v. U.S. Congress,* 328 F. 3d 466 (9th Cir. 2003), the Court of Appeals held that teacher-led recitation of the Pledge of Allegiance violated the establishment clause because of its reference to God. In *Elk Grove Unified School Dist. v. Newdow,* 542 U.S. 1 (2004), the Supreme Court held that the plaintiff in the case lacked standing and, therefore, reversed the Court of Appeals' judgment without reaching the merits.

Vincent Blasi and Seana Shiffrin's riveting account of the controversy, by 1940, nine states had responded to this campaign by enacting statutes mandating flag salute ceremonies in public schools.[17]

These local requirements led to conflict with members of the Jehovah's Witnesses, a small religious group founded in Pennsylvania in 1870. Witnesses believed that destruction of the world was at hand and that the United States government, like all human institutions, was the instrument of Satan. In 1935, a third grader in Lynn, Massachusetts, whose parents were Witnesses, refused to salute the flag and was expelled from school. The Witnesses' leader, Joseph Rutherford, gave a radio address supporting the child and, over the next year, some one-hundred twenty Witnesses were expelled from schools for refusing to recite the Pledge.[18]

Within one week of Rutherford's address, the two Gobitas* children refused to salute the flag. They were subsequently expelled from school and threatened with assignment to a reformatory. With the help of the American Civil Liberties Union, the Gobitas family challenged the expulsion. The lower courts ruled in their favor, but in an 8–1 decision, the Supreme Court reversed.[19]

Justice Felix Frankfurter, then newly appointed to the Court, wrote the majority opinion.[20] As he formulated the issue, the Court was required to decide whether the First Amendment's free exercise clause entitled individuals with religious objections to an exemption from a generally valid statute. Frankfurter's opinion begins with an early example of the kind of rhetorical hand wringing that became a hallmark of his judicial career. For our purposes, we can think of him as torn between competing liberal and republican approaches. His ambivalence is apparent in the very first paragraph of the opinion: "A grave responsibility confronts this Court whenever in the course of litigation it must reconcile the conflicting claims of liberty and authority. But when the liberty invoked is liberty of conscience, and the authority is authority to safeguard the nation's fellowship, judicial conscience is put to its severest test."[21]

---

* The Gobitas's name is misspelled in the U.S. Reports. In the discussion that follows, I use "Gobitis" when referring to the case and "Gobitas" when referring to the family.

Frankfurter was prepared to give liberalism its due. Thus, "the affirmative pursuit of one's convictions about the ultimate mystery of the universe and man's relation to it is placed beyond the reach of law."[22] This "precious right" could be brought into question only when "the conscience of individuals collides with the felt necessities of society."[23] In this case, however, there was just such a collision. This was so because the exercise from which the Gobitas family sought exemption was "required of all the other children in the promotion of national cohesion" and because "[n]ational unity is the basis of national security."[24] According to Frankfurter, the promotion of these goals was no small matter: "The ultimate foundation of a free society is the binding tie of cohesive sentiment. Such a sentiment is fostered by all those agencies of the mind and spirit which may serve to gather up the traditions of a people, transmit them from generation to generation, and thereby create the continuity of a treasured common life which constitutes a civilization."[25]

After telling the reader at considerable length just how difficult this dilemma was, Frankfurter ultimately resolved the tension between liberty and solidarity by collapsing one into the other. It turns out, he tells us, that

personal freedom is best maintained, so long as the remedial channels of the democratic process remain open and unobstructed, when it is ingrained in the people's habits and not enforced against popular policy by the coercion of adjudicated law. . . .

[T]o the legislature no less than to courts is committed the guardianship of deeply-cherished liberties. . . . Where all the effective means of inducing political changes are left free from interference, education in the abandonment of foolish legislation is itself a training in liberty. To fight out the wise use of legislative authority in the forum of public opinion and before legislative assemblies rather than to transfer such a contest to the judicial arena, serves to vindicate the self-confidence of a free people.[26]

Thus, although the opinion begins by worrying over a difficult trade-off between liberal and republican values, it ends with a triumphant embrace of republicanism. Indeed, republicanism is victorious on two different levels. First, we have the substantive question whether the Gobitas's claim of individual right should prevail over that of the state interest in solidarity. Here, Frankfurter relies on the familiar republican argument for a state responsibility to instill "civic virtue" in citizens, especially through the process of public education. Like many republicans before him, Frankfurter expresses the view that freedom cannot survive if citizens see themselves as nothing more than individual and isolated preference maximizers. This is so because "[t]he ultimate foundation of a free society is the binding tie of cohesive sentiment."[27] According to standard republican dogma, such sentiment can be maintained only so long as communities are relatively homogeneous, at least with regard to basic values. The Pledge contributes to achieving this homogeneity by "gather[ing] up the traditions of a people, transmit[ing] them from generation to generation, and thereby creat[ing] the continuity of a treasured common life which constitutes a civilization."[28]

Frankfurter administers the coup de grace when he turns to the second level of his argument. Suppose that not everyone is convinced by the first-level argument and that some of these unconvinced citizens retain liberal, rather than republican values? How should the conflict between republican and liberal citizens be resolved? Frankfurter's answer is that the conflict between liberalism and republicanism must, itself, be settled by republican deliberation. In his words, "democratic processes [must] remain open and unobstructed," and freedom must be "ingrained in the people's habits and not enforced against popular policy by the coercion of adjudicated law."[29]

This argument brilliantly turns the Gobitas's objection to coercion in the opposite direction. Frankfurter switches our attention from the school board's use of coercive power against the Witnesses to the Witnesses' attempt to use "the coercion of adjudicated law" against the popular will. This rhetoric, in turn, invokes the republican conception of freedom. Instead of an individual right to do whatever one wants, true freedom on the republican view involves active engagement with fellow citizens to determine the common good. In Frankfurter's words, it is the right "[t]o fight out the wise use of legislative authority in the forum of public opinion and before legislative assemblies"[30]

Not surprisingly, then, Frankfurter's republican stance privileges speech over silence. The remedy for the Witnesses is not to remain passively mute while the Pledge is recited and then to depend upon judges for protection. Instead, their remedy lies in active engagement in politics undertaken with the "self-confidence of a free people." If the Witnesses are to prevail, they cannot insist upon isolated silence; they must speak to their fellow citizens in an effort to vindicate their claims through a process of collective, democratic deliberation among an engaged citizenry.

Later commentators have not been kind to Frankfurter's defense of the mandatory flag salute,[31] but there is more to his argument than is generally recognized. Perhaps the most refreshing aspect of the opinion is its refusal to accept the liberal equation between freedom and a private sphere. As Frankfurter expressly recognizes, the preferences of the children of Jehovah's Witnesses do not come from nowhere. Preferences and beliefs are inevitably grounded in and constrained by sources outside the individual, here, most obviously, the religious beliefs of the parents. Thus, for Frankfurter, the real issue in the case was whether school authorities should be allowed "to awaken in the child's mind considerations as to the significance of the flag contrary to those implanted by the parent."[32] By resolving the question in favor of public authority, Frankfurter spoke for a tradition that culminated in cases like *Brown v. Board of Education*[33] that refused to take private preferences as the starting point for constitutional analysis.

Frankfurter's reasoning is prescient and generative in a second respect as well. Although he does not quite put the point this way, his argument suggests that there is a hidden cost to allowing the Witnesses to opt out of the Pledge. Permitting an "exit" option diminishes the incentive to engage in public deliberation, thereby jeopardizing key republican goals. In our own time, a similar point has been made by scholars like Bruce Ackerman, who have argued that when groups have the option of exit (the phenomenon of the closet for gay men and lesbians is the obvious example), political outcomes are distorted.[34]

Still, there are serious problems with a republican approach to the Pledge. One problem is that even though both levels of Frankfurter's argument support republicanism, the two levels are also at war with each other. On the first level, he defends the Pledge on the ground that it inculcates "cohesive sentiment." On the second level, he claims that opponents of the Pledge should "fight out" their case "in the forum of public opinion and before legislative assemblies." The difficulty is that if the Pledge is really successful in forming "cohesive sentiment[s]," then there will be nothing left to "fight out." Deliberative engagement by public citizens begins to look much less attractive if the state brainwashes people into "cohesive sentiment" before the engagement begins.

This problem is aggravated by another difficulty: The second level of the argument begs the very question at issue. Is it really fair to insist upon a republican solution to a struggle between liberalism and republicanism? Put differently, the *Gobitis* case poses a conflict between a right to private silence and an obligation of public speech. Frankfurter resolves the conflict by insisting that people defend their right to private silence by speaking publicly. But such a resolution will be satisfactory only to people who reject a right of silence in the first place. One can hardly expect Witnesses, who declined to take the Pledge precisely because they believed that involvement with secular government was sinful, to be persuaded by this resolution.

These are serious problems. We cannot assess how serious they are, however, until we compare them to the problems posed by the liberal approach.

THE LIBERAL TRIUMPH

Gobitis was followed by a period of ugly attacks directed against Witnesses. In different parts of the country, Witnesses were castrated, tarred and feathered, abused, beaten, and shot. In 1940, according to reports collected by the ACLU, almost 1,500 Witnesses were attacked in 335 incidents in forty-four states. Over 2,000 children were expelled from schools throughout the country for refusing to participate in the Pledge.[35] Meanwhile, two members of the original *Gobitis* majority—Chief Justice Charles Evans Hughes and Justice James McReynolds—retired. For reasons that remain mysterious, three other justices, Hugo Black, William O. Douglas, and Frank Murphy, came to regret their vote.

The signal that the *Gobitis* majority had disintegrated came in *Jones v. City of Opelika*,[36] a case decided two years later. A majority of the Court upheld a licensing tax as applied to written material distributed by Witnesses, but four justices dissented. Chief Justice Stone, the sole dissenter in *Gobitis,* also wrote a long dissent in *City of Opelika.*[37] More significant, however, was a short dissenting statement signed by Justices Black, Douglas, and Murphy, all of whom had been in the *Gobitis* majority. They wrote that the outcome in *City of Opelika* was a "logical extension" of *Gobitis,* but that they "now believe[d] that [*Gobitis*] was also wrongly decided."[38]

Emboldened by this dissent, a three-judge district court at the behest of the Barnett family* enjoined the enforcement of a West Virginia flag salute requirement in the teeth of the *Gobitis* precedent.[39] When the case reached the Supreme Court, Justices Stone, Black, Douglas, and Murphy were joined by newly appointed Justices Jackson and Wiley Rutledge in voting to affirm the district court and overrule *Gobitis.*

The doctrinal move made by the *Barnette* majority was to switch the focus of analysis from the free exercise claim that *Gobitis* had resolved to a free speech claim that it had ignored. Whereas Frankfurter's *Gobitis* opinion was preoccupied with the question whether religious believers were entitled to an exemption from a statute that Frankfurter tacitly assumed was facially valid, Jackson's *Barnette* opinion problematized the statute's validity. It concluded that the free speech clause prevents the government from imposing a general duty to salute the flag even if objections to doing so are not grounded in religious belief.[40]

As a matter of formal analysis, this shift of focus is less than fully successful. The Jackson approach poses the same basic question answered in *Gobitis,* namely, whether particular groups are entitled to special exemptions because of conscientious objection to a general requirement, albeit in a free speech rather than a free exercise context. Jackson does not explain why free speech and free exercise claims should be differently treated. The real work of the opinion, however, lies in its theoretical shift of focus. Instead of emphasizing republican obligation, the Jackson opinion defends liberal rights.

---

* The Supreme Court managed to misspell not only Gobitas's name, but also Barnett's. In what follows I will use "Barnett" to refer to the family and "Barnette" to refer to the case.

Jackson attacked both levels of Frankfurter's argument. On the first level, he relied on the traditional liberal position regarding personal autonomy. It was important that "[t]he freedom of these appellees does not bring them into collision with rights asserted by any other individual."[41] State intervention might be justified when there was such a conflict, but here "the refusal of these persons to participate in the ceremony does not interfere with or deny rights of others to do so."[42] For Jackson, freedom was not aligning oneself with a community that one belonged to as republicans maintained, but deciding for oneself how to act so long as that decision did not interfere with the rights of other individuals. From this perspective, education in citizenship that included compulsory group ceremonies would "strangle the free mind at its source."[43] Public schools should not be a site where children were encouraged to transcend their individuality for the sake of the community, but a forum designed to strengthen "individual freedom of mind in preference to officially disciplined uniformity."[44]

Jackson was also skeptical of Frankfurter's republican insistence on homogeneity and cohesion as a precondition for freedom. For Jackson, true national unity, to the extent that it could be achieved at all, arose not from coercion but from "persuasion and example."[45] But, perhaps more significantly, the teachings of history were that efforts to achieve such unity ended in tyranny rather than freedom. "As first and moderate methods to attain unity have failed, those bent on its accomplishment must resort to an ever-increasing severity. . . . Those who begin coercive elimination of dissent soon find themselves exterminating dissenters. Compulsory unification of opinion achieves only the unanimity of the graveyard."[46]

On the second level, Jackson rejected outright a republican solution to liberal/republican conflict. On his view,

The very purpose of a Bill of Rights was to withdraw certain subjects from the vicissitudes of political controversy, to place them beyond the reach of majorities and officials and to establish them as legal principles to be applied by the courts. One's right to life, liberty, and property, to free speech, a free press, freedom of worship and assembly, and other fundamental rights may not be submitted to vote; they depend on the outcome of no elections.[47]

Taken together, these two sets of arguments lead to the conclusion that Justice Frankfurter was wrong to privilege speech over silence. True, the first amendment is written in terms of freedom of "speech," but, on a liberal understanding, its ultimate purpose is to protect individual autonomy rather than public engagement. Silence as well as speech may be necessary to protect such autonomy. Justice Jackson writes that "[t]o sustain compulsory flag salute we are required to say that a Bill of Rights which guards the individual's right to speak his own mind, left it open to public authorities to compel him to utter what is not in his mind."[48] On liberal (but not republican) assumptions, such a conclusion is nonsensical, and the Court's newly formed majority emphatically rejected it.

SILENCE AND COERCION

At first it may seem that the conflict between the Frankfurter and Jackson opinions poses the familiar dilemma of choosing between incompatible republican and liberal political theories. How can we make such a choice in a neutral way when the choosing mechanism itself must be located within republicanism or liberalism? Notice in this regard that just as Frankfurter begs the question by holding liberal values hostage to a collective, republican veto, so too Jackson insists that liberal values be withdrawn from "the vicissitudes of political controversy," and thereby shielded from republican attack. Perhaps there is no way to avoid this reproduction of the essential conflict on the metalevel that is supposed to resolve the conflict.

It turns out, though, that the conflict may be less intractable than it first seems. This is so because the implications of the liberal argument are not as obvious as Justice Jackson makes them appear. In fact, it is far from clear that the liberal argument really supports a right to silence, at least as that right is articulated in *Barnette*. The problem is that here, as in the case of self-incrimination and confession, liberals have misunderstood the effect of coercion.[49]

To see the problem it is useful to compare *Barnette* with *Wooley v. Maynard*,[50] a case decided a quarter century later. New Hampshire license plates are embossed with the state's motto, "Live Free or Die." A New Hampshire statute made it a crime to obscure "the figures or letters on any number plate."[51] Maynard (also a follower of the Jehovah's Witness faith) found the motto offensive and covered it with tape. Relying upon *Barnette,* the Supreme Court, in an opinion written by Chief Justice Warren Burger, held that Maynard could not be punished for this conduct. Although the lower court had upheld Maynard's claim on the theory that he was engaging in symbolic speech when he obscured the message, Chief Justice Burger found it unnecessary to rule on this issue, since "the more appropriate First Amendment grounds" for decision were that the New Hampshire statute, as applied to Maynard, violated his right to silence.[52]

[T]he right of freedom of thought protected by the First Amendment against state action includes both the right to speak freely and the right to refrain from speaking at all. . . . A system which secures the right to proselytize religious, political and ideological causes must also guarantee the concomitant right to decline to foster such concepts. The right to speak and the right to refrain from speaking are complementary components of the broader concept of "individual freedom of mind."[53]

Suppose we assume with Chief Justice Burger and other liberals that a right to silence should indeed be recognized as the flip side of a right to speak. This is not a concession that republicans would be willing to make, but even if they were, the concession alone does not win the case for Maynard. He is entitled to ignore the New Hampshire statute only if it violates his right to silence. That right, in turn, would be violated only if his display of the unobstructed plate counted as Maynard's speech. But as Justice Rehnquist points out in a powerful dissent,[54] it seems quite doubtful that it should so count. Of course, the motto is *someone's* speech. No doubt the New Hampshire government wished to express a sentiment by reproducing the motto on the license plate. But in what sense is display of the plate *Maynard's* speech? As an empirical matter, it is deeply implausible that many people viewing Maynard's car with an unobstructed plate believed that he was expressing his own views about the relative merits of freedom and life. Indeed, it is the very existence of the coercion that he objects to that prevents attributing the view to him.

Imagine that New Hampshire responded to the Court's decision by instituting a system under which people could choose license plates with a wide variety of different slogans, or even, perhaps, with any slogan they wished. Under this regime, there is much less doubt that a person displaying a "Live Free or Die" plate would be expressing this sentiment. The absence of coercion makes it fair to attribute the sentiment on the chosen plate to the driver. In contrast, if everyone must display the "Live Free or Die" motto on pain of criminal prosecution, it is hardly reasonable to attribute the motto to people who are simply complying with the law. Just as coercion distances individuals from the self-betrayal that concerns liberals in the Fifth Amendment context, so too it eliminates ownership of the compelled statements in the free speech context.

Indeed, the Court itself seems to have endorsed something close to this point in one of its more recent encounters with compelled speech. In *Johanns v. Livestock Marketing Association*,[55] the Court rejected a claim by beef producers that mandatory contributions to a fund used to produce generic beef advertising violated their First Amendment rights. The Court held that the right to silence was not implicated by the program because the advertising in question was attributable to the government, rather than to the producers.

Strikingly, the Court reached this conclusion precisely because the government dictated the content of the advertising.[56] One might suppose that government control over the content of the speech made the program more, rather than less, vulnerable to a First Amendment challenge. In fact, though, it is just this government direction that insulates the speech from the individuals who do not wish to be associated with it. Because government officials dictated the content of the speech, it was government speech rather than individual speech and therefore not prohibited by an individual right to silence.

To be sure, as a formal matter, the Court distinguished the beef program from New Hampshire's use of the "Live Free or Die" slogan in *Wooley*. The beef program, the Court tells us, involves a compelled *subsidy*, which is analytically different from the compelled *speech* in *Wooley*.[57] But this distinction is difficult to maintain. The very question at issue in *Wooley* was whether the required use of the license plate was Maynard's compelled speech or merely a compelled subsidy of the government's speech. The correct categorization, in turn, depends upon whether the slogan constitutes Maynard's speech or the government's. As the *Johanns* Court instructs us, the answer to that question is substantially influenced by whether the government controls the content of the speech. Since the government controlled the slogan on the license plate, it might be thought that Maynard's forced display of the plate constituted no more than a subsidy.

Once this much is established, the last step in the argument leads us to a remarkable paradox: it turns out that it is actually *coerced speech* that best protects a right to silence, and that it is the Court's embrace of a right to avoid coerced speech in cases like *Barnette* and *Wooley* that threatens the silence right.

Consider the perspective of an outside observer watching the flag salute ceremony in *Barnette*. This observer knows that the ceremony is compelled, so she will naturally suppose that an indeterminate number of children are participating because they want to, while a similarly indeterminate number are participating because they have to. In an important sense, this regime allows the dissenting children to remain silent. True, they are mouthing words, but surely the mere mouthing of words does not constitute "speech" in the constitutional sense.

For example, we have seen that there is a serious issue as to whether compelled voice exemplars taken from criminal suspects for identification purposes violate the self-incrimination clause,[58] but no one has suggested the possibility that they violate the free speech clause. The suggestion strikes us as silly because speech, for First Amendment purposes, is about communication. In the context of a compelled Flag Salute ceremony, individual students are communicating nothing about agreement with the sentiments expressed by the Pledge because the outside observer cannot know which students are acting out of conviction and which are merely acquiescing to authority. Just as Doe's forced execution of a "consent" form tells us nothing about his actual consent and therefore does not violate the Fifth Amendment privilege,[59] so, too, a compelled Pledge fails to communicate in the First Amendment sense.

Compare this regime to the regime mandated by the *Barnette* decision. Now, dissenting students no longer retain a right to silence. Either they must participate in the ceremony or opt out. Because their participation is no longer coerced, it communicates to outside observers that they believe in the Pledge's sentiments, and, so, constitutes speech. If they instead choose to opt out, they must identify themselves as individuals opposed to those sentiments, which, again, constitutes a form of speech. A liberal believer in a right to silence could hardly be happy with this choice. It is the very freedom to opt out that makes both alternatives a form of speech and undermines a right to silence.*

RESCUING *BARNETTE*

Some liberal defenders of the *Barnette* result have noticed that there are problems with the Court's reasoning and, so, have attempted to find alternative, less troublesome rationales for the decision. Unfortunately, none of these efforts has been completely successful. Friends of *Barnette* have made three separate arguments.

First, some liberals have shifted attention from the external effect of compelled speech to its effect on the speaker herself. In an important and subtle article building on her prior work, Seana Shiffrin has argued that the problem with compelled speech is that it fails to treat citizens as rational and autonomous agents.[60] Even if such speech communicates nothing to outsiders, it does not respect "the autonomous agent's control over her mind" and "the virtue of sincerity.[61] The worry, in other words, is not that the compelled speaker will convince others, but that the speaker herself will become convinced. On this view, the government is free to

---

* Indeed, the Supreme Court seems to have endorsed something like this view in the school prayer context. In the course of rejecting the opt-out option as sufficient to solve the constitutional problem with such prayers, the Court observed that "[f]inding no violation under these circumstances would place objectors in the dilemma of participating, with all that implies, or protesting." *Lee v. Weisman,* 505 U.S. 577, 593 (1992). On the other hand, the Court does not seem to have grasped the way in which coercion blunts the communicative impact of participation. For the Court, there was "no doubt that for many, if not most, of the students at the graduation, the act of standing or remaining silent was an expression of participation in the Rabbi's prayer. . . . [G]iven our social conventions, a reasonable dissenter in this milieu could believe that the group exercise signified her own participation or approval of it." Id.

try to influence its citizens, but it must do so by offering "ideals, visions, reasons and arguments . . . for their evaluation, deliberation and assessment,"[62] rather than by forcing rote repetition.

There is surely something to this position, but there are also serious problems with it. To begin, some may doubt whether compelled speech really threatens the ideal of autonomous decision making. Interestingly, the *Barnette* Court seems to have objected to the Pledge in part for the opposite reason—because it thought that mandatory displays of patriotism were likely to be *ineffective* in creating true devotion to country.[63] There is reason to believe that compulsion of this sort actually triggers dissent that might otherwise remain latent. It certainly had this impact in the case of the Jehovah's Witnesses, where the disciplining of Witness children produced a contagion of disobedience. Recall, as well, Professor Ackerman's argument that allowing an "exit" option will blunt political opposition to the measure in question.[64]

Shiffrin may nonetheless be right when she argues that the well known mechanism of cognitive dissonance, together with the nonsalience of background coercion, at least sometimes cause people to come to believe what they are required to say.[65] Certainly, proponents of the mandatory Pledge hope that this is the case. But Shiffrin is unduly optimistic in assuming that in the absence of the government-compelled speech, students will form their views through a rational process of "evaluation, deliberation and assessment." In effect, she adopts the usual liberal assumption that people are free when the government does not act. But at least in this context, the assumption is undefended and unwarranted.

At this point in the argument, it is useful to take cognizance of the pervasive determinist insight concerning the importance of background coercion. Of course, Felix Frankfurter was hardly a pervasive determinist. Yet I take Frankfurter to be making a kind of determinist point when he observes that the compelled pledge is designed to do no more than "awaken in the child's mind considerations as to the significance of the flag contrary to those implanted by the parent."[66] There is no reason to suppose that these parents influenced their children through a process of rational argumentation. It seems more likely that the state's insistence on rote repetition does no more than counteract parental coercion.* Indeed, even when applied to adults, Shiffrin's theory could use a healthy dose of determinist skepicism. It is simply naive to suppose that any of us come to our views through unmediated ratiocination. The process of opinion formation is shot through with subtle forms of coercion and manipulation.

Shiffrin's insistence on rational persuasion seems especially odd in the context of the effort to instill feelings of patriotism. Her argument proceeds as if patriotism were justified only when supported by evidence that can be critically evaluated. As she puts it, when teachers engage in "legitimate educational efforts," they "teach or persuade students of the contents of the Pledge, its vision of America, and the worthiness of allegiance."[67] But surely this is not the way that most of us come to, or think about, love of country. Many people think patriotism is a virtue irrespective of the country to which it attaches, at least so long as the country satisfies minimal standards of decency. This conception of patriotism is inconsistent with a view that holds that people should be patriotic only when they are convinced by logical argument that their country is in fact deserving of a special and higher regard not accorded to other countries.

To put this proposition in the context of discussion in the previous chapters, patriotism, at least as commonly understood, is a specific

---

* To her credit, Shiffrin seems to recognize that state inaction with regard to the education of children may not automatically produce the virtue of critical reflection that she admires. Thus, she is troubled by the Court's decision upholding the constitutional right of the Boy Scouts to dismiss a gay scoutmaster because, in her view,

> the state may reasonably judge that children may be required to interact with a wide range of people in their social activities and to confront and assess the validity of their and others' biases toward unpopular groups. This may ensure that children have a wide informational base to inform their subsequent, adult exercises of autonomy and to ensure that children enjoy equal opportunities that might otherwise be denied by other children's untutored discriminatory choices. (Seana Valentine Shiffrin, *What Is Really Wrong with Compelled Association?*, 99 N.W. U. L. REV. 839, 883 [2005])

Surprisingly, however, Shiffrin shifts gears when discussing the Pledge. The two situations are different, she claims, because "[u]nlike compelled recitation, inclusion-oriented membership regulations do not amount to a direct effort at mind control with a specified content" (Id., at 884). True enough, but Shiffrin does not focus on the possibility that private groups, including families, might, themselves, engage in "direct effort[s] at mind control with a specified content." To the extent that they do, it is unclear why the state cannot counteract these efforts by using similar tactics.

instance of particularism. People love their country not because publicly accessible reason convinces them that it is the "best" country, but simply because it is theirs, just as love for family or friends is not held hostage to logical argumentation.

We have already seen that in general, liberals have defended particularism against imperialistic forays by universalists.[68] The association between liberalism and particularism, in turn, suggests once again that liberals may have things backward when they embrace *Barnette*. Perhaps there is a reason why particularist attachment to religion should trump particularist attachment to country. It will not do, though, simply to object to patriotic exercises because they do not constitute rational argumentation. Liberals insist that we should not be made to choose our families or lovers on the basis of universalist criteria, and neither do most of us choose our country on this basis. But if patriotism is indeed about familiarity and nonrational belonging, then ceremonies of rote repetition are an entirely appropriate means of instilling it. It is just the fact that, say, the Pledge or the National Anthem, or the American flag are omnipresent and repeatedly ceremonially honored that makes them familiar and, so, creates the mystical, nonrational bond that patriotism amounts to.

To be sure, there is a republican objection to patriotism. This assertion may seem odd, given the historic association between republicanism and allegiance to the nation state. Still, a thoroughgoing republican might think of himself as a citizen of the world. Such a citizen would treat all countries, and all people within them, with equal affection and would insist on publicly accessible, universalist argument to justify a seeming preference for one over the other. This ideal may be attractive in a certain sense, and, if one adopted it, it might lead one to object to the Pledge in particular, and patriotism more generally, precisely because neither is supported by publicly accessible argument.

I doubt whether Shiffrin really means to embrace a position like this. Even if she does, this republican stance fits uneasily with a legal doctrine that protects Jehovah's Witnesses from coerced participation in the Pledge. After all, the Witnesses were hardly objecting to the ceremony because of their allegiance to world government. For all that appears, their objection to international institutions would be at least as strong as their objection to local and national government. Their allegiance instead was to a kingdom of God. In one sense, of course, this amounts to the ultimate universalism. When it is translated into the secular realm, however, the claim cashes out as an assertion of a right of separation from earthly institutions. That right fits most easily with liberal arguments for privacy and particularism, the very arguments that also support the fostering of patriotism through rote ceremony. Making a particularist argument for the Witnesses therefore requires a theory for why religious particularism should trump patriotic particularism.

A second effort to salvage *Barnette* emphasizes the risk that compelled government speech will distort the free market of ideas. The argument here is neither that coerced participants will come to believe what they say nor that outside observers will confuse government speech with private speech. Rather, it is that government speech has the capacity to overwhelm private channels of communication and, so, control debate in a fashion that is inconsistent with First Amendment values.

There is an extensive scholarly literature on the issue of government speech, which I will not try to summarize here.[69] For our purposes, the debate is relevant only to the extent that it bears on a right to silence. A useful focus for this aspect of the debate is Gregory Klass's recent, thoughtful article on compelled subsidization.[70] Klass adopts what he calls a "forum theory" of the First Amendment, which stands in contrast to a "liberty theory" by emphasizing the protection of expressive forums rather than an individual's freedom of expression.[71] Borrowing a phrase from Robert Kamenshine's earlier work,[72] he argues that forum theory might entail an "implied political establishment clause," which would prohibit the state from "participating in public debate on contentious political issues."[73] As Klass defines these terms, they would prohibit the state from taking an official stand on matters of current controversy that are directly related to public policy.[74]

There is surely some force to this point. Klass's theory helps explain the widely shared intuition that there would be something deeply wrong if, for example, the government funded the Republican but not the Democratic convention or required every family to put a "support our troops" sign on their front lawn.

The argument is also quite clever because it turns Justice Frankfurter's republican theory on its head. Recall that Frankfurter associated political freedom with a truly inclusive public debate about our collective actions and goals, rather than with the rights of individual dissenters. But, as Klass points out, the problem with compelled subsidization is not that it suppresses the speech of individual dissenters, as liberals fear, but that it pollutes and distorts the overall outcomes of this debate. As such, it interferes with the sort of deliberative democracy that republicans favor.

Perhaps because of its republican pedigree, however, Klass's argument does not fare well along the "fit" dimension. Klass' argument is quite powerful when he defends an undistorted public sphere of debate, but less effective in tying that defense to an individual right to remain silent.* On the narrowest level, the theory as he articulates it does not justify the results in cases like *Barnette* and *Wooley*. It seems doubtful that either the sentiments expressed in the Pledge or on New Hampshire license plates amount to official stands on matters of current controversy that are directly related to public policy. They fit more easily within the category of what Klass calls "ideological" speech, and Klass is much more doubtful that his "implied establishment clause" should apply to such speech.[75]

More broadly, there is no clear nexus between the concern about government forum distortion on the one hand and the commandeering of private speech or subsidization on the other. Even if paid for wholly out of general revenues, government speech distorts the speech market.[76] Why is there a special problem with such speech when individuals are compelled to associate themselves with it? While liberals have an answer to this question, a republican response is much more difficult.

Relatedly, there is a disjunction between Klass's theory and the actual injury that people like Barnett complain of. Their point, at least as I

---

* In fairness to Klass, it must be noted that he presents his theory as a solution to the compelled subsidization problem, which he distinguishes from the compelled speech problem. *See* Gregory Klass, *The Very Idea of a First Amendment Right Against Compelled Subsidization*, 38 U.C. DAVIS L. REV. 1087, 1110 (2005). For an argument that the line between these two problems is unstable, see pp. 155–56, *supra*.

understand it, is not that public debate was insufficiently inclusive or that political outcomes had been distorted. Indeed, as we have already seen, the opt-out possibility that they insist upon might, itself, distort public debate. The essence of their claim is a right to secede from political involvement, not a right to participate in it. As I argue above, they may have misunderstood what measures best protect that right, but the right itself is grounded in liberal rather than republican theory.

Perhaps it should come as no surprise that forum theory is inconsistent with results that the courts have reached using liberal premises. What is more surprising is that it is also in deep tension with the republican theory that animates it in the first place. Republicans want free debate on matters of public interest precisely because they value public outcomes, which are an expression of the common sentiments of the community as a whole. This is a stance that supports, rather than undermines, government speech. As noted above, when the Court has succeeded in attributing speech to the government, it has held that it is *not* subject to constitutional restrictions that would otherwise apply,[77] a stance that is precisely the opposite of the result that forum theory would require but that is quite consistent with republican premises. Similarly, there is much recent scholarship explaining and defending the "expressive" function of much of what government does.[78] When Congress enacted the Civil Rights Act of 1964, it prohibited certain conduct, but perhaps more significantly, it also expressed and forcefully communicated a public determination, reached after years of struggle and debate, that racial segregation was deeply wrong. Liberals might object to this sort of collective judgment because it arguably overrides individual freedom, but it is an outcome that most republicans would applaud. After all, what is the point of public deliberation over the good if it does not in the end produce a public resolution followed by action that is consistent with that resolution?

Finally, as Klass himself acknowledges, forum theory might well support rather than condemn certain forms of government speech. Here, once again, republicans will urge us to resist the equation of freedom with the private sphere. Of course, there is some potential that government will distort the speech market, but there is no reason to suppose that the market is "undistorted" in the absence of government intervention. Differences in education, in incentives, in wealth, and in articulateness create a private baseline that is normatively problematic. Why should we presume a priori that government intervention will make matters worse rather than better?

A third effort to resurrect *Barnette* returns to the decision's liberal roots, but argues that free speech is the wrong analytic framework for understanding the problem. Instead, on this view, the decision protects a more general right to autonomy and personhood that is unconnected to freedom of expression. At the conclusion of a thorough and convincing analysis of the compelled speech problem, Abner Greene suggests a solution along these lines.[79] For him, the right to remain silent during the Pledge is analogous to reproductive rights, the right to refuse medical treatment, the right to teach children a foreign language, and the right to control family membership and living arrangements. He claims that all these cases share two characteristics: a strong personal claim of liberty conjoined with a weak justification for government regulation.[80]

Greene's argument from autonomy and personhood is much less well developed than the other arguments in his article, and he provides no basis for his conclusion that the compelled Pledge satisfies either of the criteria he sets forth. It is at least contestable whether the government interest in the compelled Pledge is weak. Certainly, this was not Justice Frankfurter's view. If the Pledge and similar forms of patriotic indoctrination really do cement the "binding ties of cohesive sentiment" that form the "ultimate foundation of a free society," then the government's interest would seem to be strong indeed. Oddly, in other work, Greene has been quite eloquent in defending what he calls "thick perfectionism," a view of the state that endorses collective embrace of contestable values.[81] Given this endorsement, it is a bit puzzling why collective judgments are given short shrift in the context of the Pledge.

Of course, there is a difference between state endorsement of values that is noncoercive and state endorsement that compels dissenters to agree. That difference, though, relates to the other criterion that Greene enunciates—the requirement that the individual interest be strong. If the compelled Pledge stifled dissent or closed avenues of communication, then it would be easy to see why this interest would be powerful. But Greene's argument proceeds on the assumption that it does neither, and the argument I have set forth above explains why he is right on that score. The question, then, is what other basis there might be for an autonomy interest in not mouthing the words of the Pledge.

In thinking about that question, it is instructive to focus on the differences between a right to opt out of the Pledge and the other supposedly analogous rights that Greene mentions. Laws that regulate reproductive freedom, family arrangements, or learning a foreign language all limit activity that is thought to be especially worthy of protection. But what activity does the compelled Pledge interfere with? Of course, the Pledge compels children to put their bodies, here their lips and vocal cords, to a certain use, but for as long as jaywalking and trespass statutes are on the books, it will remain deeply implausible that there is some general constitutional right to avoid government control over one's body. To be sure, we usually think of speech as different, but that is because it is usually true that speech involves expression and communication. Once we have taken this off the table, it is quite mysterious what remains of a "personhood" argument.

Greene's error, if he has indeed made one, resembles the error that bedevils arguments for a right to silence more generally: It mischaracterizes the effect of coercion on dignity and personhood. It is simply a mistake to suppose that application of coercion always invades personal dignity. There is no disgrace in being forced to do something against one's will.

A confusion comes about because coercion is often accompanied by a kind of self-betrayal or insincerity. Sometimes, when people are faced with coercion, they give in when they ought to resist. Perhaps, there is a disgrace in that. But for reasons outlined above, opponents of the coerced Pledge have failed to explain why this particular form of coercion results in either self-betrayal or insincerity. At least on the account we have discussed so far, the only people demeaned by the Pledge are the officials who insist upon it. They must explain to themselves and others why they are preoccupied with a ceremony that obstructs, rather than facilitates, the communication of patriotic sentiment. In contrast, their victims can take solace in the silent anonymity of compelled speech.* There is no disgrace in nonresistance because there is nothing to resist. They have not betrayed their ideals precisely because their compelled participation expresses nothing about those ideals.

RADICAL LIBERTARIANS AND *BARNETTE*

If the argument I have made above is correct, then there should be a kind of "overlapping consensus" that *Barnette* is wrongly decided regardless of whether one is grounded in republican, pervasive determinist, or liberal thought. From a republican perspective, the state has the right and duty to inculcate the "cohesive sentiment" expressed by the Pledge. Although some republicans might object to the "distortion" of public debate that occurs when the government uses private individuals to express its views, this concern is too inconsistent with other strands of republican thought for republicans to worry seriously about it. Republicans, after all, favor the inculcation of "civic virtue" in private individuals and believe in collective action to implement community values and aspirations.

For pervasive determinists, the liberal obsession with coercion and brainwashing will seem pointless and silly. In a world where coercion is everywhere, requiring a few school children to mouth some words is the least of our troubles. Here, as elsewhere, the unadulterated determinist view is deeply unappealing, but more moderate determinists have a useful reminder for liberals: the elimination of government coercion should not be confused with the elimination of coercion more generally. Abandon-

---

* I put to one side here the views of people who believe that they can be disgraced by conduct they cannot avoid. For example, in some societies, some women feel disgraced by rape that they lack the physical capacity to resist. In some religious traditions, even involuntary noncompliance with religious commands are condemned. So, too, even a compelled recitation of the Pledge that communicates nothing might violate certain religious norms. If one thinks that there is a government duty to respect beliefs of this sort, that duty might give rise to an objection to a compelled Pledge. The important point for present purposes, though, is that this objection cannot rest upon the kind of argument from personhood that Greene advances, since that argument is premised on the voluntarism that the beliefs described above reject. The kind of personhood protected by, say, the abortion right or the right to die equates dignity with liberal conceptions of freedom and human choice. In contrast, the set of beliefs described in this footnote are deeply illiberal and reject the relevance of choice.

ing the compelled Pledge does not produce a world of perfect freedom; on the contrary, compelled public education may be a useful corrective for compelled parental brainwashing.

Finally, although the liberal view seems most compatible with the result in *Barnette*, I have tried to show that liberals, too, should be troubled by that result. If one really believes in a private right to silence, then the best way to protect it is by a policy that prevents the disaggregation of group speech. So long as the speech is compelled, observers will be unable to distinguish between sincere and insincere speakers. Ironically, it is the opt out, rather than the compulsion that allows disaggregation and, so, breaks the silence.

So far, I have said nothing about the radical libertarian stance. At first, it may appear that radical libertarian thought provides an especially infertile ground to support the *Barnette* right. As we have seen in previous chapters, radical libertarians are mostly indifferent to the presence of legal coercion. To be sure, where the coercion is so severe that no real choice is possible, as in the case of torture, libertarians might worry that the possibility of resistance has been eliminated as a practical matter. Short of this, radical libertarians will claim that the legal coercion is just another excuse for denying the existence of a choice that we cannot avoid. For this reason, I have argued that in the self-incrimination context, radical libertarians should not favor a legal privilege that permits suspected criminals to avoid the choice between particularist and universalist values. At first blush, one might suppose that the *Barnette* problem should be resolved in the same way.

Consider, for example, *Rumsfeld v. Forum for Academic and Institutional Rights, Inc (FAIR).*[82] A federal statute required academic institutions to give military recruiters equal access to students on pain of losing federal funding for the entire institution. The plaintiffs claimed that putting them to this choice violated their First Amendment rights, but the Supreme Court rejected the argument. The Court concluded that the government was not really forcing universities to "speak," by requiring them to allow the presence of recruiters on campus. A radical libertarian might reach the same conclusion by focusing on the coercion rather than the speech. Surely an institution truly committed to gay rights would not abandon the cause simply for the sake of federal funding, he might say. Indeed, in an odd way, the government coercion provides an opportunity for universities to demonstrate the depth of their commitment. So, too, the Witnesses can communicate the seriousness with which they take their religious obligation by accepting expulsion. Providing an easy way out softens the choice and, so, reduces the possibility of truly taking a stand.

All this makes sense if the victim of government coercion chooses to stand and fight, as indeed the Barnett children did. Suppose, though, that they instead give in to the coercion, as universities have when faced with a fund cutoff? Once it becomes apparent that at least some people will give in, then the radical libertarian argument cuts in the opposite direction. Indeed, it turns out that radical libertarians are positioned to provide the best argument for the *Barnette* right.

This is so because the radical libertarian argument, in effect, turns the liberal perspective inside out. For the very reason that liberals should oppose *Barnette*, radical libertarians should favor it. As I have already explained, the opt-out solution forces a choice that compelled participation avoids. In a world where participants can choose whether to say the Pledge, it is much more obvious that they must choose. Either they participate or they don't, and either way, they are committing themselves to a position.

Now, to be sure, a radical libertarian will claim that there is also an unavoidable choice when the state coerces everybody into participation. One is always free to stand with the Barnett and Gobitas children and defy authority, and the denial of this freedom (the kind of denial that universities have engaged in) amounts to radical libertarian "bad faith." Still, for many, the possibility of choice is much less salient in a coercion regime. It will seem to them that there really is no choice, that there is simply an obligation to obey the law. In the best of worlds, a radical libertarian would want to disabuse people of this belief, but we do not live in the best of worlds. In the world we actually live in, the law should structure social situations in a fashion that brings home to people the possibility and obligation of choice. The opt-out regime mandated by *Barnette* does just this.

Consider, for example, the position of universities faced with fund cutoffs if they exclude military recruiters from campus. If they have no opt out, they need not face the hard choice of whether to oppose military policy during a time of war. They can fuzz the issue up (indeed, they *have* fuzzed the issue up) by claiming that they have no real option but to accede to government pressure. We cannot know how many universities have reluctantly acceded to government demands, because they would literally be destroyed if they resisted, and how many were secretly delighted to use this as an excuse for action they wanted to take anyway. In contrast, if FAIR had come out the other way, there would have been no refuge in coercion. Universities would have had to either allow the military to recruit or bar it from their campuses. Either way, they would have been taking a clear stand on the military's homophobic policies.

Superficially, it may seem that this stance is inconsistent with radical libertarian opposition to the Fifth Amendment privilege. In fact, though, the two positions are perfectly consistent. The radical libertarian argument against the privilege is premised on the belief that individuals "own" and are responsible for acts that they perform under legal compulsion. It follows that no privilege is necessary to confront individuals with the choice between universalist and particularist values that is typically presented by the risk of self-incrimination. Even without the privilege, individuals must decide what to do, and that decision inevitably confronts them with the hard choice between community obligation and self-preservation.

In contrast, self-preservation is not at stake in the compelled Pledge. The difference lies in the fact that whereas in the self-incrimination context, the risk to self comes from what the state does to criminals, in the Pledge context, the risk arises only because of what the ceremony communicates to others. When a person incriminates herself, the state puts her in prison or, perhaps, even takes her life, but when a person recites the Pledge, she does no more than move her lips. As I have argued above, the mere moving of lips that communicates nothing invades no private sphere worth protecting. Because the compelled Pledge communicates nothing, the person who recites it can take refuge in the silence of coerced speech and, so, avoid rather than confront the dilemma. We can make people confront the dilemma only if the Pledge is meaningful, and it will be meaningful only if dissenters are allowed to opt out.

What are the implications of the radical libertarian argument in other instances where the government compels speech? It is important to understand that the argument holds only in circumstances where the compelled speech is uncommunicative. Consider, for example, *Boy Scouts of America v. Dale*,[83] where the Court held that it was unconstitutional for a state to prevent the Boy Scouts of America (BSA) from dismissing a gay scoutmaster. Most reasonable observers will understand that the coerced Pledge communicates nothing about the actual belief of the individuals coerced, but there is more risk that observers will attribute the scoutmaster's speech and conduct to BSA. To be sure, the Scouts are not powerless to counteract that risk. They might go much further than they have to publicize their opposition to homosexuality. Still, state coercion is likely to fade into the background in the daily, nonritualized contact between the scoutmaster and the scouts.

One might suppose that this fact would strengthen BSA's argument, but because radical libertarian thought offers a through-the-looking-glass perspective on liberalism, it actually weakens its position. To the extent that retaining a gay scoutmaster amounts to self-betrayal, BSA is confronted with the choice that radical libertarians demand. They do not need an opt out to force that choice. Of course, just because radical libertarian and liberal approaches are mirror images of each other, the liberal argument becomes more powerful as the radical libertarian argument fades. If BSA is communicating views it does not hold, then it can no longer be said that their employment of a gay scoutmaster is meaningless in the sense that forced participation in the Pledge ritual is meaningless. What remains, then, is the liberal worry that government interference with private communication through "expressive association" is sufficiently troublesome to outweigh Dale's equality claim.

Just as the radical libertarian argument holds only when the compelled speech is uncommunicative, so too, the argument loses force when the opt out is uncommunicative. Consider, for example, the requirement that beef producers fund a generic advertising campaign.[84] I must confess that I have some trouble imagining how paying for advertising asserting that beef is "what's for dinner" will often involve deep libertarian self-betrayal, at least among the population of beef producers. Even if we put this problem to one side, though, there is a good radical libertarian reason why no opt out should be allowed. Whereas virtually all students who opt out of the Pledge will do so for reasons of conscience, even a beef producer who favors the advertisements will have an incentive to a free ride by not paying his share. Oddly, this fact means that coercion plays the opposite role in the generic advertising and Pledge situations. In the Pledge case, coercion prevents us from disaggregating the speakers into dissenters and advocates of the Pledge sentiments. In contrast, in the generic advertising case, it is the opt out that prevents disaggregation. Because we cannot know how many people are opting out for ideological reasons and how many are simply free riding, the opt out does not force people to take a stand.

The same point applies to other efforts by the Court to apply a right of silence in a commercial context. Perhaps fund-raisers opt out of the requirement to tell donors the percentage of contributions that actually go to charities because they have some deep moral objection to conveying this information.[85] Again, I must confess that this possibility strikes me as quite unlikely, but even if some fund-raisers are so motivated, surely many others fail to convey the information because they fear that doing so will reduce contribution levels. Because permitting opt outs does not force disaggregation, radical libertarians should oppose it.

Finally, what are we to make of the current insistence by Pledge opponents that an opt out is insufficient? Their claim is that implicit and informal coercion makes the opt out an unattractive choice for many dissenters and that, therefore, the ceremony should be prohibited altogether.[86] As we have seen, the Court has accepted this argument in the context of school prayer.[87] Should it have, and should it apply the argument to the Pledge as well?

If critics of the Pledge are right that opting out is not a real possibility, then the Pledge loses its meaning and, with it, the reasons for objecting to it. Oddly, then, from a radical libertarian perspective, if the argument of Pledge critics were to prevail, the result might well be what these critics fear most—not only the Pledge, but also the end of the opt-out possibility.

But radical libertarians are unlikely to think that the argument should prevail. They are likely to have limited sympathy at best for those who find it difficult to opt out. To be sure, a pervasive determinist would be alive to the possibility of informal coercion of this sort, but for a radical libertarian, our obligation, always and everywhere, is to choose and act in the face of the situation in which we find ourselves.

Of course, nothing that I have said above provides arguments for why we should be radical libertarians. Because radical libertarians believe that choice is no more constrained by argument than by more overt forms of coercion, it is awkward, to say the least, to make such an argument. It is at just this point that the right to silence has deep force. One can at least say this much, however: if one chooses to believe in *Barnette,* then one might well choose to be a radical libertarian as well.

CHAPTER 8

Silence and Death

ONE DAY, "DIANE," A FORTY-FIVE-YEAR-OLD WOMAN, walked into the office of her doctor, Timothy Quill.[1] She was feeling tired and had a rash. As Dr. Quill later described her, Diane was no ordinary patient. Raised in an alcoholic family, she had suffered from vaginal cancer, her own alcoholism, and depression. Gradually, through luck, determination, and hard work, she had overcome these problems. For the previous three years, she had been healthy and sober. She was happily married, with a college-age son and a successful career. In Dr. Quill's words, she was also "an incredibly clear, at times brutally honest, thinker and communicator."[2] And, it turned out, she was suffering from acute myelomonocytic leukemia.

Standard treatment for the disease at the time of Diane's illness began with induction chemotherapy, which involved three weeks in the hospital, hair loss, and probable infections. About 75 percent of the patients respond favorably to this treatment, but 25 percent die. If the treatment works, the patient then undergoes consolidation chemotherapy with the same side effects. The 50 percent of the patients who make it through these two stages must undergo bone marrow transplantation, which involves two months of hospitalization, whole body irradiation, and a high risk of disease. About half the remaining patients survive this ordeal. Thus, Diane's overall chance of survival was one in four. In contrast, if she did nothing, her maximum life expectancy was a few months.

Diane decided that all she wanted to do was to go home and be with her family. After extensive discussion with Dr. Quill, her husband, and son, she remained very clear that she did not want to undergo chemotherapy and did not want hospitalization. Quill was disturbed by her choice, but gradually came to terms with it and eventually "understood the decision from her perspective and became convinced that it was the right decision for her."[3]

Then Diane asked for something else: she wanted drugs so that, when the time came, she could decide upon death on her own terms. Dr. Quill asked her to come to his office to talk the matter over. Quill describes their conversation as follows:

It was clear that she was not despondent and that in fact she was making deep, personal connections with her family and close friends. I made sure that she knew how to use the barbiturates for sleep, and also that she knew the amount needed to commit suicide. We agreed to meet regularly, and she promised to meet with me before taking her life, to ensure that all other avenues had been exhausted.[4]

At the end of the appointment, Dr. Quill wrote the prescription.

Given the circumstances, the next several months went relatively well. Her son stayed home from college, and they were able to be with one another and say much that had not been said earlier. Her husband did his work at home so that he and Diane could spend more time together. She spent time with her closest friends. . . . She had periods of intense sadness and anger. Several times she became very weak, but she received transfusions as an outpatient and responded with marked improvement of symptoms. She had two serious infections that responded surprisingly well to empirical courses of oral antibiotics. After three tumultuous months, there were two weeks of relative calm and well being, and fantasies of a miracle began to surface.[5]

But there was to be no miracle. Diane began to suffer from bone pain, weakness, fatigue, and fevers. To Dr. Quill, it was obvious that the end was coming and that what lay ahead was increasing discomfort, sedation, and dependence. Diane met with her closest friends to say goodbye and, as she had promised, had a final consultation with Quill. "When we met, it was clear that she knew what she was doing, that she was sad and frightened to be leaving, but that she would be even more terrified to stay and suffer. In our tearful goodbye, she promised a reunion in the future at her favorite spot on the edge of Lake Geneva, with dragons swimming in the sunset."[6]

Two days later, Diane said her final goodbyes to her husband and son and asked to be left alone. An hour later, they found her dead on the couch, covered by her favorite shawl.

Did Diane, Dr. Quill, and her family do the right thing? Should the law say anything about whether it was right or not?

Among other things, death is silence. It irrevocably and permanently severs communication. Moreover, when we think about death, we confront the vast, unimaginable, and terrifying silence of the universe. Thus, the question naturally arises: if there is a right to silence, is there a right to death?

Not only is death silence; as the gay rights movement has taught us, silence can sometimes mean death. In some contexts, when we hold our tongues, we passively and cravenly acquiesce in our own destruction. And so the question also arises: if there is a right to life, is there an obligation to speak?

Diane chose the silence of death but, before it came, she chose to speak. The occasion of her approaching death led to renewed and deepened communication with her husband, her son, her friends, and her physician. More broadly and paradoxically, her suicide, her decision to bring eternal silence upon herself, was itself a kind of speech. Her affirmation of human will and choice in the face of inevitable death communicates with us the living long after her passing. And Dr. Quill, too, chose speech. True, in the immediate wake of her death, he did not report her suicide to the medical examiner. Had he not been silent, there might have been an effort at resuscitation followed, perhaps, by criminal prosecution of Quill and the family.[7] Later, though, he wrote courageously and movingly about the case in the *New England Journal of Medicine,* a decision that triggered a grand jury investigation of his conduct.*

These speech acts undertaken in the face of a silent void strike me as brave and right. They are acts of defiance—defiance of conventional thought, of the law, and of the meaninglessness of endless time and space. And yet, silence, too, has its claim. In this chapter, I argue that the questions confronting Diane and Dr. Quill are not subject to the usual protocols for rational decision making. What speaks to us about their actions

---

* The grand jury ultimately decided not to file charges against him. *See* Lawrence K. Altman, "Jury Declines to Indict a Doctor Who Said He Aided in a Suicide," N.Y. TIMES, July 27, 1991, at 11.

is their insistence on the inevitability of unmediated choice that is unbounded by the usual demands of morality and rationality. Ultimately, there simply is no "argument" that supports the choice of either life or death. Because there is nothing to say about that choice, silence with respect to it is more than just a right; it is a necessity.

THE LEGAL REGIME

These assertions raise very deep philosophical questions. Perhaps it is wise at this point to note again the limits of my expertise. Although I have tried to think hard and read widely about these issues, I am not trained as a philosopher, a medical ethicist, or a theologian. My excuse for writing about the issues is that the law, too, must respond in some way to the choice between life and death. This means that lawyers, as well as philosophers, medical ethicists, and theologians, must think about that choice. In what follows, I attempt to embed the problem in the specific questions that lawyers face.

The first step in this analysis is to understand the current legal regime regarding suicide and euthanasia. This section briefly describes that regime. In the sections that follow, I examine it critically through the familiar lens of liberal, republican, pervasive determinist, and radical libertarian thought.

For centuries the law treated suicide as a crime,[8] but, obviously, prosecution for its successful completion was impossible.* For this and other reasons, suicide has now been widely decriminalized.[9] This hardly means that the law passively accepts the practice, however. Persons who are mentally ill and dangerous to themselves are subject to civil commitment. Be-

---

* Which is not to say that people didn't try. There is a long history, extending through the early nineteenth century, of degradation of the corpses of suicide victims. See A. ALVAREZ, THE SAVAGE GOD: A STUDY OF SUICIDE 46–47 (1972). Around 1860, a London man attempted to cut his throat, but was rescued before he died. He was sentenced to death for the crime of suicide. Although a doctor warned that he could not be hanged because his throat would burst open and he would breath through the hole, the officials nonetheless proceeded with the execution. Just as the doctor predicted, the victim survived the hanging. After lengthy deliberation, the officials responded by binding up the neck below the wound until the man died. These events are recounted in, id, at 45. which, in turn, cites E. H. CARR, THE ROMANTIC EXILES 389 (1949).

cause suicidal ideation is often treated as prima facie (indeed, sometimes conclusive) evidence of mental illness,[10] people who want to take their own lives often find that their liberty has been taken instead.

Moreover, although suicide has been decriminalized, euthanasia and assisted suicide have not. Dr. Jack Kevorkian is now serving a ten- to twenty-five-year sentence for second degree murder for administering a lethal injection to Thomas Youk, a fifty-two year old man suffering from Lou Gehrig disease.[11] Dr. Quill, and conceivably Diane's husband and son as well, might have been charged with murder for their involvement with Diane's death.

To calibrate how serious legal jeopardy is, it is necessary to make several distinctions. First, there is the fundamental distinction between life and death. If a person is already dead, then his doctor can hardly be responsible for killing him. Until fairly recently, the law treated individuals as alive so long as they maintained heart and lung function, but the development of "artificial" means for maintaining these functions together with the growth of organ transplantation put pressure on this definition. Today, it has been rejected in many places. Instead, an individual whose brain is no longer able to maintain heart beat and pulmonary ventilation unaided is treated as "dead."[12] A physician who disconnects the machines "artificially" maintaining heart and lung function in a "brain-dead" patient therefore does not risk legal liability.

At the other end of the spectrum from individuals who are legally dead are conscious and competent individuals who for a variety of reasons that may strike us as sensible or not want to end their own lives. With respect to these individuals, it is necessary to distinguish between active euthanasia and assisted suicide on the one hand and the foregoing of life-sustaining medical treatment (sometimes called "passive euthanasia") on the other. Active euthanasia and assisted suicide typically involve the administration of a lethal dose of a drug, although there are also other methods. A person is said to be euthanized when the drug is administered by another (the conduct for which Kevorkian was convicted), whereas she commits assisted suicide when someone else supplies the drug, but the patient administers it (the conduct that Quill describes).

In general, both of these practices are illegal. The statement must be qualified in two respects, however. First, the law is more ambiguous with respect to "indirect" euthanasia: A doctor who administers a drug for the purpose of reducing pain may be acting legally even if the drug has the unintended but anticipated side effect of shortening life.[13]

Second, in 1994, the voters of Oregon enacted a ballot initiative permitting doctor-assisted suicide. The Death with Dignity Act, which was reaffirmed by another ballot measure in 1997, applies to individuals diagnosed with a terminal illness that will lead to death within six months.[14] The statute contains detailed procedural safeguards, including a fifteen day waiting period, a requirement of two oral and one written request for the medication, consultation with a second physician, and referral for psychiatric counseling if there is evidence that the patient suffers from depression or other mental illness.[15] In 2005, thirty-nine physicians wrote sixty-four prescriptions for lethal doses of medication. Thirty-two patients took the medicine and died.[16]

Most jurisdictions distinguish between active euthanasia and assisted suicide on the one hand and the foregoing of life-sustaining medical treatment (passive euthanasia) on the other. At common law, unconsented treatment was considered a battery, and today as well competent individuals usually have the right to refuse or discontinue treatment.[17] It follows that consensual passive euthanasia is permissible even in circumstances where treatment would lead to a full recovery. Thus, Dr. Quill did not risk legal liability when he respected Diane's wish not to undergo chemotherapy.

In the space between the legally dead on the one hand and competent decision makers on the other are people who are alive but for one reason or another are incompetent. These individuals may, for example, be in a coma, in a persistent vegetative state (meaning that they are awake but lack the higher brain function that produces consciousness), mentally ill, or retarded. When individuals have made their wishes known before becoming incompetent by, for example, executing a "living will" or a durable power of attorney authorizing a surrogate decision maker, most jurisdictions purport to follow their directives.[18] When the previous wishes of the incompetent patient are less clear, a legal proceeding may be necessary to resolve a factual dispute about the patient's prior intentions.

Suppose the patient had or expressed no prior intentions? In this situation, jurisdictions face two questions: Who should decide, and what should the standard be for decision. With respect to the first question, some jurisdictions give final decision-making authority to a close relative, while others use a neutral fact finder like a judge or a hospital ethics board. With regard to the second, jurisdictions are arrayed along a continuum between those using relatively subjective tests (what this person would have wanted) and relatively objective tests (what a "reasonable" person would have wanted).

Overlaid on top of these statutory and common law rules is an emerging set of constitutional requirements. To date, the United States Supreme Court has decided three cases concerning the constitutional status of suicide and euthanasia. In *Cruzan v. Director, Missouri Department of Public Health,*[19] the Court faced a constitutional challenge to Missouri's insistence on continuing artificial nutrition and hydration procedures on a woman in a persistent vegetative state in the face of a demand by the woman's parents that the treatment be terminated. In a 5–4 decision, the Court held that Missouri's requirement of proof by clear and convincing evidence that the patient would have wanted termination was constitutionally permissible.* However, in dicta, Chief Justice William Rehnquist implied, without quite holding, that a competent person would have a constitutional right to refuse life-saving hydration and nutrition.[20]

Justice Sandra Day O'Connor's concurring opinion was much more explicit in asserting that "the liberty guaranteed by the Due Process Clause must protect, if it protects anything, an individual's deeply personal decision to reject medical treatment, including the artificial delivery of food and water."[21] In addition, O'Connor noted that this liberty interest may require a state to give effect to the decisions of a surrogate decision

---

* After the Supreme Court had ruled, the state court permitted Ms. Cruzan's parents to introduce further evidence about expressions of her intent before she lost competence. Based upon this new evidence, the court found that the "clear and convincing" standard had been met and permitted discontinuation of hydration and nutrition. Shortly thereafter, Ms. Cruzan died. *See* Susan Tiffl, "Life and Death," TIME MAGAZINE, Jan. 21, 1991, at http//www.time.com/time/magazine/article/0,9171,9721768,00.html (site visited 8/28/06) (noting that Nancy Cruzan died twelve days after a Missouri probate judge heard additional testimony and permitted the family to stop nurishment).

maker. When her views are combined with those of the four dissenters, it appears that a majority of the justices believed that competent patients have a constitutional right to avoid state obstruction of passive euthanasia and that incompetent patients may have a constitutional right to have the decisions of their surrogates respected.

In *Washington v. Glucksberg*,[22] the Court turned its attention to the question of doctor-assisted suicide for competent patients. The majority opinion, again written by Chief Justice Rehnquist, rejected a facial challenge to a Washington statute that criminalized the causing or aiding of a suicide. However, in separate concurring opinions, five justices emphasized the facial nature of the challenge and suggested that doctor assistance might be constitutionally protected in a narrower range of cases. For example, Justice O'Connor wrote that while she agreed that there was "no generalized right to 'commit suicide,'" the Court was not deciding "the narrower question whether a mentally competent person who is experiencing great suffering has a constitutionally cognizable interest in controlling the circumstances of his or her imminent death."[23]

Finally, in *Vacco v. Quill*,[24] a suit initiated by the same Dr. Quill who served as Diane's physician,* all nine justices agreed that New York's distinction between passive euthanasia (which it permitted) and doctor-assisted suicide (which it prohibited) was at least sufficiently rational to withstand equal protection attack. Once again, however, the Court's superficial unanimity cloaked a range of views. In separate concurring opinions, Justices Stephen Breyer, Sandra Day O'Connor, David Souter, Ruth Ginsburg, and John Paul Stevens all indicated some unease with a flat ban on doctor assistance in taking one's life.[25]

As this brief summary makes clear, current constitutional doctrine leaves open key questions about the extent of constitutional protection for decisions about death. Moreover, even if the doctrine were perfectly clear, it does no more than establish a constitutional floor. So long as states remain above that floor, for the most part they are free to alter their present rules about suicide and euthanasia. Finally, it must be noted that actual medical practice may well deviate from the formal rules. On

---

* The suit was a facial challenge and did not involve Diane's particular case.

the one hand, doctors, who are trained to preserve life, who are paid for the care they administer, and who may worry about liability for "causing" death, have been known to ignore living wills mandating treatment termination and "do not resuscitate" orders. On the other hand, the distinction between administering a drug for the purpose of causing death and administering it to eliminate pain while knowing that it will cause or hasten death is sufficiently porous as to permit a fair amount of active euthanasia under the guise of pain management.

Given the unsettled nature of both law and practice, there is more than enough room along the "fit" dimension for debate about what the rules should be, indeed, about whether there should be any rules. As usual, thinking about the problem from the perspective of liberals, republicans, pervasive determinists, and radical libertarians helps to clarify what is at stake.

LIBERAL FREEDOM AND ITS PROBLEMS

Here, as elsewhere, the liberal position seems clear at first, but becomes more ambiguous under closer analysis. Liberals favor a right to choose silence and so, it would seem, they should favor a right to choose death. As we have seen, silence is a method of resisting entanglement with others. A person who is silent does not expose her thoughts and beliefs to public scrutiny and, so, resists the pull toward the universalism that results from public exposure. From a liberal perspective, silence can also symbolize freedom. Precisely because a person who remains silent avoids entanglement with others, she can act autonomously. Thus, when the law respects a right to silence, it vindicates the right to autonomous and particularistic judgments, or at least so liberals claim.

A right to choose death, the ultimate disentanglement from others, follows naturally from this orientation. The force of particularistic judgment is nicely captured by Dr. Quill's observation that he believed Diane's decision was wrong, but that eventually he came to "[understand] the decision from her perspective and [to be] convinced that it was the right decision for her." Because people should be allowed to weigh for themselves their obligations to their community, their loved ones, and themselves, we should insist upon individual decisions that work for the people who make them. The alternative to these decisions, state coercion, substitutes deadening universalism for the individual struggle between the universal and particular that is the hallmark of human freedom.[26]

These are powerful arguments, but, even if they are right, it is far from clear that they support the conclusions that liberals draw from them. In particular, it does not follow from the arguments that liberals should necessarily support decriminalization of suicide. After all, as things currently stand, there is a kind of silence that cloaks many decisions about assisted suicide and euthanasia. Whatever the law says, doctors and patients regularly make judgments like the one that Diane and Dr. Quill made.[27] These decisions are private, individualized, intimate, and discreet, just as liberals would want them to be.*

In contrast, as the Oregon experience demonstrates, decriminalization usually means regulation. Just as providing a "safe harbor" for apologies corrupts rather than vindicates the value that liberals attach to apologetic speech,[28] so too the very effort to provide legal protection for suicide makes the decision public rather than private. Proposals to change existing law inevitably put the question in the political arena where public considerations dominate. It is certain that the outcome of this debate, even if it leads to liberalization, will be a heavily qualified and regulated right. There will be limitations on who can exercise the right, onerous procedural requirements imposed on those who seek to exercise it, and careful review by outsiders. The result may be what liberals fear most, a government bureaucracy with standardized rules making decisions according to universalist criteria.

These are problems about the appropriate strategy for accomplishing liberal goals, but there are also problems from within liberalism about whether those goals should include establishment of a right to suicide. A perennial problem for liberals is created by the effort to turn liberal theory on itself. Should liberal freedom include the freedom to make decisions that are illiberal? Perhaps suicide, like selling oneself into slavery,

---

* Of course, liberals would prefer that the decisions be legally permissible. Liberals may face hard choice because legalization (which they favor) may also entail regulation (which they oppose).

is such a decision. In his well known argument against suicide, Immanuel Kant maintained that,

> If a man destroys his body, and so his life, he does it by the use of his will, which is itself destroyed in the process. But to use the power of a free will for its own destruction is self-contradictory. If freedom is the condition of life it cannot be employed to abolish life and so to destroy and abolish itself. To use life for its own destruction, to use life for producing lifelessness, is self-contradictory.[29]

Later in this chapter, I will return to this problem of comparing life to lifelessness. For now, it is sufficient to note that even if the liberal position does not suffer from the global contradiction that Kant detected, it remains vulnerable to a similar contradiction in particular cases. This is so because liberal theory must necessarily recognize exceptions to its general opposition to government interference for cases where private decision making is not free. When an individual does not act autonomously, because of fraud, coercion, or lack of competency for example, liberals can hardly defend private choice on autonomy grounds. Liberals must also come to grips with addictive behavior, and situations where there is a conflict between short-term and long-term desires. The difficulty, of course, is that these exceptions immediately demand some sort of theory to distinguish between factors that must be weighed in rational decision making on the one hand and pressures that produce coerced decision making on the other. Liberals have had notorious difficulty in coming up with such a theory.

It is just this problem that has given many of the justices pause when they have been asked to recognize a broad right to die. Their concern is that economic factors, mental illness, and pressure from family members or doctors may make many acts of "consensual" suicide and euthanasia less than fully autonomous.[30] It hardly need be added that, without a good theory for evaluating these claims, determinist skepticism about the possibility of any free choices quickly rears its ugly head. For example, at least some psychiatrists treat suicidal ideation as, itself, strong (perhaps conclusive) evidence of the sort of mental illness that makes the decision nonautonomous.[31] Moreover, even psychiatrists who reject this view are bound to take into account the "rationality" of the decision when they decide whether it is the product of such illness. The difficulty is that, at least in this context, judgments about rationality inevitably involve the sort of generalizations over broad populations that particularist liberals want to resist.

These problems, which are quite serious when dealing with competent persons, become more serious still when dealing with incompetents. Consider, for example, Justice William Brennan's defense of the liberal position in his dissenting opinion in *Cruzan*.[32] As discussed above, Chief Justice Rehnquist wrote for the Court's majority to uphold a Missouri statute that prohibited termination of nutrition and hydration for a patient in a persistent vegetative state unless there was clear and convincing evidence that the patient had wanted this result while competent. Justice Brennan dissented, claiming that biasing the decision in this way violated a constitutional right to die, which Justice Brennan grounded in liberal values.

Unfortunately, Justice Brennan's opinion is dominated by a single, puzzling analytic failure. His analysis is organized around the assertion that Ms. Cruzan is a person who has a right to die and that the decision should therefore be located in the private sphere. Yet most of his argument supports the claim that she is a person who has no right to live and that public decision making is therefore appropriate.

Consider, first, the graphic statement of Ms. Cruzan's predicament with which the opinion begins: "[Nancy Cruzan] is oblivious to her surroundings and will remain so. Her body twitches only reflexively, without consciousness. The areas of her brain that once thought, felt, and experienced sensations have degenerated badly and are continuing to do so. . . . Nancy will never interact meaningfully with her environment again. She will remain in a persistent vegetative state until her death."[33] Now consider the right that the opinion defends: "The right to be free from unwanted medical attention is a right to evaluate the potential benefit of treatment and its possible consequences according to one's own values and to make a personal decision whether to subject oneself to the intrusion."[34]

This juxtaposition poses an obvious problem for Justice Brennan. How does he suppose that Ms. Cruzan, unconscious and "oblivious to her surroundings," is going to "evaluate the potential benefit of treatment" and make a "personal decision" in accord with her "own values"?

Of course, whatever her status now, Ms. Cruzan once had the capacity for decison making. Much of Brennan's opinion is devoted to discussing Ms. Cruzan's past desires. Thus, the dissent argues that "[f]or many, the thought of an ignoble end, steeped in decay, is abhorrent," and that such a death is "for many, humiliating to contemplate, as is visiting a prolonged and anguished vigil on one's parents, spouse, and children."[35]

But surely the dissent is not asserting that Ms. Cruzan currently has thoughts of "an ignoble end" or that she is now feeling humiliated. Perhaps the claim is that Ms. Cruzan would have had these thoughts if, at some time in the past, she had known that the desire she then had to avoid an ignoble end would be frustrated. The dissent is on solid ground in believing that many people, whether rightly or wrongly, feel that they are somehow connected to the entity that they become when they lose consciousness. And there can be no doubt that many people, while conscious, care deeply about what will happen to their loved ones after they are no longer conscious and, indeed, after they are no longer alive.

But these observations, while true, do not do the work that Justice Brennan needs them to do. It is obvious that no resolution of the *Cruzan* case will affect what Ms. Cruzan thought, or what she might have thought, in the past. If she once feared a prolonged and undignified death, removing the feeding tube now will not retroactively provide mental peace. Conversely, if she once experienced satisfaction because she believed that she would not burden her family in death, no prolongation of her parents' current agony can now deprive her of that past tranquility.

If there is a reason for respecting Ms. Cruzan's prior wishes, it is not that this respect will make things different for her now. It is, rather, that respecting them will make things different for other persons, persons who are now capable of feeling anxiety, fear, and impotence, and who might now experience these emotions if they think that, should they become incompetent, their wishes will be ignored.

Perhaps these ancillary effects of disregarding Ms. Cruzan's former desires justify recognition of a "right to die." For present purposes, the important point is that this cannot be the kind of "right" that liberals value. It is not a right premised on individualized, particularist, and private choice. Instead, recognition of the right grows out of a public decision based upon generalizations about the welfare of the whole population of people who worry about their future incapacity. It is, in short, the kind of right appropriately subject to public debate, the contours of which should be determined by universalist values.

Given these difficulties, the question arises why Justice Brennan placed so much emphasis on Cruzan's permanent lack of consciousness. Almost certainly, the answer is that he did not want to be put in the position of defending a broader right of physically healthy, but perhaps depressed, individuals to take their own lives. We see this same tendency among other justices, who have emphasized that the right they are defending is only for very sick people in great pain and at the end of their lives. The concern is apparent as well in the carefully cabined right to suicide established by Oregon's voters.

Unfortunately, however, this effort to defend only "rational" or "sensible" suicides pushes liberals into yet another contradiction. Rational according to whom? Individuals hardly need protection from public power when their conduct conforms to what the public believes in any event to be sensible. A truly liberal and individual right to suicide makes a difference in precisely those cases where the general public would disapprove. A liberal right to suicide, then, is a right to take one's own life in circumstances where people like Justice Brennan (after all, a government official) view the choice as irrational and not sensible.

But, of course, there is no mystery why liberals do not want to recognize such a right. Precisely because the choice is irrational and not sensible, liberals are likely to think that it is also not autonomous—that it is the product of mental illness, or coercion, or imperfect information. In this way, the autonomy requirement at the core of liberalism pushes the liberal argument toward the very universalism and paternalism that liberals want to escape.

REPUBLICANS AND SUICIDE

For republicans, it is no accident that Justice Brennan's defense of liberal rights ends up in difficulty. Nor is the problem limited to the killing of incompetents. Republicans claim that even in the case of competent individuals, liberals underestimate the extent to which we are bound to each other and, so, the extent to which the choice for suicide involves much more (and much less) than an exercise of individual freedom. The initial impulse of republicans is to reject an individual right to suicide for just these reasons, but, as we shall see, their position, like the liberal view, is less clear cut than it might first seem.

Recall that republicans are attracted to speech rather than silence because speech connects us to each other. This organic connection, in turn, leads to the development of the public, universalist values by which we define ourselves and our society. For republicans, human freedom consists of the ability to engage actively in collective self-governance. In contrast, individual, willful choice, especially a choice for silence, reflects merely alienation and selfishness. Because true freedom is always manifested by embeddedness within a community, it cannot exist when we remain isolated from each other.

It is easy to see how this perspective might lead to opposition to a right to suicide. On the simplest level, suicide reflects a violent break with community. A person who chooses death chooses, among other things, to absent himself from the rest of us. There is no such thing as collective deliberation beyond the grave.

There is also a more subtle sense in which suicide is in deep tension with republican impulses. In a path-breaking work written in the nineteenth century, the great French sociologist Emile Durkheim argued that suicide was primarily a social phenomenon and not merely a manifestation of individual weakness or disease, much less a manifestation of individual freedom and choice.[36] In modern society, Durkheim argued, many suicides are the product of a breakdown in solidarity, produced either by the alienation of individuals from the connective tissue of society (which he called "egoistic suicide")[37] or by the failure of society to provide regulatory norms for the individual (which he called "anomic suicide").[38]

Durkheim himself avoided drawing strong normative conclusions from these observations, but modern republicans have been less reticent. Consider, for example, the views eloquently expressed by the contemporary philosopher Daniel Callahan:

The general repugnance most societies, and religions, have to suicide stems from the perception that it represents a profound failure to cope with life. But it is a social and not just individual failure: it breaks the solidarity that people should have in the face of the evils and tragedies of life.

[W]e have been socially tutored that, despite pain, suffering, and tragedy, life ought to go on, and that we owe it to each other not to despair in the face of evil and misfortune. We are implicitly asked by our fellow human beings to give witness to the possibility of human endurance and the need to transcend evil by bearing it in our own lives. We need the help of other people in coping with what life throws our way, and one of the most fundamental goods that others can give us is the example of their lives in enduring pain and misery. If others can do it, so can I. And if I cannot do it, I will thereby be failing in my duty to others, failing to give them the kind of help that they, by simply enduring, have given me.[39]

This argument resonates deeply with republican theory, as well as with Catholic social thought. Instead of emphasizing liberal rights, Callahan speaks of social obligation. For him, suicide is a manifestation of community failure rather than of individual freedom. It is a selfish choice of silence when we have an obligation to speak to each other.

This view is a useful corrective to the liberal insistence on isolated, individualistic choice, but, like the liberal position, it is subject to both an internal and external critique. First, if one considers the argument from within republicanism, it is not obvious that resisting suicide is always the best way to meet our social obligations. Importantly, Durkheim wrote not just of egoistic and anomic suicide, but also of what he called "altruistic suicide."[40] Consider, for example, the soldier who goes on a suicide mission, the elderly and sick grandfather who cannot justify to himself the consumption of medical resources that might go to younger patients, the terminally ill patient who takes a drug overdose to avoid a crushing financial burden for his family, or the martyr who dies so as not to betray his cause.

Of course, one can play definitional tricks to escape calling some (all?) of these acts suicide. From within republicanism, the suicide ban can be made merely tautological if one arbitrarily defines "suicide" as only those self-killings that are proscribed by republican principles. But if we try to avoid tautology, it quickly becomes apparent that some self-killings demonstrate our commitment to others rather than our alienation from them.

Nor is it true that the occasion of self-inflicted death is always marked by isolation and alienation. Think again of Diane's death. Her suicide may not have been altruistic in the Durkheimian sense, but it nonetheless triggered a deeper communication with her community. Does her choice of death really betray her obligations to the rest of us? There is no evidence that those around her believed this. On the contrary, for many, her choice sets an example of courage, determination, and, importantly, human connection in the shadow of inevitable death.

There are further difficulties with Callihan's argument if one is prepared to move outside of republicanism. His argument is powerful because he invokes an image of shared community life that many of us find attractive. It is a mistake, however, to confuse an ideal with reality. Just as liberals criticize republicans for assuming that political institutions are necessarily public regarding, so too they might criticize thinkers like Callihan for assuming the actual existence of a utopian community. In the society we actually inhabit, sick and unhappy people are often also isolated and lonely. We can all resolve to work for the kind of world that Callihan envisions, but these individuals must live (or die) in the world that exists now. In the absence of reciprocal bonds, is it really fair to hold them morally obligated to undergo continuing misery for the sake of a society that has abandoned them?

Moreover, even if we posit a person (like Diane) who is not alienated and alone, republican insistence on universalist obligation has a disturbingly self-referential quality. Suppose it is true that, by universalist standards, Diane's public duties outweighed her private duties. That fact does no more than to raise yet again the recurring question why she should be bound by universalist standards in the first place. Perhaps, instead, Diane should count her private obligations, to herself, her family, and her loved ones, for more than obligations to an abstract and anonymous community.

For most of us, confronting the choice between universalist and particularist obligation creates internal struggle and ambivalence. Republicans would settle that struggle by fiat and government coercion. But even if liberals are wrong to think that particularist norms necessarily define the realm of freedom, don't they have a point when they insist that the struggle itself is an aspect of freedom?

PERVASIVE DETERMINISM

The discussion above already makes clear why both the liberal and the republican position are vulnerable to determinist criticism. Consider first the liberal position. Liberals confront the usual problem posed by their conflation of privacy and freedom. If, as pervasive determinists insist, coercion is omnipresent in the private as well as the public sphere, then a right to die amounts to a license to kill.

This point is most obvious when patients choose death because, for example, a managed care company refuses to pay for treatment or scheming relatives pressure them for selfish reasons. But the pervasive determinist argument goes beyond the obvious cases. For example, a pervasive determinist might take a much darker view of Dr. Quill's interaction with Diane than Quill's self-justificatory account would suggest. Are we really to believe that Quill's lengthy conversations had no influence on Diane? What, after all, was the point of the conversations if not to influence her in some way?

If the conversations did, in fact, influence Diane, then we are confronted with the disquieting possibility that Dr. Quill's interests were not perfectly aligned with hers. No doubt Quill's self-perception was that he was merely helping her work through a problem for herself. As hard as we try, though, we are never simply ciphers when we interact with others. We always have our own agenda whether we are conscious of it or not. Moreover, it is precisely when we are unconscious of our agenda—when we perceive ourselves and are perceived by others as acting altruistically—that the danger of imposing our will on others is the greatest. Consider, for example, the possibility that, perhaps unconsciously, Dr. Quill was motivated by a desire to appear as a courageous doctor crusading for patient rights. Perhaps, even as he was counseling Diane, in some corner of his mind, he was also imagining the article he might later write for the *New England Journal of Medicine*, the trial at which he would bravely face punishment, and the case he would litigate all the way to the Supreme Court. Can we really be sure that his interaction with her was not "infected" by these motives and that her decision was not, in turn "infected" by his advice?*

Republicans, too, must explain why the solidarity they value is not just a cover for the exercise of power. Here, pervasive determinists align themselves with liberal critics of republicanism. Whatever might be true in some ideal world, in our own world, governments seldom act pursuant to universalist values arrived at through unforced and disinterested deliberation. As public choice theorists have taught us, public policy is often crucially influenced by selfishly motivated, highly organized, minorities determined to use public institutions for private gain.

At first blush, it might seem that the assisted suicide debate actually presents a counterexample. Political debate about a right to die seems less about interest group politics and more about an authentic search for public values. Pervasive determinists are unlikely to be fooled, however. Just as our private interactions are most dangerous when we manage to convince ourselves and others that we are acting altruistically, so too government power is most insidious when it is cloaked in the rhetoric of public interest.

Consider in this regard Congress's actions in the Terri Schiavo case. For pervasive determinists, Congress's hasty and ill-informed intervention was hardly a stirring example of deliberative democracy in action. Instead of convening the good-faith, town-meeting-style debate that republicans (here, emphatically with a small *r*) favor, the congressional leadership decided to act in a symbolic and hasty fashion that would pay off the evangelical base on which it depended. The very embrace of seemingly public values was a ploy to maintain political power, or, at least, so pervasive determinists will suspect. For the individuals on both sides of the actual case who more or less randomly found their lives caught up in this political struggle, the result was a tragedy. Despite all the sanctimonious talk of concern over their fate, they ended up as props in a melodrama staged for a different audience.

---

* The point of the quotation marks is that, for a pervasive determinist, there is no pure state of affairs that is not infected by some sort of power relationship.

Of course, people who are not pervasive determinists will doubt that the world is always quite this bleak. They will insist on the possibility of both authentic individual connection and good faith public debate. Even if they are wrong and pervasive determinists are right, though, it is once again unclear what precisely follows from the determinist critique. It is useful here to distinguish between hard and soft pervasive determinists. Consider, first, the stance of the hard liners who insist that power is literally everywhere. Hard liners will, of course, greet liberal assertions of a right to suicide with derision. It does not follow, however, that they will insist on an obligation to remain alive. In fact, there is an important sense in which choosing pervasive determinism amounts to an embrace of death. Once human agency and connection are gone, what, after all, is the point of life? People who are merely cogs in an all-powerful machine might as well be dead.

At first, it might seem that soft liners offer a more positive contribution to the debate. Without reducing everything to power relationships, they might still caution us to be aware of the risk that seemingly autonomous conduct is actually coerced. A majority of the justices seem to have taken something like this stance with regard to the suicide debate. They are hardly global skeptics about the possibility of free will, but they are nonetheless cautious in assuming that the removal of government constraints on suicide will necessarily produce autonomous choice.

This caution may be useful, but the problem for soft liners is that they must find a way to resist the drift toward the hard version of the theory. In this context, that means figuring out a reason why exercise of the "right" to die is somehow more vulnerable to private pressure than the exercise of other putative rights. Surely, the justices are not unaware that voters are sometimes manipulated by campaign commercials, that some pregnant women "choose" abortion because of financial pressures or coercion from other family members, or that religious choice sometimes results from family indoctrination or social pressure. If the rights to free speech, reproductive autonomy, and free exercise are not to fall victim to the same analytic juggernaut that demolishes the right to die, soft pervasive determinists, like liberals, need a theory to distinguish problematic surrender to coercion from unproblematic free choice. Our failure to develop such a theory is an open scandal.

RADICAL FREEDOM, SILENCE, AND SUICIDE

Just as pervasive determinism offers an escape from liberal and republican conundrums, radical libertarian thought can rescue us from determinist despair. Radical libertarians will remind us, in yet another context, of the inevitability of choice, even in an absurd and purposeless universe and even in a world where coercion is all around us. Because I have already set out the attractions and problems with this view, I focus my attention here on what follows from it with regard to a putative suicide right.

In this context, as elsewhere, there is some embarrassment in claiming that anything at all follows from it. For a radical libertarian, no argument can shield us from the unmediated choices that confront us, whether that choice is about committing suicide or allowing it. Still, even if radical libertarian thought fails to dictate an outcome, it throws light on how we might (if we choose to do so!) think about the problem. In particular, it problematizes several of the distinctions that are central to legal analysis of suicide.

We can start with the fundamental distinction between life and death. As we have seen, most jurisdictions treat a patient as "dead" when there is a cessation of lower brain function.[41] It is important to understand that there is nothing natural or inevitable about this definition. Indeed, it has changed over time. The definition was created by human beings to serve human purposes. One important purpose it serves is to shield us from the inevitability of choice. When we say that the patient is already dead, it appears that we do not have to decide whether to kill him. Instead, we have merely allowed nature to take its course. Because it is easy to forget the earlier choice of definition, we manage to hide our own freedom from ourselves.

There is a similar difficulty with the distinction between passive euthanasia on the one hand and active euthanasia or doctor assisted suicide on the other. Recall that the law generally permits the former while outlawing the latter, and that the Supreme Court upheld this distinction in *Vacco v. Quill*.[42] The usual justification for the distinction is that the underlying disease causes death in the case of passive euthanasia, while the doctor's intervention causes death in the case of active euthanasia or assisted suicide.[43] The distinction serves to efface the fact that in both cases, the relevant actors have a choice between life and death. It is, after all, merely arbitrary to say that the underlying disease, rather than the doctor's failure to treat it, causes death in the case of passive euthanasia. As Justice Antonin Scalia has written, "It would not make much sense to say that one may not kill oneself by walking into the sea, but may sit on the beach until submerged by the incoming tide; or that one may not intentionally lock oneself into a cold storage locker, but may refrain from coming indoors when the temperature drops below freezing."*

But although the distinction is analytically problematic, the function it serves is, once again, all too obvious. Because passive euthanasia requires no positive intervention and seems "natural," it allows the participants to obscure the fact that they are making a choice. Cowardice has consequences. In this case, the price of pretense is paid in the currency of human suffering for individuals who must undergo deaths that are slow and painful when they might have been quick and painless.

Most significantly, radical libertarians highlight the problems with categorizing suicides along the dimensions of morality and rationality. Radical libertarian analysis can help us to see not only that suicide is a choice, but also that it is only a choice. There is no argument, logical necessity, overriding moral principle, or cost-benefit analysis that can dictate an outcome. It is here that the issue of silence takes hold. Radical libertarian theory cannot tell us whether to choose eternal silence, but it does counsel silence about choosing silence. On this view, it is hardly surprising that liberal and republican arguments are unpersuasive or contradictory.

---

* These words appear in Justice Scalia's concurring opinion in *Cruzan. See* 497 U.S., at 296. In the same opinion, he noted that although the due process clause had "nothing to say" about the suicide issue, he thought that the equal protection clause did impose limits on differential treatment of different sorts of suicide. Id., at 300. Yet remarkably, in *Vacco v. Quill,* 521 U.S. 702 (1997), where the Supreme Court rejected an equal protection attack on New York's distinction between passive and active killing, Justice Scalia joined the majority opinion without comment.

Liberals and republicans have failed to speak convincingly about suicide because, on this topic at least, there is nothing to say.

In making this argument, I want to start by distinguishing between theistic and nontheistic approaches to the suicide question. Although my organization obviously oversimplifies, I want to use theistic approaches to focus our attention on the issue of morality, and nontheistic approaches to highlight the issue of rationality.

Consider first theistic views. Most (although certainly not all) approaches to suicide grounded in religious tradition treat the practice as immoral. This rejection is something of a puzzle given the large number of religious martyrs in a variety of faith traditions who have sacrificed their lives for their religious beliefs.* One might also suppose that a belief in an afterlife would make suicide more palatable. Justice Scalia has recently reminded us, albeit in a different context, that earthly life matters less if one can bring oneself to believe that it is followed by an eternal existence.[44]

Despite these considerations, religious condemnation of suicide is widespread. I will not here rehearse the various textual and theological arguments against the practice except as they bear on my general thesis. One such argument distinguishes between "natural" and "unnatural" responses to impending death. Many people with religious sensibilities seem to believe that God's will is manifest in the natural progression of things and that suicide is evil because it interferes with this natural progression. For example, thinkers in the Catholic tradition make a sharp distinction between allowing a disease to follow its natural course by forgoing extraordinary treatment (permissible) and suicide or the foregoing of ordinary treatment (impermissible).[45] And although this distinction is especially important for Catholics, it corresponds to intuitions shared by many non-Catholics as well.

Almost two hundred years ago, the Scottish philosopher David Hume mounted a powerful attack on this argument.[46] Hume wondered why human choice was not, itself, part of the natural order of things. He pointed

---

* Once again, it is possible to gerrymander the definition of suicide to take care of many of these cases. No suicide can be justified within a religious tradition if suicide is defined as self-killings that are not so justified. Tautological definitions are simply another way of maintaining silence, albeit a misleading one.

out that human beings constantly and unproblematically disturb nature. A person who deflects a rock about to fall on his head or builds a shelter to shield himself from the elements changes "natural" arrangements with regard to life and death. If human beings do not violate God's will by diverting powerful rivers, Hume asked, in what sense do they defy Him when they divert their own blood from its usual arterial route?*

Of course, Hume's argument, standing alone, is not powerful enough to dislodge the intuition that some states of affairs are natural and some are not. Most of us can still tell the difference between unspoiled arctic wilderness and Disneyland. But the argument does demonstrate a radical libertarian point: What we treat as natural is, itself, contingent and constructed by human choice. As the shifting definition of death illustrates, in different cultures and different times and places different states of affairs seem natural or artificial. We must therefore choose what we treat as natural, and that choice cannot, itself, be grounded in nature.

This problem might seem much less serious if God has somehow spoken to us about what parts of nature should not be disturbed. Consider for example, Thomas Aquinas's position: "[W]hoever takes his own life, sins against God, even as he who kiss another's slave, sins against that slave's master, and as he who usurps himself judgment of a matter not entrusted to him. For it belongs to God alone to pronounce sentence of death and life, according to Deut. xxxii 39, *I will kill and I will make to live.*[47] Even for readers with religious sensibilities, Aquinas's use of slave imagery is bound to seem jarring and, perhaps, unintentionally revealing. What are we to make of human freedom in a world where God is a slavemaster? Moreover, this argument will have no purchase at all for people who do not believe in God, or who do not believe that God spoke in Deuteronomy, or who do not believe that Deuteronomy must be interpreted in the way that Aquinas suggests. Suppose, though, that we accept all of Aquinas's premises. What exactly follows from his argument? Consider what he says next.

---

* Hume, himself, was a religious skeptic. In light of this fact, it seems probable that he meant to suggest that even if one assumes arguendo the existence of God, opposition to suicide does not follow.

St. Augustine says . . . *not even Samson is to be excused that he crushed himself together with his enemies, under the ruins of the house, except the Holy Ghost, Who had wrought many wonders, through him, had secretly commanded him to do this.* He assigned the same reason in the case of certain holy women, who at the time of persecution took their own lives, and who are commemorated by the Church.[48]

There is a large risk in attempting to interpret a text written hundreds of years ago by a person grounded in a very different tradition from one's own. Still, if one takes Aquinas's words at face value, this is no small qualification.* Suicide is usually against God's will, but sometimes, it turns out, it is not. If God is truly unconstrained, this will hardly come as a surprise, since no prior rule can limit his will. As soon as this much is conceded, however, we are faced with a daunting question: Just how do we know when the Holy Ghost has secretly commanded suicide? This problem is all the more pressing because, as Aquinas formulates the qualification, it is not merely one additional factor to be weighed in an overall judgment. Rather, it trumps the rest of his argument.** Even if everything else he says is true, suicide might still be required if there is a "secret command" from the Holy Ghost.

Of course, it does not follow that most, or even many suicides are justified by divine intervention. Presumably, the Holy Ghost does not frequently command self-destruction. On the other hand, Aquinas clearly does not believe that Samson's situation is completely unique. After all, the Holy Spirit also commanded "certain holy women" to take their lives. If Aquinas's argument is correct, then, no matter what other considerations

---

* Even if I am misinterpreting Aquinas, the argument in text stands or falls on its own merits. Whether or not it is what Aquinas believed, it is an important problem for theists to consider.

** Thus, Aquinas might have said that, for one reason or another, the factors that generally make suicide impermissible were not present in Samson's case. Importantly, instead of making this argument, he begins by conceding that not even Samson should be excused, except for the intervention of the Holy Ghost. The clear implication of this way of formulating the point is that, but for that intervention, Samson would have acted wrongly and that, therefore, the intervention trumps the rest of the argument.

counsel against suicide, the possibility of divine intervention requiring it is always on the table and always must be considered.

We can put the same point in more secular terms: It turns out that the rightness of human action is never fully reducible to syllogistic reasoning. However convincing a moral argument might be, the argument alone cannot fully resolve the problem. When we are finished arguing, there always remains the option of simply ignoring everything that has been said (as, indeed, Aquinas does with respect to Samson), and there always remains the possibility that ignoring it is simply the right thing to do. At this point, an infinite regress takes hold. The reasons for our decision to act in the teeth of the previous argument might, themselves, be reduced to an argument. But then there is the option to ignore this argument. It would be silly to pretend that Aquinas was a radical libertarian. Still, at the end of the regress that his qualification suggests lies a radical libertarian choice and silence about that choice.

Although theistic approaches have a residual effect on public discourse about suicide, they are less important today than nontheistic approaches that focus on rationality rather than morality. From the perspective of radical libertarians, this is hardly an advance. At least theists take the decision to commit suicide seriously; that is, after all, why it is worth condemning. In contrast, the modern medicalization of suicide is a way of trivializing the act. Because it is the result of a breakdown of rationality produced by disease, suicide need not, or at least often need not, be treated as a serious choice, worthy of even the backhanded respect that condemnation provides.

Perhaps Camus exaggerated when he famously wrote that suicide posed the only "truly serious philosophical problem,"[49] but surely it is a graver mistake not to treat it as a serious problem at all. To see why it is a problem worth taking seriously, we need to focus more carefully on what liberals mean when they distinguish between rational and irrational suicide choices.

There is, of course, much dispute about how to define rationality. Because liberals believe in a right to individual choice about the nature of the good, they will push for a thin conception of rationality that leaves this choice intact. Suppose, then, that we adopt such a thin conception by saying that a decision is rational when chosen means are better adapted to whatever end the actor has than other, readily available means. How, then, do we know when a suicide is rational, or, indeed, whether it can be?

The utilitarian philosopher Richard Brandt claims that a rational person thinking about suicide would decide whether he "now prefer[s], or shall later prefer, the outcome of one world-course to that of another."[50] This is another way of stating that the means (here the suicide) are best adapted to the end of producing the preferred world course. But there is an obvious objection to this way of thinking about suicide. It is easy enough to imagine what results a suicide produces for the survivors, but thinking about the result for the person who commits suicide runs into what philosopher Philip Devine has called the "opaqueness of death."[51] Brandt asks us to compare two states of the world, but we can know very little about one of the states. As Devine puts it, "[w]hat I am contemplating is much more intimate than a world course. It is my own (self-chosen) death, and such a choice presents itself inevitably as a leap in the dark."[52] From this fact, Devine concludes that suicide can never be rational.

If left in this form, Devine's argument is subject to two objections. First, people regularly make what we think of as rational choices in the face of incomplete facts. The choice of law school over medical school is also, in some sense, a leap in the dark. Second, Devine's insight does not argue for life over death, as he seems to suppose. Even if he is right that the choice of death is irrational, on his argument, the choice of life is equally irrational.

Devine's argument might be reformulated so as to take account of these objections, however. The problem with the choice between life and death is not just that death is unknowable, but that there is no subject to know it. For this reason, life and death are not just different choices, but on different planes. In most other situations, when people try to make sensible decisions, they do something like what Brandt suggests: they imaginatively place themselves in two alternative worlds and think about which one is better. Of course, we cannot know fully what it is like to be in either alternative world, but we can make guesses informed by probability judgments. In contrast, it makes no sense at all to ask whether I would be better off if I were alive or dead. There is no "I" once I am dead and, therefore, there is no better or worse for me. Instead of comparing two alternative states of existence, one is comparing existence with non-existence. Imagining what it is like to be dead is like imagining what it is like to be a rock. Because rocks do not have consciousness and are not alive, there is no "being" to imagine. It is only our difficulty in comprehending the fact that we will one day turn into rocks that prevents us from seeing this truth about death as well.

Of course, this is not to deny that people, while alive, care about the state of the world after they die. It is actually something of a mystery why people care. My own suspicion is that the feeling is, once again, rooted in our difficulty in comprehending the full implications of our own annihilation. I will not insist on this point, however, especially since I cannot rid myself of my own concern for events likely to occur after my death. But whether or not it makes sense to care about a postdeath state of the world, it surely makes no sense to care about the welfare of *oneself* once one dies. The supposed rationality or irrationality of many, although not all, suicides seems to turn on just such a comparison. For example, it is sometimes said of a person in severe pain that death will bring the person peace. The implicit assumption behind this suggestion is that one is trading life for relief from pain. Yet if there is to be peace for the sufferer, then there must be a postdeath person who is at peace. But, obviously, there is not.

Moreover, even when suicide is motivated by a concern for others, an individual's choice between life and death always involves himself. Imagine, for example, a person who is willing to give up his life to protect his family from financial ruin. If the person chooses life, he will feel pain in seeing his loved one's suffer. If he chooses death, he will experience, while still alive, the satisfaction that comes from the knowledge that they will not suffer after he dies. Still, there is a sense in which the trade cannot be judged by rationality criteria. The trade is his life for his family's happiness after his death. But there is no way to compare the traded states of affairs because we cannot measure how he will "be" when he gives up his life.

It does not follow from this argument alone that suicide decisions are immune from rationality judgments. As philosopher Margaret Battin has pointed out,[53] sometimes suicides seem irrational precisely because people fail to understand that death is nonexistence. Think, for example, of the teenager who imagines how happy she will be when she sees all the people crying at her funeral.* Moreover, although it makes no sense to compare life with death, it does make sense to make predictions about future life events, and sometimes these predictions are mistaken or even crazy. Thus, a profoundly depressed individual who wrongly assumes that the future is bleak, a person who mistakenly thinks that he has a fatal disease, and a person who walks out of a twenty-story window supposing that he is entering a hallway have made mistakes about what the future holds. Surely, one might think, there is no need to remain silent about errors like these.

Perhaps some of these cases can be disposed of by distinguishing between "mistakes" about the choice for death and "mistakes" about whether one is choosing death. For example, the person mistaking a window for a hallway has not chosen death. One might also want to distinguish between "mistakes" about how it is to be dead and "mistakes" about how it is to be alive. Although it makes no sense to talk of mistakes in the former context (at least from a secular perspective), we regularly make judgments about mistakes in the latter context.

Still, even in the latter context, the problem is more difficult than it might at first seem. Imagine that at the time an individual makes a choice, the individual is certain that he will not regret the choice, and imagine further that this prediction is correct. Is it possible to say that the choice is irrational from the individual's point of view? At least so long as we maintain a secular perspective, we can be certain that no one ever regretted committing suicide. To be sure, others who know of the mistake may think it a shame that the individual died prematurely, and the individual himself may feel regret if he learns of his mistake between the time when he irrevocably commits to death and the time when he dies. But there is no regret after death.

The impossibility of regret is simply another manifestation of the fact that we are trying to compare things on different planes. Even if, while

---

* Think, too, of Diane's promise to meet Dr. Quill at Lake Geneva, with dragons swimming in the sunset.

alive, I make a palpably crazy error that leads to death, it makes no sense to say that I am "worse off" because of that error. Once again, there is no "I" to be worse off. The most that can be said is that if I knew of the error while alive, I would not have made the same choice, but this is quite different from saying that I am worse off because of making it.

At this point, many readers are likely to think that my argument has gone badly off track. Does it follow that we should not intervene to stop a person about to drink poison that he has mistaken for grape soda? It does not follow, but to see why not, we need to correct the second error in Devine's argument. Devine seems to suppose that if he can demonstrate that it is not rational to commit suicide, then one should not do so. Conversely, one might suppose, if it is rational to commit suicide, then perhaps it is at least permissible to do so. As we have seen, however, neither life nor death can be defended according to our thin rationality standard. An argument from rationality therefore has no consequences. But the debunking of rationality is about how, if at all, we should speak, not about how we should act. Here, as elsewhere, the failure of rational argument cannot, itself, be an argument for inaction. It cannot be an argument for anything. It follows that suicide, as well as the decision to stop a suicide, involve choice rather than argument. In both cases, what is required is action. Argument gets in the way of effective action when what we really need is silent resolve.*

What, then, is the legal payoff of a radical libertarian perspective? One payoff is that the law should stop worrying about the morality and rationality of suicide. Perhaps that is all that can be said and that what remains is silence, choice, and action. And yet, at the risk of breaking an appropriate silence, I want to say something more. If suicide is just a choice, then, perhaps the legal regime should confront us with that choice and, more to the point, with our status as choosing beings.

---

* Of course, this is not to say that speech designed to establish human connection, rather than to compel by argument, is inappropriate. Human connection can sometimes ward off death when argument cannot. There may even be some people (law professors come to mind) for whom argument is an important form of human connection, but then the argument is valuable because of the connection it creates, not because of the conclusions it compels.

Our previous discussion of torture provides a model for how this might be accomplished. Recall that the best case for the torture prohibition rests on the need to retain the illusion that we are not merely corporeal machines.[54] Torture is evil because it confronts us with the fact that we will do anything for our bodies. The torture ban allows us to avoid confronting this fact. It reflects a choice to conceive of ourselves as capable of choice.

Legalized assisted suicide can play a similar role. The analogy is clearest when we are talking about cases like Diane's, when a patient chooses controlled death in the face of terminal disease. Disease, like torture, is relentlessly physical, painful, uncontrolled, and, for exactly these reasons, terrifying. Like torture, it can be deeply dehumanizing. It, too, reminds us that we are ultimately only body.

The availability of suicide has the capacity to transform this experience. It preserves the possibility of mental control even as the body asserts its ultimate power over us. Interestingly, this may be true even if the control is never asserted. The Oregon experience is instructive here. Apparently, some terminally ill patients fill prescriptions for lethal medication but never use the medicine.[55] They nonetheless appear to be comforted by its availability. The mere existence of an option to use the medicine, even if it is never used, creates a sense of control over a process marked by the progressive loss of control.[56] Of course, even under the best of circumstances, dying is not exactly enjoyable. Still, the Oregon experience suggests that it does not have to be dehumanizing in the way that torture is dehumanizing. We have the potential to be more at peace with the loss of control that is dying when we retain the illusion that we can take control.*

---

* I take this to be a central theme of Norman Mailer's great novel *The Executioner's Song* (1979). The novel's antihero, condemned killer Gary Gilmore, manages to wrest control, or at least the illusion of control, of his own death from the state when he makes the choice not to appeal his conviction. Id. at 489–90, 509. Near the end of the novel, Gilmore appears to metaphorically "orchestrate" the firing squad as its bullets pierce his body, just as, in life, Gilmore had been a skilled thief, able to go "through everything like a guy leading an orchestra." Id. at 987. For a modern replay of the Gilmore drama, see William Yardley, *Even in Facing the Needle, a Killer Is Master of His Fate*, N.Y. TIMES, MAY 12, 2005, at B5 (reporting on convicted murderer Michael Ross's decision to end the appeals and hasten the execution of his death sentence).

Interestingly, this argument suggests that doctor-assisted suicide is most justifiable before the patient has reached the stage of excruciating pain, precisely the opposite of the common intuition.[57] When the patient is in severe pain, opting for death is giving in to torture in the most literal sense. It is analogous to the decision of a political prisoner, subjected to unbearable pain, to betray her comrades. Of course, I do not mean to suggest that there should be a prohibition against people giving in to torture, or, by extension, that severe pain should disqualify a person from receiving lethal medication. We are doing no one a favor by making people put up with agony. But although people should have the right to relief from this sort of pain, their exercise of the right hardly represents a victory of mind over body. That victory can only be won at an earlier stage when the decision reflects real choice. It follows that the right to suicide is most significant when it is available to people who still have some control over their bodies.

Obviously, the torture analogy is much less powerful when the subject is not suffering from physical illness. There is nonetheless a strong radical libertarian argument for emphasizing choice in this context as well. Many suicides are deeply angry acts. They constitute rebellions against existence. As our own Declaration of Independence emphasizes, when one gets angry enough at one's country, there is a natural right of revolution. True allegiance to country must be against the backdrop of this right, for it is only the presently rejected possibility of revolution that makes the allegiance authentic. So, too, there is a natural right of revolution against life. Life's fragility and the ever present possibility of choosing against it is what makes our hold on it poignant and powerful. It is just because we walk in the valley of the shadow of death that we can fear no evil. Once we summon the courage to bring into consciousness and face the choice we make every day between life and death, no other decision can frighten us. On a radical libertarian account, the law makes us truly free when it emphasizes, rather than obscures, that choice.

CHAPTER 9

Conclusion: A Little Less Noise, Please

TO LIVE IN MODERN AMERICA is to be surrounded by noise. We inhabit a world of 24/7 talk radio, an infinite blogosphere, and ubiquitous
cell phones and MP3 players. With a few keystrokes on the computer, we
can communicate with the world, and the world answers back.

From one perspective, this cacophony is the mark of a free and vibrant
society. Yet there is also a desperate quality to all of this speech. Could
it be that endless argument is the way that we ward off boredom while
we inexorably advance toward oblivion? Or that conversation distracts
us from the meaninglessness of our lives?

Of course, sometimes distraction is not such a bad thing, but if the
thesis of this book is correct, we should also worry that, paradoxically
enough, all this talking is a threat to our liberty. Our culture is so preoccupied with the right of self-expression and the fear of government
control that we have not noticed the problems that can be produced by
too much speech. As the variety and volume of communication has expanded, speakers have found that they must shout louder and louder to
a smaller and smaller audience if they are to be heard at all. The result
has been a gradual ratcheting up of rhetoric and a segmentation and po-
larization of our communications market that threatens the possibility
of compromise and civil public discourse.

If there is to be any hope of reversing or controlling these trends, we
must reassert and think carefully about the value of silence. That has
been the project of this book. I have tried to show in a variety of contexts, ranging from apologetic speech, to self-incrimination, to compelled
public ceremonies, to the regulation of suicide, that silence indeed has
value. Although it turns out that the value it has differs in different settings, it is possible to extrapolate some general points from these disparate contexts.

Silence is important to our freedom because we need to think in quiet before we decide what to say. It is important because we can only hear others when we are silent ourselves.

Silence has value because it preserves our privacy and our ability to shield ourselves from public criticism. We need silence because we need to resist the dangerous and seductive illusion that we can break through the tragic barrier that separates us from each other. Yet silence can also foster the deepest, most private communication that is sometimes obstructed by speech.

We need silence because we need to choose and to act, because endless speechifying can be a substitute for choice and action, and because forced speech undermines our self-conception as choosing agents. Yet we also need silence because sometimes we do not know what to say.

Most of all, we need silence because all the noise will eventually stop, and then we will be left alone with ourselves. If we are to be any good at it at all, we must practice being with ourselves, and silence is necessary for that.

Still, it must be acknowledged that there is an ultimate futility and contradiction in asserting the value of silence. Someone who yells out "be quiet!" is, himself, contributing to the noise. The right to silence is a right to be free from words that purport to compel action, when we really have an inalienable ability to choose, no matter what others say. Yet an argument for a right to silence is, itself, a set of words that purports to compel action. Silence needs speech to defend itself, but any defense necessarily contradicts what is being defended.

There is no escape from that contradiction, and, for that reason, silence must be our only response to it.

Notes

CHAPTER ONE

1. 384 U.S. 436 (1966).
2. Herman Melville, "Bartleby, The Scrivner," in LEGAL FICTIONS: SHORT STORIES ABOUT THE LAWYERS AND THE LAW (JAY WISINGRAD, ED.) 224 (1992).
3. MELVILLE'S BILLY BUDD (F. BARRON FREEMAN, ED. 1948).
4. "Silver Blaze" in II ARTHUR CONAN DOYLE, THE ANNOTATED SHERLOCK HOLMES 250 (WILLIAM S. BARING-GOULD, ED. 1967).
5. JOHN IRVING, THE WORLD ACCORDING TO GARP: A NOVEL (1978).
6. For an account, see DIANE JOHNSON, DASHIELL HAMMETT: A LIFE 238–52 (1983).

CHAPTER TWO

1. 274 U.S. 357, 372 (1927).
2. Id., at 375–76.
3. For a defense of deliberative democracy, see AMY GUTMANN & DENNIS THOMPSON, DEMOCRACY AND DISAGREEMENT 39–49 (1996). *See also* JOSEPH M. BASSETTE, THE MILD VOICE OF REASON: DELIBERATIVE DEMOCRACY AND AMERICAN NATIONAL GOVERNMENT (1994).

On republican influence on the drafting of the American Constitution, see, *e.g.,* J. G. A. POCOCK, THE MACHIAVELLIAN MOMENT: FLORENTINE POLITICAL THOUGHT AND THE ATLANTIC REPUBLICAN TRADITION (1975); GORDON S. WOOD, THE CREATION OF THE AMERICAN REPUBLIC 1776–1787 (1969).

On the "republican revival" and its influence on contemporary constitutional thought, see, *e.g.,* MARK V. TUSHNET, RED, WHITE, AND BLUE: A CRITICAL ANALYSIS OF CONSTITUTIONAL LAW (1988); Frank I. Michelman, *Foreword: Traces of Self-Government,* 100 HARV. L. REV. 4 (1986); Morton J. Horwitz, *Republicanism and Liberalism in American Constitutional Thought,* 29 WM. & MARY L. REV. 57 (1987).
4. For the classic defense of the free speech clause of the First Amendment along these lines, see ALEXANDER MEIKLEJOHN, FREE SPEECH AND ITS RELATION TO SELF-GOVERNMENT (1948). For a contemporary restatement, see Steven J. Heyman, *Righting the Balance: An Inquiry into the Foundations and Limits of Freedom of Expression,* 78 B. U. L. REV. 1275, 1344–52 (1998).
5. 277 U.S. 438, 471 (1928).
6. Id., at 478.
7. In John Rawls's famous formulation, "[P]olitical liberalism tries to answer the question: how is it possible that there can be a stable and just society, whose free and equal citizens are deeply divided by conflicting and even incommensurable religious, philo-

sophical, and moral doctrines?" JOHN RAWLS, POLITICAL LIBERALISM (EXPANDED EDITION 2005).

8. The most famous argument for liberal freedoms in a private sphere is in JOHN STUART MILL, ON LIBERTY (ELIZABETH RAPAPORT, ED. 1978). *See also* I WILLIAM BLACKSTONE, COMMENTARIES ON THE LAWS OF ENGLAND 120 (1979) ("the principal aim of society is to protect individuals in the enjoyment of those absolute rights which were vested in them by immutable laws of nature"). For a discussion of liberal autonomy, the contractarian tradition said to support it, and its influence on American constitutional law, see DAVID A. J. RICHARDS, TOLERATION AND THE CONSTITUTION (1986). *Compare* Anita L. Allen, *Social Contract Theory in American Case Law,* 51 FLA. L. REV. 1 (1999) *with* Heidi Li Feldman, *Rawls Political Constructivism as a Judicial Heuristic: A Response to Professor Allen,* 51 FLA. L. REV. 67 (1999). For Rawls's argument in favor of government neutrality as between "reasonable comprehensive doctrines," see POLITICAL LIBERALISM, note 7, *supra,* at 134.

9. One might, e.g., contrast Meiklejohn's republican defense of free speech as necessary for collective self-government, see note 4, *supra,* with Thomas Emerson's liberal defense of free speech: "[F]reedom of expression is essential as a means of assuring individual self-fulfillment. The proper end of man is the realization of his character and potentialities as a human being. For the achievement of this self-realization, the mind must be free. Hence, suppression of belief, opinion, or other expression is an affront to the dignity of man, a negation of man's essential nature." THOMAS I. EMERSON, THE SYSTEM OF FREEDOM OF EXPRESSION 6 (1970).

10. *See* POLITICAL LIBERALISM, note 7, *supra,* at 134.

11. *See* Richard L. Hasen, *Voting without Law?,* 144 U. PA. L. REV. 2135, 2169 (1996).

12. *See, e.g.,* JERRY L. MASHAW, GREED, CHAOS, AND GOVERNANCE: USING PUBLIC CHOICE TO IMPROVE PUBLIC LAW 15 (1997).

13. *See* Richard L. Hasen, note 11, *supra,* at 2138 ("Enactment of a compulsory voting law in the United States, even if desirable as a method of overcoming collective action problems, and even if proven effective as a means of increasing turnout in other states, is unlikely to occur because of a widely held libertarian belief against government interference in the decision to vote").

14. *See, e.g.,* JOHN STEWART MILL, note 8, *supra,* at 9.

15. The Supreme Court has elevated this solution to the status of constitutional principle. *See Pierce v. Society of Sisters,* 268 U.S. 510 (1925).

16. Consider, e.g., the explicitly republican justifications offered for public education around the time of the Constitution's framing. *See* Benjamin Rush, "Plan for the Establishment of Public Schools" in ESSAYS ON EDUCATION IN THE EARLY REPUBLIC (FREDERICK RUDOLPH, ED. 1965) 3 ("[Public education] is favorable to liberty. A free government can only exist in an equal diffusion of literature. Without learning, men become savages or barbarians and where learning is confined to a *few* people, we always find monarchy, aristocracy, and slavery"; "A Bill for the More General Diffusion of Knowledge," in THOMAS JEFFERSON, WRITINGS (1984) ("experience has shown that even under the best forms [of government] those entrusted with power have . . . perverted it into tyranny; and . . . the most effectual means of preventing this would be, to illuminate, as far as practicable, the minds of the people at large").

17. *See, e.g., Wisconsin v. Yoder,* 406 U.S. 205, 245 (1972) (Douglas, J., dissenting in part) ("If a parent keeps his child out of school beyond the grade school, then the

child will be forever barred from entry into the new and amazing world of diversity that we have today.")

18. *See, e.g.,* GORDON WOOD, *supra,* note 3; GEOFFREY R. STONE, LOUIS MICHAEL SEIDMAN, CASS R. SUNSTEIN, MARK V. TUSHNET, & PAMELA S., KARLAN, CONSTITUTIONAL LAW 12–14 (5TH ED. 2005).

19. As Brandeis also wrote, "publicity is justly commended as a remedy for social and industrial diseases. Sunlight is said to be the best of disinfectants." LOUIS BRANDEIS, OTHER PEOPLE'S MONEY 62 (1933).

20. *See, e.g.,* James M. Buchanan & Gordon Tullock, "The Calculus of Consent" in III THE COLLECTED WORKS OF JAMES BUCHANAN 282–302 (1990).

21. Holmes, e.g., thought that just because "time has upset many fighting faiths" therefore the government should not regulate speech. *Abrams v. United States,* 250 U.S. 616, 630 (1919) (Holmes, J., dissenting).

22. Richard Rorty, e.g., defends "minimalist" liberalism based upon antifoundationalist premises. *See* Richard Rorty, "A Defense of Minimalist Liberalism" in DEBATING DEMOCRACY'S DISCONTENT: ESSAYS ON AMERICAN POLITICS, LAW, AND PUBLIC PHILOSOPHY 117–125 (ANITA L. ALLEN & MILTON C. REGAN, JR., EDS. 1998). Liberal arguments along these lines have their roots in early twentieth-century pragmatism. *See, e.g.,* John H. Dewey, "Logical Method and Law" in AMERICAN LEGAL THEORY 17–27 (ROBERT SAMUEL SUMMERS, ED. 1992).

23. Consider, e.g., Justice Douglas's defense of a constitutional right of a married couple to use contraception: "Marriage is a coming together for better or for worse, hopefully enduring, and intimate to the degree of being sacred. It is an association that promotes a way of life, not causes; a harmony in living, not political faiths; a bilateral loyalty, not commercial or social projects. Yet it is an association for as noble a purpose as any involved in our prior decisions." *Griswold v. Connecticut,* 381 U.S. 479, 486 (1971).

24. I take this point to be central to the plurality's argument when it affirmed the abortion right in *Planned Parenthood of Southeastern Pennsylvania v. Casey:* "[A woman's] suffering is too intimate and personal for the State to insist, without more, upon its own vision of the woman's role, however dominant that vision has been in the course of our history and our culture. The destiny of the woman must be shaped to a large extent on her own conception of her spiritual imperatives and her place in society." 505 U.S. 833, 852 (1992). For a book-length defense of the abortion right along these lines, see ROBERT D. GOLDSTEIN, MOTHER-LOVE AND ABORTION: A LEGAL INTERPRETATION (1988).

25. 50 U.S.C. '1861 (a) (1) (2005).

26. For an introduction, see ACTION AND FREEDOM, 2000 (JAMES E. TOMBERLIN, ED. 2000).

27. For a modern reconceptualization of American constitutional law along these lines, see RANDY E. BARNETT, RESTORING THE LOST CONSTITUTION: THE PRESUMPTION OF LIBERTY (2004).

28. For a well-known political theory built around "encumbered" selves, see MICHAEL J. SANDEL, DEMOCRACY'S DISCONTENT: AMERICA IN SEARCH OF A POLITICAL PHILOSOPHY (1996). For an introduction to communitarian thought, see NEW COMMUNITARIAN THINKING: PERSONS, VIRTUES, INSTITUTIONS, AND COMMUNITIES (AMITAI ETZIONI, ED. 1995).

29. *See* Duncan Kennedy, *The Structure of Blackstone's Commentaries,* 28 BUFF. L. REV. 205, 211–13 (1979). For Kennedy's second thoughts, see Peter Gabel & Duncan Kennedy, *Roll over Beethoven,* 36 STAN. L. REV. 1, 16–17 (1985).

30. David Luban, *A Theory of Crimes against Humanity,* 29 YALE J. INT. L. 85, 110 (2004).

31. Duncan Kennedy has categorized this view as a species of "organicism." For a description and citations to the relevant literature, see Duncan Kennedy, *A Semiotics of Critique,* 22 CARDOZO L. REV. 1147, 1149 & n. 3 (2003).

32. *See, e.g.,* MICHEL FOUCAULT, DISCIPLINE AND PUNISH: THE BIRTH OF THE PRISON (1977); MICHEL FOUCAULT, THE HISTORY OF SEXUALITY (1990).

33. The canonical work is EDWARD O. WILSON, SOCIOBIOLOGY: THE NEW SYNTHESIS (1975). For an example of the application of these concepts to legal problems, see Owen D. Jones, *Law and Behavioral Biology,* 105 COLUM. L. REV. 405 (2005).

34. For a collection of readings making this point, see AMERICAN LEGAL REALISM 98–120 (WILLIAM W. FISHER III, MORTON J. HORWITZ, & THOMAS A. REED, EDS. 1993).

35. *See, e.g.,* AMITAI ETZIONI, RIGHTS AND THE COMMON GOOD: THE COMMUNITARIAN PERSPECTIVE iv (1995). John J. DiIulio, Jr., *A Lack of Moral Guidance Causes Juvenile Crime and Violence,* in WHAT CAUSES JUVENILE CRIME AND VIOLENCE? 115 (ANDREA NAKAYA, ED. 2005). *Cf.* Susan J. Stabile, *Using Religion To Promote Corporate Responsibility,* 39 WAKE FOREST L. REV. 839 (2004).

36. This idea goes back at least to Roger Williams. *See* Edward J. Eberle, *Roger Williams' Gift: Religious Freedom in America,* 4 ROGER WILLIAMS U. L. REV. 425, 452 (1999). For Madison's articulation of the same argument, see "Letter from James Madison to Edward Livingston," in V THE FOUNDERS CONSTITUTION (PHILIP KURLAND & RALPH LERNER, EDS. 1987) 106. For a modern restatement of the position, see STEVEN GOLDBERG, SEDUCED BY SCIENCE: HOW AMERICAN RELIGION HAS LOST ITS WAY 92–97 (1999).

37. On the rise of American Legal Realism, see EDWARD A. PURCELL, JR., THE CRISIS OF DEMOCRATIC THEORY: SCIENTIFIC NATURALISM & THE PROBLEM OF VALUE 74–95 (1973). On the connection between Realism and Critical Legal Studies, see Elizabeth Mensch, "The History of Mainstream Legal Thought" in THE POLITICS OF LAW: A PROGRESSIVE CRITIQUE 13–37 (DAVID KAIRYS, ed. 1990).

38. *See, e.g.,* note 34, *supra.*

39. For examples of work in this tradition, see POWER, DOMINANCE, AND NONVERBAL BEHAVIOR (STEVE L. ELLYSON & JOHN F. DOVIDIO, EDS. 1985); PERSONALITY, ROLES AND SOCIAL BEHAVIOR (WILLIAM ICKES & ERIC S. KNOWLES, EDS. 1982).

40. *See* note 33, *supra.*

41. In his helpful (and brilliant) typology, Duncan Kennedy characterizes these thinkers as "decisionists." For a discussion and collection of sources, see Duncan Kennedy, *A Semiotics of Critique,* note 31, *supra,* at 1161–1164 & nn. 26–33.

42. *See* Jean-Paul Sartre, BEING AND NOTHINGNESS: AN ESSAY ON PHENOMENOLOGICAL ONTOLOGY 47–70 (HAZEL E. BARNES, TRANS. 1956).

CHAPTER THREE

1. Clinton actually stopped short of a formal, full-scale apology for slavery, apparently because it would have "angered some centrist white voters who [had] been dependable supporters." James Bennet, "Clinton in Africa: The Overview; In Uganda Clinton

Expresses Regret on Slavery in U.S.," N.Y. TIMES, March 25, 1998, at A1. Instead, Clinton expressed "regret" for slavery. Id.

2. At first, Clinton issued what critics called an "unapologetic public apology" for the Lewinsky affair. *See* Walter Goodman, "Critics Notebook; Covering and Covering the Clinton Story, Oh So Apologetically," N.Y. TIMES, Sept. 1, 1998, at E3. When this stance met with public criticism, he more overtly asked for forgiveness. *See* Katherine Q. Seelye, "'Embraced by the Forgiving,'" Clinton Talks of Forgiveness," N.Y. TIMES, Aug. 29, 1998, at A1.

3. *See, e.g.,* Sheryl Gay Stolberg, "Leading Democrat Apologizes for Prisoner Abuse Remark," N.Y. TIMES, June 22, 2005, at A14 (Sen. Richard Durbin apologizes for likening American mistreatment of detainees to acts of Nazis, Soviets, and other mad regimes); Sheryl Gay Stolberg, "Under Fire, Lott Apologizes for His Comments at Thurmond's Party," N.Y. TIMES, Dec. 10, 2002, at A28 (Sen. Trent Lott apologizes for statement that seemed to endorse racial segregation).

4. *See, e.g.,* PETE ROSE, MY PRISON WITHOUT BARS (2004). It must be said that Rose offers something less than a full-throated apology. His book might better be characterized as a failed apology because it attempts to mix apology with account. *See* pp. 28–29, *infra*.

5. *See, e.g.,* "Report: Christie Brinkley's Husband Apologizes," http://www.cnn.com/2006/SHOWBIZ/07/25/people.brinkley.ap/index.html (husband apologizes publicly for infidelity) (site visited 7/27/06); Todd S. Purdum, "And Now for Her Third Act: Jane Fonda Looks Over the First Two," N.Y. TIMES, April 5, 2005, at E1 (apology for "being photographed laughing and clapping while sitting on an antiaircraft gun in Hanoi").

6. *See, e.g.,* David Firestone, "Billy Graham Responds to Lingering Anger over 1972 Remarks on Jews," N.Y. TIMES, March 17, 2002, at 129 (apology for antisemitic remarks); Pam Belluck & Frank Bruni, "Scandals in the Church: The Overview; Law, Citing Abuse Scandal, Quits as Boston Archbishop and Asks for Forgiveness," Dec. 14, 2002 at A1 (apology for allowing priests accused of sexual abuse to remain in ministry).

7. *See* Sara Rimer, "Harvard President Apologizes Again for Remarks on Gender," N.Y. TIMES, Jan. 20, 2005, at A14 (Harvard President Lawrence Summers issues two-page apology for comments sending "unintended signal of discouragement to talented girls and women.")

8. *See* David J. Garrow, "Aftermath: The Rule of Fear; Another Lesson from World War II Internments," N.Y. TIMES, Sept. 23, 2001, at 46 (referring to congressional apology to Japanese-Americans for World War II internment); Sheryl Stolberg, "The Nation; The Senate Apologizes, Mostly," N.Y. TIMES, June 19, 2005, at 43 (Senate apologizes to lynching victims and their descendants).

9. *See, e.g.,* "The Pope's Apology, "N.Y. TIMES, March 14, 2000, at A22 (referring to Pope John Paul II's acknowledgment of "mistakes and cruelty imbedded in church history, including the Inquisition, the forced conversions of native peoples in Africa and Latin America, and support for the Crusades").

10. *See* "Panel I Day Two of the Eight Public Hearings of the National Commission on Terrorist Attacks upon the United States," http://www.9-11commission.gov/archive/hearing8/9-11Commission_Hearing_2004-03-24.pdf (site visited 6/27/06): "I . . . welcome the hearings because it is finally a forum where I can apologize to the loved

ones of the victims of 9/11 . . . Your government failed you. Those entrusted with protecting you failed you. And I failed you. We tried hard, but that doesn't matter because we failed. And for that failure, I would ask, once all the facts are out, for your understanding and for your forgiveness."

11. It did so even though the commission did not demand apologies from those who came before it. *See, e.g.,* Donald G McNeil, Jr., "South African Tycoons Apologize for Gaining from Apartheid," N.Y. TIMES, Nov. 14, 1997, at A13 (apologies by "chief executives of the nation's biggest corporations and banks"); "De Klerk Blames Rogue Security Units for Apartheid Terror," N.Y. TIMES, Aug. 22, 1996, at 5 ("South Africa's former President F. W. DeKlerk, formally apologized today for the miseries of apartheid"). *See gen.* KENNETH CHRISTIE, SOUTH AFRICAN TRUTH COMMISSION (2000).

12. *See* AARON LAZARE, ON APOLOGY 7 (2004) (noting radio and television programs addressing subject of private apology).

13. Lee Taft characterizes our era as a time of "apology mania." *See Lee Taft, Apology Subverted: The Commodification of Apology,* 109 YALE L. J. 1135, 1135 (2000). For an effort to document the proposition that "apologies [are] on the rise," see AARON LAZARE, ON APOLOGY 6–8 (2004).

14. *See, e.g.,* BEVERLY ENGEL, THE POWER OF APOLOGY: HEALING STEPS TO TRANSFORM ALL YOUR RELATIONSHIPS (2001).

15. *See id.,* at 23–25.

16. P. G. WODEHOUSE, THE MAN UPSTAIRS AND OTHER STORIES 10 (2004).

17. On the gender valence of apologies, see AARON LAZARE, ON APOLOGY 27–31 (2004); NICHOLAS TAVUCHIS, MEA CULPA: A SOCIOLOGY OF APOLOGY AND RECONCILIATION 127 n. 2 (1991); Donna L. Pavlick, *Apology and Mediation: The Horse and Carriage of the Twenty-First Century,* 18 OHIO ST. J. ON DISP. RES. 829, 852 (2003).

18. *See* WILLIAM IAN MILLER, FAKING IT 79 (2003) ("[In the case of apology] the anxiety belongs less to the apologizer for faking it, which he often knowingly is doing, than to the person apologized to, for being taken in or for having to accept an apology he knows is false").

19. AMBROSE BIERCE: THE DEVIL'S DICTIONARY 9 (1957).

20. *See* LENORE E. WALKER, THE BATTERED WOMAN 65–66 (1979) ("[The batterer] truly believes he will never again hurt the woman he loves; he believes he can control himself from now on"). Walker's "cycle theory" has been vigorously attacked. *See, e.g.,* David L. Faigman, *Note: The Battered Woman Syndrome and Self-Defense: A Legal and Empirical Dissent,* 72 VA. L. REV. 619, 630–44 (1986). For a collection of the critical literature, see Robert F. Schopp, Barbara J. Sturgis, & Megan Sullivan, *Battered Woman Syndrome, Expert Testimony, and the Distinction between Justification and Excuse,* 1994 U. ILL. L. REV. 45, 53–64.

21. *See, e.g.,* Donna L. Pavlick, *Apology and Mediation, supra,* note 17, at 830 (arguing that apology "can help make injured parties whole in a way that legal remedies and economics cannot"). For a summary of the empirical literature on the effects of apologies on settlement rates, see Jennifer K. Robbennolt, *Apologies and Legal Settlement,* 102 MICH. L. REV. 460 (2003).

22. *See, e.g.,* Jonathan R. Cohen, *Advising Clients to Apologize,* 72 S. CAL. L. REV. 1009 (1999).

23. *See, e.g.,* COLO. REV. STAT. ' 13-25-135 (2003):

In any civil action brought by an alleged victim of an unanticipated outcome of medical care, or in any arbitration proceeding related to such civil action, any and all statements, affirmations, gestures, or conduct expressing apology, fault, sympathy, commiseration, condolence, compassion, or a general sense of benevolence which are made by a health care provider or an employee of a health care provider to the alleged victim, a relative of the alleged victim, or a representative of the alleged victim and which related to the discomfort, pain, suffering, injury, or death of the alleged victim as the result of the unanticipated outcome of medical care shall be inadmissible as evidence of an admission of liability or as evidence of an admission against interest.

See also Ill. Comp. Stat. Ann. ch. 710 (405 (establishing "Sorry Works!" pilot program providing for reimbursement to hospital that promptly apologizes for mistakes in patient care and offers fair settlement for costs to hospital that exceed costs that would have been incurred if case had been handled by traditional means).

For an example of a statute providing less comprehensive protection, but extending beyond medical malpractice suits, see Mass. Gen. Laws ch. 233 ' 23D (2002).

For academic commentary arguing for safe apology legislation, see, *e.g.*, Jonathan R. Cohen, *Legislating Apology: The Pros and Cons,* 70 U. CIN. L. REV. 819 (2002); Aviva Orenstein, *Apology Excepted: Incorporating a Feminist Analysis into Evidence Policy Where You Would Least Expect It,* 28 SW. U. L. REV. 221 (1999).

24. *See* United States Sentencing Guidelines '3E.1(a) ("If the defendant clearly demonstrates acceptance of responsibility for his offense, decrease the offense level by 2 levels.") In *United States v. Booker,* 543 U.S. 220 (2005), the Supreme Court invalidated mandatory use of the Guidelines but upheld their voluntary use by sentencing judges.

25. *See, e.g., State v. Gaultney,* slip op. (Wis., June 13, 2006) (sentencing judge may consider defendant's "remorse, repentance, and cooperativeness"); *People v. Wesley,* 411 N.W. 2d 159 (Mich. 1987) (consideration of remorsefulness as it bears on rehabilitation proper in sentencing).

26. For collections of readings on the movement, see RESTORATIVE JUSTICE (DECLAN ROCHE, ED. 2D ED. 2004); RESTORATIVE JUSTICE AND CIVIL SOCIETY (HEATHER STRANG & JOHN BRAITHWAITE, EDS. 2001). For a discussion of assessment studies showing some reason to believe that the movement is achieving its goals, see KEVIN REITZ & HENRY RUTH, THE CHALLENGE OF CRIME: RETHINKING OUR RESPONSE 56–66 (2003).

27. For a description of the project and its work, see "Georgia Justice Project: Changing Our Community One Person at a Time" http://www.gjp.org/about (visited 6/21/06). *See also* Stephen P. Garvey, *Punishment as Atonement,* 46 U.C.L.A. L. Rev. 1801 (1999). For a more skeptical account, see Cheryl G. Bader, *"Forgive the Victim for I Have Sinned": Why Repentance and the Criminal Justice System Do Not Mix, A Lesson from Jewish Law,* 31 FORDHAM URB. L. J. 69, 71–79 (1999).

28. *See* Martin Tolchi, "Packwood Offers Apology Without Saying for What," N.Y. TIMES, Dec. 12, 1992, at A24.

29. *See* Address to the Nation Announcing Decision to Resign the Office of President of the United States, August 8, 1974.

30. *See* Wit and Wisdom of Benjamin Disraeli, Earl of Beaconsfield: Collected from his Writings and Speeches 12 (1886) (quoting from Speech in House of Commons [order of business], July 28, 1871).

31. *See* note 20, *supra.*

32. *See* NICHOLAS TAVUCHIS, MEA CULPA: A SOCIOLOGY OF APOLOGY AND RECONCILIATION 31 (1991).

33. *See* id., at 23.

34. As Tavuchis puts it, when we apologize "we stand unarmed and exposed, relying, in a manner of speaking, on our moral nakedness to set things right." Id., at 18.

35. For an account of the affair, *see* id., at 104–05.

36. Id., at 21.

37. *See* p. 18, *supra.*

38. For a brilliant exploration of this problem, *see* WILLIAM IAN MILLER, FAKING IT 11–30 (2003).

39. For a related discussion, *see* George P. Fletcher, *Paradoxes in Legal Thought,* 85 COLUM. L. REV. 1263, 1280–82 (1985).

40. *See, e.g.,* MODEL PENAL CODE ' 3.02 (providing that conduct actor believes to be necessary to avoid harm is justifiable if harm avoided is greater than that sought to be prevented by law defining the offense charged).

41. 947 P. 2d 681 (Utah 1997).

42. Id., at 684.

43. Id., at 686.

44. *See* p. 30, *supra.*

45. *See* note 23, *supra.*

46. For an argument that there ought to be consistent rules for treating apologies at both stages, *see* Erin Ann O'Hara & Douglas Yarn, *On Apology and Consilience,* 77 WASH. L. REV. 1121, 1129–30 (2002).

47. *See* note 10, *supra.*

48. Oliver Wendell Holmes, Jr., *The Path of the Law,* 10 HARV. L. REV. 457, 459 (1897).

49. As usual, William Miller makes the point with cynical perspicacity: "We will never properly understand apology rituals and their requirement of humiliation and compensation if we do not understand that the ritual form is largely necessitated by how easy it is to fake remorse, and by how hard it is to distinguish genuine remorse that arises as a moral response to the harm done to the other from equally genuine amoral regret that arises from the discomfort the whole fiasco is causing the wrongdoer." WILLIAM IAN MILLER, FAKING IT 94 (2003).

50. *See* Lee Taft, *Apology Subverted: The Commodification of Apology,* 109 YALE L. J. 1135 (2000). *See also* Lee Taft, *On Bended Knee (with Fingers Crossed),* 55 DE PAUL L. REV. 601 (2006); Lee Taft, *Apology and Medical Mistake: Opportunity or Foil,* 14 ANN. OF HEALTH LAW 55 (2005); Lee Taft, *Apology Within a Moral Dialectic: A Reply to Professor Robbennolt,* 103 MICH. L. REV. 1010 (2005).

51. Lee Taft, *Apology Subverted: The Commodification of Apology,* note 50, *supra,* at 1157.

52. Id., at 1153.

53. The most frequently cited realist texts making this point are Morris R. Cohen, *Property and Sovereignty,* 13 CORN. L. Q. 8 (1927) and Robert L. Hale, *Coercion and Distribution in a Supposedly Non-Coercive State,* 38 POL. SCI. Q. 470 (1923).

54. *See, e.g.,* Seiji Takaku, Bernard Weiner, & Ken-Ichi Ohbuchi, *A Cross-Cultural Examination of the Effects of Apology and Perspective Taking on Forgiveness,* 20 J. LANG. & SOC. PSYCH. 144, 144 (2001) and sources cited therein (noting that "most

researchers regard accounts as a form of strategic communication, which are motivated by the instrumental concerns of evading punishment or obtaining favorable reactions from others"),

55. ERVING GOFFMAN, RELATIONS IN PUBLIC (1971).

56. Id., at 108.

57. Id., at 113–14.

58. *See* Jeffrie Murphy "Forgiveness and Resentment" 17–18 in JEFFRIE G. MURPHY & JEAN HAMPTON, FORGIVENESS AND MERCY (1988).

59. *See, e.g.,* Ken-Ichi Ohbuchi et al., *Apology as Aggression Control: Its Role in Mediating Apparaisal of and Response to Harm,* 56 J. PERSONALITY & SOC. PSYCH. 219 (1988).

60. *See,* Hiroshi Wagatsuma & Arthur Rosett, *The Implication of Apology: Law and Culture in Japan and the United States,* 20 LAW & SOCY. REV. 461, 473 (1986) (according to Japanese norms, self-denigration and submission restores harmony). *Cf.* Avivia Orenstein, *Apology Excepted: Incorporating a Feminist Analysis into Evidence Policy Where You Would Least Expect It,* 28 SW. U. L. REV. 221 (1999) (exploring gender differences in readiness to apologize).

61. The "truth and reconciliation" process by which a new regime establishes itself without punishing all wrongdoers from the old one might be said to achieve this goal. *See* note 11, *supra.*

62. Erin Ann O'Hara & Douglas Yarn, *On Apology and Consilience,* 77 WASH. L. REV. 1121 (2002).

63. Id., at 1146.

64. Id., at 1167–68.

65. Id., at 1180.

66. *See, e.g.,* LOUIS KAPLOW & STEVEN SHAVELL, DECISION ANALYSIS, GAME THEORY, AND INFORMATION 1 (2004) (arguing that "proceeding through the decision-making process in an organized and methodical way" is best means of achieving a chosen goal); A. MITCHELL POLINSKY, AN INTRODUCTION TO LAW AND ECONOMICS 7 (2D ED. 2004) ("Economists traditionally concentrate on how to maximize the size of the pie, leaving to others—such as legislators—the decision of how to divide it").

67. ALBERT CAMUS, THE STRANGER (MATHEW WARD, TRANS. 1988).

68. On the problem of consciously forgetting, see George Fletcher, *Paradoxes in Legal Thought,* 85 COLUM. L. REV. 1263, 1283 (1985); JON ELSTER, SOUR GRAPES: STUDIES IN THE SUBVERSION OF RATIONALITY 46 (1983).

CHAPTER FOUR

1. *See* LOUIS MICHAEL SEIDMAN, OUR UNSETTLED CONSTITUTION: A NEW DEFENSE OF CONSTITUTIONALISM AND JUDICIAL REVIEW (2001).

2. *See, e.g.,* RANDY E. BARNETT, RESTORING THE LOST CONSTITUTION: THE PRESUMPTION OF LIBERTY 118–30 (2003) (explaining that the public meaning of constitutional text often allows for construction); Akhil Reed Amar, *Foreword: The Document and the Doctrine,* 114 HARV. L. REV. 26, 28 (2000) (conceding that "the document, itself, will often be indeterminate over a wide range of possible applications").

3. The most famous defense of this position is Robert H. Bork, *Neutral Principles and Some First Amendment Problems,* 47 IND. L. J. 1 (1971). For more sophisticated and nuanced versions, see note 2, *supra;* Richard S. Kay, *Adherence to the Original*

Intentions in Constitutional Adjudication: Three Objections and Responses, 82 Nw. U. L. REV. 226 (1988); Frederick Schauer, *Easy Cases,* 58 S. CAL. L. REV. 399 (1985).

4. For criticisms along these lines see Paul Brest, *The Misconceived Quest for the Original Understanding,* 60 B.U. L. REV. 204 (1980).

5. *See* RONALD DWORKIN, FREEDOM'S LAW: THE MORAL READING OF THE AMERICAN CONSTITUTION (1996); RONALD DWORKIN, LAW'S EMPIRE (1986).

6. For my own criticisms, see OUR UNSETTLED CONSTITUTION, note 1, *supra,* at 48–54.

7. U.S. CONST., AMEND. V.

8. *See, e.g., Kansas v. Hendricks,* 521 U.S. 346 ((1997) (civil commitment of sex offenders); *International Union, United Mine Workers of America v. Bagwell,* 512 U.S. 821, 828 (1994) ("The paradigmatic coercive, civil contempt sanction . . . involves confining a contemnor indefinitely until he complies with an affirmative order"). *But cf. Kansas v. Crane,* 534 U.S. 407, 412 (2002) (the Constitution requires some lack of control determination for civil commitment of sex offender).

9. *See Kansas v. Hendricks,* note 8, *supra, at* 361 ("only the 'clearest proof' will suffice to override legislative intent and transform what is denominated a civil remedy into a criminal penalty" (quoting *Hudson v. United States,* 522 U.S. 93 [1997]).

10. At least there is no constitutional excuse. Conceivably, a witness might be able to invoke state common law duress principles. For an effort to explain the constitutional self-incrimination privilege by reference to these principles, see William Stuntz, *Self-Incrimination and Excuse,* 88 COLUM. L. REV. 1227 (1988).

11. *See Counselman v. Hitchcock,* 142 U.S. 547, 562 (1892).

12. *See, e.g., Emspak v. United States,* 349 U.S. 190 (1955).

13. *See Counselman v. Hitchcock,* 142 U.S. 547 (1892).

14. *See Chavez v. Martinez,* 538 U.S. 760, 768–69 (2003).

15. *See United States v. Doe,* 465 U.S. 605 (1984).

16. *See Kastigar v. United States,* 406 U.S. 441 (1972).

17. *See, e.g., Garner v. United States,* 424 U.S. 642, 654 (1976).

18. *See, e.g., id.,* at 654 n. 9 ("an individual may lose the benefit of the privilege without making a knowing and intelligent waiver").

19. According to the International Centre for Prison Studies, the United States currently imprisons 2,186,230 people. We have the highest total in the world, with more than three-quarters of a million more prison inmates than China, which is in second place. See King's College, London, International Centre for Prison Studies, http://www.kcl. ac.uk/depsta/rel/icps/worldbrief/highest_to_lowest_rates.php (site visited 7/10/06).

20. For a systematic debunking of the various arguments advanced for the privilege, see David Dolinko, *Is There a Rationale for the Privilege Against Self Incrimination?,* 33 U.C.L.A. L. Rev. 1063 (1986).

21. *See, e.g., New York v. Quarles,* 467 U.S. 649, 674 (1984) (O'Connor, J., concurring in the judgment in part and dissenting in part) (noting that the trend in some other countries is to admit compelled self-incriminatory statements if corroborated by non-testimonial evidence).

22. *See* Peter W. Tague, *The Fifth Amendment: If an Aid to the Guilty Defendant, an Impediment to the Innocent One,* 78 GEO. L. J. 1 (1989).

23. *See* pp. 11–12.

24. *See* p. 8, *supra.*

25. JEREMY BENTHAM, A TREATISE ON JUDICIAL EVIDENCE 241 (1825). Bentham is one of a long line of famous legal scholars who have disparaged the privilege. *See, e.g., Palko v., Connecticut,* 302 U.S. 319, 326 (1937) (Cardozo, J) ("Justice . . . would not perish if the accused were subject to a duty to respond to orderly inquiry"); HENRY J. FRIENDLY, THE FIFTH AMENDMENT TOMORROW: THE CASE FOR CONSTITUTIONAL CHANGE, 37 U. CIN. I. REV. 671 (1968).

26. *See, e.g., Murphy v. Waterfront Commn. of New York Harbor,* 378 U.S. 52, 55 (1964) ("[The privilege] reflects many of our fundamental values and most noble aspirations [including] our preference for an accusatorial rather than an inquisitorial system of criminal justice").

27. For an argument that it is not, see LLOYD WEINREB, DENIAL OF JUSTICE: CRIMINAL PROCESS IN THE UNITED STATES (1977).

28. AKHIL REED AMAR, THE CONSTITUTION AND CRIMINAL PROCEDURE: FIRST PRINCIPLES 71 (1997).

29. A study of sixty-two cases of convicted defendants subsequently exonerated that was conducted by the Innocence Project found that perjured informant testimony was a factor in 21 percent of them. See JIM DWYER, PETER NEUFELD, & BARRY SHECK, ACTUAL INNOCENCE: FIVE DAYS TO EXECUTION AND OTHER DISPATCHES FROM THE WRONGLY CONVICTED 246 (2000).

30. *See, e.g.,* ELIZABETH LOFTUS, EYEWITNESS TESTIMONY (1979). On the even more serious problem of crossracial identification, *see* Sheri Lynn Johnson, *Cross-Racial Identification. Errors in Criminal Cases,* 69 CORN. L. REV. 934 (1984).

31. *See, e.g., Green v. United States,* 718 A.2d 1042 (D.C. 1998).

32. *See* AKHIL REED AMAR, THE CONSTITUTION AND CRIMINAL PROCEDURE: FIRST PRINCIPLES 48–49 (1997) ("Modern understandings of the clause deviate far from its early American implementation, from plain meaning, and from common sense").

33. *See* Daniel J. Seidmann & Alex Stein, *The Right to Silence Helps the Innocent: A Game-Theoretic Analysis of the Fifth Amendment Privilege,* 114 HARV. L. REV. 430 (2000).

34. Id., at 458.

35. Id., at 461.

36. As Stephanos Bibas points out, the Seidmann-Stein theory predicts that rational, guilty suspects will exercise their right to silence, but in fact 80–90 percent of suspects talk to the police. This is so, Bibas argues, because even if they have a right to remain silent, successful lying nonetheless has a tremendous payoff for guilty defendants. *See* Stephanos Bibas, *The Right To Remain Silent Helps Only the Guilty,* 88 IOWA L. REV. 421, 421–22 (2002).

37. 380 U.S. 609 (1965).

38. I am grateful to Mark Tushnet for suggesting this point to me.
    The argument in text is weakened to the extent that the *Griffin* Court anticipated that its own rule would not be fully obeyed. When applied to the real world, *Griffin* may result in no more than jurors giving less probative weight to the defendant's failure to testify.

39. *Cf.* Gordon Van Kessel, *Quieting the Guilty and Acquitting the Innocent: A Close Look at a New Twist on the Right to Silence,* 35 IND. L. REV. 925, 935 (2002) (arguing that criminal trials are a "one-shot process where factfinders do not accumulate market-savvy by continuous exposure to the marketplace of exonerating statements").

40. In fairness to Seidmann and Stein, the "brilliance" problem affects more than their work alone. For a brilliant analysis, see Daniel A. Farber, *The Case Against Brilliance*, 70 MINN. L. REV. 917 (1986).

41. *See, e.g.,* TOM BUCKE, ROBERT STREET, & DAVID BROWN, THE RIGHT OF SILENCE: THE IMPACT OF THE CRIMINAL JUSTICE AND PUBLIC ORDER ACT OF 1994 (2000) discussed in Daniel J. Seidmann & Alex Stein, *The Right to Silence Helps the Innocent: A Game-Theoretic Analysis of the Fifth Amendment Privilege*, 114 HARV. L. REV. 430, 501 (2000).

42. *See* Paul G. Cassell & Richard Fowles, *Handcuffing the Cops? A Thirty-Year Perspective on Miranda's Harmful Effects on Law Enforcement*, 50 STAN. L. REV. 1055, 1065–66 (1998), discussed in Daniel J. Seidmann & Alex Stein, *The Right to Silence Helps the Innocent: A Game-Theoretic Analysis of the Fifth Amendment Privilege*, 114 HARV. L. REV. 430, 500 (2000).

43. *See, e.g.,* George C. Thomas III, *Plain Talk About the Miranda Empirical Debate: A "Steady-State" Theory of Confessions*, 43 U.C.L.A. L. REV. 933 (1996).

44. *See, e.g.,* AKHIL REED AMAR, THE CONSTITUTION AND CRIMINAL PROCEDURE: FIRST PRINCIPLES 65–70 (1997); William J. Stuntz, *Self-Incrimination and Excuse*, 88 COLUM. L REV. 1227, 1232–37 (1988); Henry J. Friendly, *The Fifth Amendment Tomorrow: The Case for Constitutional Change*, 37 CIN. L. REV. 671 (1968).

45. The liberal argument I make here is influenced by, but not identical to, arguments actual liberals have made in defense of the privilege. It most closely tracks the argument in R. Kent Greenawalt, *Silence as a Moral and Constitutional Right*, 23 WM & MARY L. REV. 15 (1981). *See also* Robert Gerstein, *Privacy and Self-Incrimination*, 80 ETHICS 87 (1970); Robert Gerstein, *Punishment and Self-Incrimination*, 16 A. J. JURIS 84 (1971).

46. *See United States v. Johnson,* 964 F. 2d 124 (2d Cir. 1992).

47. Id., at 126.

48. The *Johnson* court concluded that they did. Finding that "[t]he United States Sentencing Guidelines do not require a judge to leave compassion and common sense at the door to the courtroom," id, at 125, the court approved the trial judge's decision to award Johnson a substantial downward departure.

49. *Murphy v. The Waterfront Commn. of New York Harbor,* 378 U.S. 52, 55 (1964).

50. *Cf.* William J. Stuntz, *Self-Incrimination and Excuse*, 88 COLUM. L. REV. 1227, 1237–38 (1988) ("[T]he immunized witness . . . must testify against criminal associates, notwithstanding their threat to injure or kill him if he talks. Surely the choice this witness faces is harsher than the choice faced by a burglary suspect asked to give an account of his conduct on the day of the crime").

51. *See, e.g.,* William J. Stuntz, *Self-Incrimination and Excuse*, 88 COLUM. L. REV. 1227, 1232–34 (1988).

52. *See* p. 67, *infra.*

53. *See* William J. Stuntz, *Self-Incrimination and Excuse*, 88 COLUM. L. REV. 1227, 1232–34 (1988); AKHIL REED AMAR, THE CONSTITUTION AND CRIMINAL PROCEDURE: FIRST PRINCIPLES 65 (1997).

54. 384 U.S. 757 (1966).

55. *United States v. Wade,* 388 U.S. 218 (1967).

56. *United States v. Dionisio,* 410 U.S. 1 (1973) (voice exemplar); *United States v. Mara,* 410 U.S. 19 (1973) (handwriting exemplar).

57. 425 U.S. 391 (1976).
58. *See Senate Select Committee on Ethics v. Packwood*, 845 F. Supp. 17 (D. D. C. 1994).
59. *See, e.g., United States v. Dionisio*, 410 U.S., at 768.
60. *Fisher v. United States*, 425 U.S., at 409–11.
61. *See United States v. Hubbell*, 530 U.S. 27, 44 (2000).
62. 496 U.S. 582 (1990).
63. Id., at 591.
64. Id.
65. *See, e.g.*, Oliver Sacks, "Neurology and the Soul," N.Y. REV. BOOKS, Nov. 22 1990, at 44, 45 (rejecting "mystical" and "dualistic" explanations of human behavior). As Steven Goldberg has explained, modern science has advanced "by setting [dualism] aside, that is, by defining inquiries into the spiritual as nonscientific." Steven Goldberg, *Gene Patents and the Death of Dualism*, 5 S. CAL. INDISC. L. J. 25, 36 (1996).
66. *See, e.g.*, Paul M. Churchland & Patricia S. Churchland, "Intertheoretic Reduction: A Neuroscientist's Field Guide" in THE MIND BODY PROBLEM 53 (RICHARD WARNER & TADUSEZ SZUBKA EDS. 1994) (reporting that they are "very upbeat" about possibility of reducing psychology to neuroscience). Even neurobiologists whose work is sometimes treated as opposing strong claims of artificial intelligence nonetheless emphasize that they are not dualists. *See, e.g.*, GERALD EDELMAN, BRIGHT AIR, BRILLIANT FIRE 194–95 (1992) (arguing that material artifacts could be constructed with high-order consciousness). For a discussion, see STEVEN GOLDBERG, CULTURE CLASH: LAW AND SCIENCE IN AMERICA 165–66 (1994).
67. 414 U.S. 70 (1973).
68. *See United States v. Rylander*, 460 U.S. 752, 753 (1983).
69. Id.
70. 468 U.S. 841 (1984).
71. 335 U.S. 1 (1948).
72. *See, e.g., New State Ice Co. v. Liebmann*, 285 U.S. 262 (1932) (invalidating statute prohibiting person from manufacturing ice without government permission).
73. *See, e.g., Ferguson v. Skrupa*, 372 U.S. 726 (1963) (upholding statute prohibiting any person from engaging in business of debt adjusting except as incident to practice of law).
74. *California v. Byers*, 402 U.S. 424 (1971).
75. 493 U.S. 549 (1990).
76. *See Williams v. Florida*, 399 U.S. 78, 84 (1970) ("The pressures generated by the State's evidence may be severe, but they do not vitiate the defendant's choice to present an alibi defense and witnesses to prove it"); *United States v. Rylander*, 460 U.S. 752, 758 (1983) ("We have squarely rejected the notion . . . that a possible failure of proof an issue where the defendant has the burden of proof is a form of 'compulsion' which requires that the burden be shifted from the defendant's shoulders to that of the government").
77. *See, e.g., Brady v. United States*, 397 U.S. 742 (1970); *McMann v. Richardson*, 397 U.S. 759 (1970); *Parker v. North Carolina*, 397 U.S. 790 (1970).
78. William Stuntz has effectively made this point more globally with respect to all of criminal procedure. *See* William J. Stuntz, *The Uneasy Relationship between Criminal Procedure and Criminal Justice*, 107 YALE L. J. 1 (1997).

79. *See, e.g., Rummel v. Estelle,* 445 U.S. 263 (1980) (holding that mandatory life sentence for defendant's third felony conviction for obtaining $120.75 by false pretenses was not cruel and unusual punishment); *Harmelin v. Michigan,* 501 U.S. 957 (1991) (life sentence without possibility of parole for possession of 672 grams of cocaine was not cruel and unusual punishment even though defendant had no prior felony convictions).

80. *See* pp. 59, 73, *supra.*

81. *See, e.g., Dixon v. United States,* 1265 ct. 2437 (2006) U.S. (June 22, 2006) (duress is an affirmative defense that defendant must therefore prove by preponderance of evidence); *Patterson v. New York,* 432 U.S. 197 (1977) (same for emotional distress); *Martin v. Ohio,* 480 U.S. 228 (1987) (same for self-defense)

82. 399 U.S. 78 (1970).

83. Id., at 85.

84. *See, e.g., Johnson v. United States,* 318 U.S. 189, 195 (1943).

85. 403 U.S. 573 (1971).

86. *See* p. 101, *infra.*

87. 380 U.S. 609 (1965).

88. *See Raffel v. United States,* 271 U.S. 494 (1926).

89. *See Mullaney v. Wilbur,* 421 U.S. 684 (1975) (holding that due process violated by placing burden of proof on defendant to establish "heat of passion" that reduced murder to manslaughter).

90. *See Brooks v. Tennessee,* 406 U.S. 605 (1972) (holding that requirement that defendant testify before any other defense witness is unconstitutional).

91. 487 U.S. 201 (1988).

92. Id., at 216.

93. *See* p. 48, *supra.*

94. *See* p. 86, *supra.*

95. *See* p. 51, *supra.*

96. *See* U.S. SENTENCING GUIDELINES MANUAL (§E1.1. Courts have held that this provision does not violate the Fifth Amendment privilege. *See United States v. Henry,* 883 F. 2d 1010 (11th Cir. 1989); *United States v. Gonzalez,* 897 F. 2d 1018 (9th Cir. 1989).

97. *See* pp. 67, 74–77, *supra.*

98. *See* pp. 80–87, *supra.*

99. Dworkin, himself, for example, opposes judicial articulation of a constitutional right to subsistence because such a right would violate the "fit" requirement and, therefore, the rule of law. *See* Ronald Dworkin, *The Arduous Virtue of Fidelity: Originalism, Scalia, Tribe, and Nerve,* 65 FORDHAM L. REV. 1249, 1254–55 (1997).

CHAPTER FIVE

1. Most of the facts related in the text that follows are drawn from Chief Justice Warren's majority opinion in *Spano v. New York,* 360 U.S. 315 (1959). *See also* "Surrenders in Slaying; Machinist Wanted in Killing of Boxer Gives Himself Up," N.Y. TIMES, Feb. 5, 1957, at 16; "Murder Guilt Denied; Machinist Pleads Innocence in Bronx Slaying of Boxer," N.Y. TIMES, Feb. 6, 1957, at 16; "Sentenced to Death; Spano, Killer of Palermo, to Die, Week of June 23," N.Y. TIMES, May 10, 1957, at 27; "Spano Pleads Guilty in Killing," N.Y. TIMES, Dec. 10, 1959, at 35; "Spano Is Sentenced; Gets 10–20 Years for Killing Boxer Palermo in '56," N.Y. TIMES, Jan 12, 1960, at 16.

2. *See, e.g., Ashcraft v. Tennessee,* 322 U.S. 143 (1944); *Watts v. Indiana,* 338 U.S. 49 (1949); *Culombe v. Connecticut,* 367 U.S. 568 (1961).

3. 384 U.S. 436 (1966).

4. *See Twining v. New Jersey,* 211 U.S. 78 (1908); *Adamson v. California,* 332 U.S. 46 (1947).

5. *Malloy v. Hogan,* 378 U.S. 1 (1964).

6. *See* YALE KAMISAR, WAYNE R. LaFAVE, JEROLD H. ISRAEL, & NANCY KING, MODERN CRIMINAL PROCEDURE: CASES-COMMENTS-QUESTIONS 570 (11th ED. 2005) (Fifth Amendment privilege thought not to apply in station house because compulsion was not "legal"). *But see Bram v. United States,* 168 U.S. 543 (1897) (holding that involuntariness of confessions controlled by self-incrimination clause).

7. *See, e.g., Reck v. Pate,* 367 U.S. 433, 440 (1961); *Rogers v. Richmond,* 365 U.S. 534, 544 (1961).

8. *See Brown v. Mississippi,* 297 U.S. 278 (1936).

9. *See, e.g., Leyra v. Denno,* 347 U.S. 556 (1954) (confession inadmissible because defendant's "mental freedom" interfered with).

10. *Spano v. New York,* 360 U.S. 320 (1959).

11. *Culombe v. Connecticut,* 367 U.S. 568, 601 (1961) (Frankfurter, J., announcing judgment of the Court).

12. *See* YALE KAMISAR, WAYNE R. LaFAVE, JEROLD H. ISRAEL, & NANCY J. KING, MODERN CRIMINAL PROCEDURE CASES-COMMENTS-QUESTIONS 553–55 (11TH ED. 2005). For an example of confusion between the two rationales within a single sentence, see *Watts v. Indiana,* 338 U.S. 49, 55 (1949) (emphasis added): "In holding that the Due Process Clause bars *police* procedure which violate the basic notions of our accusatorial mode of prosecuting crime and vitiates a conviction based on the fruits of such procedure, we apply the Due Process Clause to its historic function of *assuring appropriate procedure before liberty is curtailed or life is taken.*"

13. *See Wolf v. Colorado,* 338 U.S. 25 (1949).

14. This point has been made most forcefully by Yale Kamisar. *See, e.g.,* YALE KAMISAR, WAYNE R. LaFAVE, JEROLD H. ISRAEL, & NANCY J. KING, MODERN CRIMINAL PROCEDURE: CASES-COMMENTS-QUESTIONS 556–58 (11TH ED. 2005); YALE KAMISAR, POLICE INTERROGATION AND CONFESSIONS: ESSAYS IN LAW AND POLICY 75 (1980).

15. *See McNabb v. United States,* 318 U.S. 332 (1943); *Mallory v. United States,* 354 U.S. 449 (1957).

16. *See Escobedo v. Illinois,* 378 U.S. 478, 490–91 (1964).

17. *See Malloy v. Hogan,* 378 U.S. 1 (1964).

18. *See Miranda v. Arizona,* 384 U.S. 436, 461 (1966) ("We are satisfied that all the principles embodied in the privilege apply to informal compulsion exerted by law-enforcement officers during in-custody questioning").

19. Id., at 444.

20. *See Chavez v. Martinez,* 538 U.S. 760, 767 (2003).

21. *Miranda v. Arizona,* 384 U.S. 436, 479 (1966).

22. 18 U.S.C. § 3501.

23. 530 U.S. 428 (2000).

24. *See New York v. Quarles,* 467 U.S. 649, 655 (1984).

25. *Edwards v. Arizona,* 451 U.S. 477 (1981).

26. *See* id., at 489–90 (Powell, J., dissenting).

27. *See, e.g., Oregon v. Bradshaw,* 462 U.S. 1039 (1983).

28. *See, e.g., Miranda v. Arizona,* 384 U.S. 436, 511–12 (Harlan, J., dissenting).

29. *See, e.g., New York v. Quarles,* 467 U.S. 649, 682 (1984) (Marshall, J., dissenting).

30. *See, e.g., Michigan v. Tucker,* 417 U.S. 433, 444 (1974) (*Miranda* rights "were not themselves rights protected by the Constitution but were instead measures to insure that the right against compulsory self-incrimination was protected"); *Oregon v. El-sted,* 470 U.S. 298, 306 (1985) (*Miranda* exclusionary rule "may be triggered even in the absence of a Fifth Amendment violation").

31. *See, e.g.,* Henry P. Monaghan, *Foreword: Constitutional Common Law,* 89 HARV. L. REV. 1, 19–23 (1975).

32. *Compare, e.g.,* Paul Cassell, *Miranda's Social Costs: An Empirical Reassessment,* 90 Nw. U. L. Rev. 387 (1995) (costs of *Miranda* significant) *with* George C . Thomas III & Richard A. Leo, *The Effects of Miranda v. Arizona: "Embedded" in Our National Culture?,* 29 CRIM & JUS. 203 (2002) (no good evidence that *Miranda* imposed significant costs).

33. *See, e.g.,* Welsh S. White, *Miranda's Failure to Restrain Pernicious Interrogation Practices,* 99 MICH. L. REV. 1211, 1219 (2001).

34. David A. Strauss, *The Ubiquity of Prophylactic Rules,* 55 U. CHI. L. REV. 190 (1988).

35. Richard A. Fallon, *Judicial Legitimacy and the Unwritten Constitution: A Comment on Miranda and Dickerson,* 45 N.Y. L. SCH. L. REV. 119 (2000).

36. Mitchell N. Berman, *Constitutional Decision Rules,* 90 VA. L. REV. 1 (2004).

37. *See, e.g.,* Steven J. Schulhofer, *Bashing Miranda is Unjustified and Harmful,* 20 HARV. J. L. & PUB. POL. 347, 350 (1997).

38. Of course, it remains possible that *Miranda* has led police to substitute effective permissible tactics for effective impermissible tactics, thereby producing a "win-win" situation. *See* Stephen J. Schulhoffer, *Miranda's Practical Effect: Substantial Benefits and Vanishingly Small Social Costs,* 90 Nw. U. L. REV. 500, 559 (1996).

39. *See, e.g.,* Paul G. Cassell, *Miranda's Social Costs: An Empirical Reassessment,* 90 Nw. U. L. REV. 387, 390 (1996).

40. *See* pp. 70–74, *supra.*

41. *Dickerson v. United States,* 530 U.S. 428, 444 (2000).

42. *See* p. 19, *supra.*

43. *See* PETER BROOKS, TROUBLING CONFESSIONS: SPEAKING GUILT IN LAW AND LIT-ERATURE 35–87 (2000).

44. DAVID SIMON, HOMICIDE: A YEAR ON THE KILLING STREETS 209 (1991) *quoted in* PETER BROOKS, TROUBLING CONFESSIONS: SPEAKING GUILT IN LAW AND LITERA-TURE 41–42 (2000).

45. *Cf. Bloom v. Illinois,* 391 U.S. 194, 202 (1968), noting that a defendant in a criminal contempt case is entitled to a jury trial in part because "Contemptuous conduct, though a public wrong, often strikes at the most vulnerable and human qualities of a judge's temperament. Even when the contempt is not a direct insult to the court or the judge, it frequently represents a rejection of judicial authority, or an interference with the judicial process or with the duties of officers of the court."

46. *Cf.* Charles Fried, *The Lawyer as Friend: The Moral Foundations of the Lawyer-Client Relation,* 85 YALE L. J. 1060 (1976).

47. For discussion of a similar proposal, see Albert W. Alschuler, *A Peculiar Privilege in Historical Perspective: The Right to Remain Silent,* 94 MICH. L. REV. 2625, 2669 (2002). Alschuler reports that the list of commentators who have endorsed something like this solution reads "like an honor role of the legal profession." Id.

48. *See* "Spano Pleads Guilty in Killing," N.Y. TIMES, Dec. 10, 1959, at 35; "Spano Is Sentenced; Gets 10–20 Years for Killing Boxer Palermo in '56," N.Y. TIMES, Jan 12, 1960, at 16.

49. Telephone interview between Miriam Lederer and Christopher Scott, Clerk No. 1 Record Depository, New York Department of Corrections, July 12, 2005.

50. *See* Louis Michael Seidman, *Akhil Amar and the (Premature) Demise of Criminal Procedure Liberalism,* 107 YALE L. J. 2281 (1998).

51. *See* p. 94, *supra.*

52. *See* AKHIL REED AMAR, THE CONSTITUTION AND CRIMINAL PROCEDURE: FIRST PRINCIPLES 46–88 (1997).

53. *See* note 50, *supra.*

CHAPTER SIX

1. The facts that follow are drawn from JACOBO TIMERMAN, PRISONER WITHOUT A NAME, CELL WITHOUT A NUMBER (TOBY TALBOT, TRANS., 1981).

2. Id., at 11.

3. Id., at 33–34.

4. ELAINE SCARRY, THE BODY IN PAIN: THE MAKING AND UNMAKING OF THE WORLD 35 (1985).

5. *See, e.g.,* Eric A. Posner & Adrian Vermeule, *Should Coercive Interrogation Be Legal?,* 104 MICH. L. REV. 671 (2006).

6. *See* U.S. Department of Justice, Office of Legal Counsel, Memoradum for Alberto R. Gonzales, Counsel to the President: Standards of Conduct for Interrogation under 18 U.S.C. § (2340–2340A) in THE TORTURE PAPERS: THE ROAD TO ABU GHRAIB (KAREN J. GREENBERG & JOSHUA L. DRATEL, EDS. 2005). After this memorandum became public, the Bush administration disavowed it. *See* Mike Allen & Susan Schmidt, "White House Disavows Justice," WASH. POST, June 27, 2004, at A3.

7. *See, e.g.,* James Risen, David Johnston, & Neal A. Lewis, "The Struggle for Iraq: Detainees; Harsh C.I.A. Methods Cited in Top Qaeda Interrogations," N.Y. TIMES, May 13, 2004, at A1.

8. *See., e.g.,* Scott Shane, "Detainee's Suit Gains Support from Jet's Log," N.Y. TIMES, March 30, 2005, at A1.

9. *See* Douglas Jehl & Eric Schmitt, "The Conflict in Iraq: Detainees; U.S. Military Says 26 Inmate Deaths May Be Homicide," N.Y. TIMES, May 16, 2005, at A1.

10. *See, e.g.,* SLAVOJ ZIZEK, WELCOME TO THE DESERT OF THE REAL! 102–04 (2002) ("[E]ssays . . . which do not advocate torture outright, [but] simply introduce it as a legitimate topic of debate, are even more dangerous than an explicit endorsement of torture"). I was made aware of Zizek's argument by Sanford Levinson, *"Precommitment" and "Postcommitment": The Ban on Torture in the Wake of September 11,* 81 TEX. L. REV. 2013, 2042–43 (2003).

11. JACOBO TIMERMAN, PRISONER WITHOUT A NAME, CELL WITHOUT A NUMBER 3–35 (TOBY TALBOT, TRANS., 1981).

12. Convention against Torture, Art. 2(2) 1465 UNTS 85.

13. I borrow this terminology from Michael Moore's sophisticated account. *See* Michael S. Moore, *Torture and the Balance of Evils*, 23 ISRAEL L. REV. 280, 297–334 (1989). *See also* Jeremy Waldron, *Rights in Conflict*, 99 ETHICS 503, 503–04 (1989).

14. On the relationship between agent relativity and conflicts between rights, see Jeremy Waldron, *Rights in Conflict*, 99 ETHICS 503, 503–06 (1989).

15. *See* JOEL FEINBERG, SOCIAL PHILOSOPHY 87 (1973).

16. *See, e.g.,* ALAN DERSHOWITZ, WHY TERRORISM WORKS: UNDERSTANDING THE THREAT, RESPONDING TO THE CHALLENGE 140 (2002); Emanuel Gross, *Legal Aspects of Tackling Terrorism: The Balance Between the Right of a Democracy to Defend Itself and the Protection of Human Rights*, 6 U.C.L.A. J. INT. L. & FOR. AFF. 89, 102–05 (2001).

17. ALAN DERSHOWITZ, WHY TERRORISM WORKS: UNDERSTANDING THE THREAT, RESPONDING TO THE CHALLENGE 144 (2002)

18. U.S. Department of Justice, Office of Legal Counsel, Memoradum for Alberto R. Gonzales, Counsel to the President: (Standards of Conduct for Interrogation under 18 U.S.C. § 2340–2340A) in THE TORTURE PAPERS: THE ROAD TO ABU GHRAIB 176 (KAREN J. GREENBERG & JOSHUA L. DRATEL, EDS. 2005)

19. *See* p. 122, *supra*.

20. For an extended argument that it is not, see GRAEME NEWMAN, JUST AND PAINFUL: A CASE FOR THE CORPORAL PUNISHMENT OF CRIMINALS (2D ED. 1995).

21. *Dawson v. State*, 274 Ga. 327, 335, 554 S.E. 2d 137, 144 (2001) (electrocution produces "specter of excruciating pain and . . . certainty of cooked brains and blistered bodies"); Marian J. Borg & Michael L. Radelet, "On Botched Executions" in CAPITAL PUNISHMENT: STRATEGIES FOR ABOLITION 153–56 (PETER HODGLEINSON & WILLIAM R. SCHELNS, EDS. 2004) (describing severity and frequency of pain from electrocution and lethal injection). The United States Supreme Court held that a death row inmate's challenge to lethal injection on the ground that it would impose severe pain was cognizable under 42 U.S.C. § 1983 in *Hill v. McDonough*, 126 S. Ct. 2096 (2006).

22. The seminal work is Gary Becker, *Crime and Punishment: An Economic Approach*, 76 J. POL. ECON. 169 (1968). For some important qualifications, see Neil Kumar Katyal, *Deterrence's Difficulty*, 95 MICH. L. REV. 2385 (1997).

23. For an explanation, see Louis Michael Seidman, *Soldiers, Martyrs, and Criminals: Utilitarian Theory and the Problem of Crime Control*, 94 YALE L. J. 315, 321 n. 13 (1984).

24 *See,* e.g., Peter Maass, "Torture, Tough or Lite: If a Terror Suspect Won't Talk, Should He Be Made To?" N.Y. TIMES, Mar. 9, 2003, at D4 ("[M]any terrorism experts believe that in the long run torture is a losing strategy."); Philip B. Heymann, "Torture Should Not Be Authorized," BOSTON GLOBE, Feb. 16, 2002, at A 15 ("Torture is a prescription for losing a war of support of our beliefs in the hope of reducing the casualties from relatively small battles."); Alisa Solomon, "The Case Against Torture," VILLAGE VOICE, Dec. 4, 2001, at 56 (citing a CIA training manual and a study of Argentina's dirty war for the proposition that torture is ineffective).

25. *See* Sanford Levinson, *"Precommitment" and "Postcommitment": The Ban on Torture in the Wake of September 11*, 81 TEX. L. REV. 2013, 2030–2031 (2004) ("To insist that torture is *always* inefficacious is not only implausible; it also removes any element of the tragedy that may accompany an absolute precommitment not to torture under

any circumstances."); Alan Dershowitz, Why Terrorism Works: Understanding the Threat, Responding to the Challenge 137 (2002) (citing the use of torture by Philippine authorities that uncovered and helped prevent plots to assassinate the Pope, to crash eleven commercial airliners carrying approximately four thousand passengers into the Pacific Ocean, and to fly an airplane into CIA headquarters).

26. I am not the first to notice the analogy between plea bargaining and torture. See John Langbein, "Torture and Plea Bargaining" in Philosophical Problems in the Law 394–403 (David Adams ed. 1996). Langbein argues that both plea bargaining and torture were responses to breakdowns in formal methods of proof. He uses the analogy to attack plea bargaining, but, of course, the valence of the argument can be reversed: In a world where plea bargaining is accepted, opponents of torture need to explain why it is relevantly different.

27. The Supreme Court has held that these threats are constitutional. See Bordenkircher v. Hayes, 434 U.S. 357 (1978); Brady v. United States, 397 U.S. 742 (1970). See also p. 83, supra. Over ninety percent of felony convictions nationwide are obtained by guilty pleas. See Bureau of Justice Statistics, U.S. Department of Justice, Sourcebook of Criminal Justice Statistics, 1995 at 498 tbl. 5.47 (Kathleen Maguire & Ann L. Pastore eds., 1996).

28. See Santobello v. New York, 404 U.S. 257, 261 (1971); F.R.Cr.P. Rule 11(b)(3).

29. Giglio v. United States, 405 U.S. 150 (1972). But cf. United States v. Ruiz, 536 U.S. 622 (2002) (defendant can waive right to be informed of impeachment evidence against government witnesses by pleading guilty).

30. The Supreme Court has made clear that coerced statements must be suppressed even in circumstances where they are truthful. See, e.g., Rogers v. Richmond, 365 U.S. 541 (1961). See also p. 99, supra.

31. See pp. 69–72, supra.

32. See pp. 74–77, supra.

33. 530 U.S. 27 (2000).

34. 384 U.S. 757 (1966).

35. See pp. 78–79, supra.

36. U.S. Const. Amend IV provides that "[t]he right of the people to be secure in their persons, houses, papers, and effects, against unreasonable searches and seizures, shall not be violated."

37. For a well known argument along these lines, see P. F. Strawson, "Freedom and Resentment," in Free Will 66–67 (G. Watson, ed., 1982) (distinguishing between the "participant attitude" and the "objective attitude").

38. As Lloyd Weinreb put the point in a related context, "[t]he most committed behaviorist does not disregard the distinction between responsible action and nonresponsible behavior in the conduct of his life. If he did, we would lock him up." Lloyd L. Weinreb, Oedipus at Fenway Park: What Rights Are and Why There are Any 48 (1994).

39. Cf. Richard Swinburne, "Body and Soul" in The Mind-Body Problem 312 (Richard Warner & Tadeusz Szubka eds. 1994):

> There really are events which humans experience and which in consequence they can know about better than does anyone else who studies their behavior or inspects their brain. My sensations, for example, my having a red afterimage or a smell of roast beef, or my feeling of pain, are such that, while I can learn about them in the

same ways as others do (by inspecting my brain-state or studying a film of my behavior), I have an additional way of knowing about them other than those available to the best student of my behavior or brain: I actually experience them. Consequently they must be distinct from brain events, or any other physical events.

40. *Cf.* P. F. Strawson, "Freedom and Resentment," in FREE WILL 68 (G. WATSON, ED., 1982) ("A sustained objectivity of inter-personal attitude, and the human isolation which that would entail, does not seem to be something of which human beings would be capable, even if some general truth were a theoretical ground for it.")

41. ELAINE SCARRY, THE BODY IN PAIN: THE MAKING AND UNMAKING OF THE WORLD 29, 31 (1985).

42. Jean Amery, "Torture," in ART FROM THE ASHES: A HOLOCAUST ANTHOLOGY 130–31, 136 (LAWRENCE L. LANGER, ED. 1995) For additional first hand accounts of the experiences of torturers and their victims, see JOHN CONROY, UNSPEAKABLE ACTS, ORDINARY PEOPLE: THE DYNAMICS OF TORTURE (2000).

43. There is, to be sure, a Fifth Amendment right not to reveal incriminating information on a tax return, but no general right not to reveal "private" information on the return. *See United States v. Sullivan,* 274 U.S. 259 (1927) (Fifth Amendment self-incrimination clause provides no general right not to file income tax return). *Cf. Marchetti v. United States,* 390 U.S. 39 (1968) (distinguishing case where tax is directed at inherently criminal activity).

44. FYODOR MIKHAILOVICH DOSTOEVSKY, THE BROTHERS KARAMAZOV 124 (CONSTANCE GARNETT, TRANS. 1952).

45. Consider, in this regard, Martha Nussbaum's views: "Because disgust embodies a shrinking from contamination that is associated with the human desire to be nonanimal, it is frequently hooked up with various forms of shady social practice, in which the discomfort people feel over the fact of having an animal body is projected outwards onto vulnerable people and groups. These reactions are irrational, in the normative sense, both because they embody an aspiration to be a kind of being that we are not, and because in the process of pursuing that aspiration, they target others with gross harms." MARTHA C. NUSSBAUM, HIDING FROM HUMANITY: DISGUST, SHAME, AND THE LAW 74–75 (2004).

46. On the relationship between disgust and the maintenance of social hierarchy, see WILLIAM IAN MILLER, THE ANATOMY OF DISGUST 8–9 (1997). Miller nonetheless argues that disgust can reinforce opposition to cruelty when one is disgusted by the perpetrator of cruelty. Id., at 195–96. Still, a "second disgust" focusing on the degraded victim of that cruelty, inhibits the (desire to relieve the suffering of the victim." Id., at 196. *But see* MARTHA C. NUSSBAUM , HIDING FROM HUMANITY: DISGUST, SHAME, AND THE LAW 84 (2004) ("[Miller offers no] argument that cruelty always disgusts. Such argument would be difficult to produce in light of the evidence he himself cites concerning the pleasure societies take in inflicting cruel forms of subordination on powerless people and groups").

CHAPTER SEVEN

1. 319 U.S. 624 (1943).
2. *See Minersville School Dist. v. Gobitis,* 310 U.S. 586 (1940).
3. 319 U.S., at 642.
4. *Glickman v. Wileman Brothers & Elliott, Inc.,* 521 U.S. 457 (1997).

5. *United States v. United Foods, Inc.*, 533 U.S. 405 (2001).

6. *Johanns v. Livestock Marketing Assn.*, 544 U.S. 550 (2005).

7. *Riley v. National Federation of the Blind of North Carolina, Inc.*, 487 U.S. 781 (1988).

8. *Pacific Gas and Electric Co. v. Public Utilities Commn. of California*, 475 U.S. 1 (1986).

9. *Miami Herald Publishing Co. v. Tornillo*, 418 U.S. 241 (1974).

10. *Boy Scouts of America v. Dale*, 530 U.S. 640 (2000).

11. Compare *Riley v. National Federation of the Blind of North Carolina, Inc.*, 487 U.S. 781 (1988) with *Zauder v. Office of Disciplinary Counsel of the Supreme Court of Ohio*, 471 U.S. 626 (1985).

12. Compare *Wooley v. Maynard*, 430 U.S. 705 (1977) with *Pruneyard Shopping Center v. Robins*, 447 U.S. 74 (1980).

13. Compare, *e.g., Abood v. Detroit Bd. of Educ.*, 431 U.S. 209 (1972) with *Board of Regents of the University of Wisconsin System v. Southworth*, 529 U.S. 217 (2000).

14. For a survey of, and lament about, the confused state of the law, see Karen C. Daly, *Balancing Act: Teachers' Classroom Speech and the First Amendment*, 30 J. L. & EDUC. 1 (2001).

15. *See Lee v. Weisman*, 505 U.S. 577 (1992); *Santa Fe Independent School Dist. v. Doe*, 530 U.S. 290 (2000).

16. 310 U.S. 586 (1940).

17. *See* Vincent Blasi & Seana V. Shiffrin, "The Story of *West Virginia State Board of Education v. Barnette:* The Pledge of Allegiance and the Freedom of Thought," in CONSTITUTIONAL LAW STORIES 435 (MICHAEL C. DORF, ED. 2004).

18. Id., at 438–39.

19. Id., at 439–40.

20. *Minersville School Dist. v. Gobitis*, 310 U.S. 586 (1940).

21. 310 U.S., at 588.

22. 310 U.S., at 593.

23. Id.

24. 310 U.S., at 595.

25. Id.

26. 310 U.S., at 599.

27. 310 U.S., at 596.

28. Id.

29. 310 U.S., at 599.

30. Id.

31. *See. e.g.,* Zackery Heider, *Fences and Neighbors*, 17 LAW & LIT. 225, 230 n. 12 (2005) (*Gobitis* "generally regarded as completely gone, dead, overruled, so much so that Westlaw had a red flag next to its name, a badge of dishonor that even Plessy v. Ferguson has not yet earned"); Yale Kamisar, *A Look Back on a Half-Century of Teaching, Writing, and Speaking about Criminal Law and Criminal Procedure*, 20 OHIO ST. J. CRIM. L. 69 (2004) (calling Frankfurter's *Gobitis* opinion "quite disappointing"); Richard Epstein, *The "Necessary" History of Property and Liberty*, 6 CHAP. L. REV. 1, 17 (Frankfurter's *Gobitis* opinion marred by "the autocratic claim that state security depends on state domination").

32. 310 U.S., at 598.

33. 347 U.S. 483 (1954).
34. *See* Bruce A. Ackerman, *Beyond Carolene Products,* 98 HARV. L. REV. 713, 730–31 (1985). Ackerman relied upon the well-known analysis in ALBERT O. HIRSCHMAN, EXIT, VOICE, AND LOYALTY: RESPONSES TO DECLINE IN FIRMS, ORGANIZATIONS, AND STATES (1970).
35. *See* Vincent Blasi & Seana V. Shiffrin, "The Story of *West Virginia State Board of Education v. Barnette:* The Pledge of Allegiance and the Freedom of Thought," in CONSTITUTIONAL LAW STORIES 443–45 (MICHAEL C. DORF, ED., 2004).
36. 316 U.S. 584 (1942).
37. 316 U.S., at 599.
38. 316 U.S., at 623.
39. *Barnette v. West Virginia State Board of Educ.,* 47 F. Supp. 251 (D. Va. 1942).
40. *West Virginia Board of Educ. v. Barnette,* 319 U.S. 624, 632–35 (1943).
41. 319 U.S., at 630.
42. Id.
43. 319 U.S., at 637.
44. Id.
45. 319 U.S., at 640.
46. 319 U.S., at 640–41.
47. 319 U.S., at 638.
48. 319 U.S., at 634.
49. My argument in the paragraphs that follow overlaps substantially with an argument that Abner Greene first advanced over a decade ago. *See* Abner Greene, *The Pledge of Allegiance Problem,* 64 FORD. L. REV. 454 (1991).
50. 430 U.S. 705 (1977).
51. N. H. REV. STAT. ANN § 262:27-c (Supp. 1975). The statute is now codified at N. H. REV. STAT. ANN § 261:176.
52. 430 U.S., at 713.
53. 430 U.S., at 714.
54. 430 U.S., at 719.
55. 544 U.S. 550 (2005).
56. *See* 544 U.S., at 560 (noting that "The message of the promotional campaigns is effectively controlled by the Federal Government itself").
57. *See* 544 U.S., at 564–65 & n. 8.
58. *See United States v. Wade,* 388 U.S. 218 (1967) (holding that compelled voice identification does not violate the privilege against self-incrimination); pp. 74–75, *supra.*
59. *See Doe v. United States,* 487 U.S. 201 (1988); pp. 87–88, *supra.*
60. *See* Seana Valentine Shiffrin, *What Is Really Wrong with Compelled Association?,* 99 NW. U. L. REV. 839 (2005).
61. Id., at 854.
62. Id., at 883.
63. The Court thought that the "[u]ltimate futility of such attempts to compel coherence is the lesson of every such effort from the Roman drive to stamp out Christianity as a disturber of its pagan unity, the Inquisition, as means of religious and dynastic unity, the Siberian exiles as a means to Russian unity, down to the fast failing efforts of our present totalitarian enemies." West *Virginia State Board of Educ. v. Barnette,* 319

U.S. 624, 640–41 (1943). This argument has a long and distinguished pedigree. Apparently, Spinoza opposed attempts to control thought "not because it is immoral but because it is inherently self-defeating." *See* STEVEN B. SMITH, SINOZA, LIBERALISM, AND THE QUEST OF JEWISH IDENTITY 157 (1997).

64. *See* p. 149, *supra*.

65. For discussion of a well-known historical example, see Elizabeth Harmer-Dionne, *Note: Once a Peculiar People: Cognitive Dissonance and the Suppression of Mormon Polygamy as a Case Study Negating the Belief-Action Distinction*, 50 STAN. L. REV. 1295 (1998).

66. *Minersville School Dist. v. Gobitis*, 310 U.S. 586, 599 (1940).

67. Seana Valentine Shiffrin, *What Is Really Wrong with Compelled Association?*, 99 NW. U. L. REV. 839, 883 (2005).

68. *See* pp. 13–15, *supra*.

69. *See, e.g.*, MARK G. YUDOF, WHEN GOVERNMENT SPEAKS (1983); Randall P. Benanson, *The Many Faces of Government Speech*, 86 IOWA L. REV. 1377 (2001); Abner Greene, *Government Speech on Unsettled Issues*, 69 FORD. L. REV. 1667 (2001).

70. *See* Gregory Klass, *The Very Idea of a First Amendment Right Against Compelled Subsidization*, 38 U. C. DAVIS L. REV. 1087 (2005).

71. Id., at 1126.

72. *See* Robert D. Kamenshine, *The First Amendment's Implied Political Establishment Clause*, 67 CAL. L. REV. 1104 (1979).

73. Gregory Klass, *The Very Idea of a First Amendment Right Against Compelled Subsidization*, 38 U. C. DAVIS L. REV. 1087, 1128 (2005).

74. Id., at 1129–30.

75. Id., at 1136–37.

76. *See, e.g.*, David Cole, *Beyond Unconstitutional Conditions: Charting Spheres of Neutrality in Government-Funded Speech*, 67 N.Y.U. L. REV. 675 (1992).

77. *See* p. 155, *supra*.

78. *See, e.g.*, Elizabeth S. Anderson & Richard H. Pildes, *Expressive Theories of Law: A General Restatement*, 148 U. PA. L. REV. 1503 (2000). For a critique, see Matthew D. Adler, *Expressive Theories of Law: A Skeptical Overview*, 148 U. PA. L. REV. 1363 (2000).

79. *See* Abner Greene, *The Pledge of Allegiance Problem*, 64 FORD. L. REV. 451, 480–81 (1995).

80. Id.

81. *See* Abner Greene, *The Government of the Good*, 53 VAND. L. REV. 1 (2000).

82. 126 S. Ct. 1297 (2006). In the interests of full disclosure, I note that I am on the board of directors of the respondent in this case.

83. 530 U.S. 640 (2000).

84. *See Johanns v. Livestock Marketing Assn.*, 544 U.S. 550 (2005).

85. *See Riley v. National Federation of the Blind of North Carolina*, 487 U.S. 781 (1988).

86. *See Newdow v. U.S. Congress*, 328 F. 3d 466 (9th Cir. 2002), *rev'd sub nom. Elk Grove Unified School Dist. V. Newdow*, 542 U.S. 1 (2004).

87. *See Lee v. Weisman*, 505 U.S. 577 (1992); *Santa Fe Independent School Dist. v. Doe*, 530 U.S. 290 (2000).

CHAPTER EIGHT

1. The facts described in this section are taken from Timothy Quill, *Death and Dignity: A Case of Individualized Decision Making,* 324 NEW ENGLAND J. OF MED. 691 (1991).
2. Id., at 692.
3. Id.
4. Id., at 693.
5. Id.
6. Id.
7. Id., at 694.
8. *See, e.g.,* 4 WILLIAM BLACKSTONE, COMMENTARIES *189.
9. *See Cruzan v. Director, Missouri Dept. Of Health,* 497 U.S. 261, 294 (Scalia, J., concurring) (noting that although states abolished common law penalties for suicide, assisting suicide remained a criminal offense).
10. *See, e.g.,* Edwin S. Schneidman, "Preventing Suicide" in ETHICAL ISSUES IN DEATH AND DYING 354 (2D ED. ROBERT WEIR, ED. 1986)
    For an argument that this approach "serves to legitimize psychiatric force and fraud by justifying it as medical care and treatment," see Thomas S. Szasz, *The Ethics of Suicide,* 31 THE ANTIOCH REVIEW 7 (1971).
11. *See* Dirk Johnson, "Kevorkian Sentenced to 10 to 25 Years in Prison," N.Y. TIMES, April 4, 1999, at A1.
12. *See* UNIFORM DETERMINATION OF DEATH ACT (1 (1980) (providing that individual who has sustained "irreversible cessation of circulatory and respiratory functions" is dead); 2006 ELECTRONIC POCKET PART UPDATE (detailing states that have accepted definition).
13. *See Washington v. Glucksberg,* 521 U.S. 702, 737–38 (1997) (O'Connor, J., concurring) (noting that "[t]here is no dispute that dying patients in Washington and New York can obtain palliative care, even when doing so would hasten their deaths").
14. *See* Oregon Death with Dignity Act, ORE. REV. STAT. § 127.800 et seq. (2003). The United States Supreme Court upheld the Act against a claim that it was preempted by federal law in *Gonzales v. Oregon,* 126 S. Ct. 904 (2006).
15. *See* ORE. REV. STAT. § 127.815–127.850 (2003).
16. *See* DEPT. OF HUMAN SERVICES, OFFICE OF DISEASE PREVENTION AND EPIDEMIOLOGY, EIGHTH ANNUAL REPORT ON OREGON'S DEATH WITH DIGNITY ACT 4 (2006).
17. *See Cruzan v. Director, Missouri Dept. of Health,* 497 U.S. 261, 270 (1990); In re Quinlan, 70 N.J. 10, 355 A. 2d 647 (1976); *Schloendorff v. Society of New York Hospital,* 211 N.Y. 125, 129–30, 105 N.E. 92, 93 (1914) (Cardozo, J.).
18. *See Cruzan v. Director, Missouri Dept. Of Health,* 497 U.S. 261, 291 (1990) (O'Connor, J., concurring) (noting that these procedures "appear to be rapidly gaining acceptance").
19. 497 U.S. 261 (1990).
20. Rehnquist wrote that "[t]he principle that a competent person has a constitutionally protected liberty interest in refusing unwanted medical treatment may be inferred from our prior decisions." 497 U.S., at 278.
21. Id., at 289.
22. 521 U.S. 702 (1997).
23. Id., at 736 (O'Connor, J., concurring).

24. 521 U.S. 793 (1997).
25. See id at 736 (O'Connor, J., concurring); id., at 738 (Stevens, J., concurring in the judgments); id., at 752 (Souter, J., concurring in the judment); id., at 789 (Ginsburg, J., concurring in the judgments); id., at 789 (Breyer, J., concurring in the judgments).
26. For an example of the liberal position, see MARGARET PABST BATTIN, ETHICAL ISSUES IN SUICIDE 180-95 (1995) For a defense of the liberal position from within a utilitarian framework, see R. B. Brandt, "The Morality and Rationality of Suicide," in A HANDBOOK FOR THE STUDY OF SUICIDE 61(SEYMOUR PERLIN, ED. 1975).
27. For an example of the controversy that erupts when the silence is broken, see *"It's Over, Debbie,"* 259 J. AMER. MED. ASSN. 272 (1988); *Editorial: "It's Over Debbie" and the Euthanaisia Debate,* id, at 2142; *Letters,* id., at 2094.
28. See pp. 39-40, *supra.*
29. IMMANUEL KANT, LECTURES ON ETHICS 148 (LOUIS INFIELD, TRANS. 1963).
30. *See, e.g., Washington v. Glucksberg,* 521 U.S. 702, 781-85 (1997) (Souter, J., concurring in the judgment).
31. For a strong attack on this view, see Thomas S. Szasz, *The Ethics of Suicide,* 31 THE ANTIOCH REVIEW 7 (1971).
32. *Cruzan v. Director, Missouri Dept. of Health,* 497 U.S. 261, 301 (1990) (Brennan, J., dissenting).
33. Id.
34. Id., at 309.
35. Id., at 310–11.
36. *See* EMILE DURKHEIM, SUICIDE: A STUDY IN SOCIOLOGY (JOHN A, SPAULDING & GEORGE SIMPSON, TRANS. 1951).
37. Id., at 152–216.
38. Id., at 241–76.
39. Daniel Callahan, "Reasons, Rationality, and Ways of Life," in CONTEMPORARY PERSPECTIVES ON RATIONAL SUICIDE 25–26 (JAMES. L. WERTH, JR., ED. 1999)
40. *See* EMILE DURKHEIM, SUICIDE: A STUDY IN SOCIOLOGY 217–240 (JOHN A. SPAULDING & GEORGE SIMPSON, TRANS. 1951)
41. *See* p. 177, *supra*
42. 521 U.S. 793 (1997).
43. *See* id., at 801 ("when a patient refuses life-sustaining medical treatment, he dies from an underlying fatal disease or pathology; but if a patient ingests lethal medication prescribed by a physician, he is killed by that medication"). For a critique, see James Rachels, *Active and Passive Euthanaisia,* 292 NEW ENGLAND J. OF MED. 78 (1975).
44. See "A Call for Reckoning: Religion and the Death Penalty, Session Three: Religion, Politics, and the Death Penalty, http://pewforum.org/deathpenalty/resources/transcript3.php3 (site visited 8/22/06) ("Abolition [of the death penalty] has taken its firmest hold in post-Christian Europe and has least support in the church-going United States. I attribute that to the fact that for the believing Christian, death is no big deal").
45. For a short summary of the Catholic view, see Robert Barry, "The Catholic Condemnation of Rational Suicide" in CONTEMPORARY PERSPECTIVES ON RATIONAL SUICIDE 29 (JAMES L.WERTH, JR. ED. 1999).
46. David Hume, "Reason and Superstition," in SUICIDE: RIGHT OR WRONG? 43 (2D ED. JOHN DONNELLY, ED. 1998)

47. 2 St. Thomas Aquinas, Summa Theologica 1469 (Trans. Fathers of the English Dominican Province 1947).

48. Id., at 1470.

49. Albert Camus, The Myth of Sisyphus and Other Essays 3 (Justin O'Brien, trans. 1961). Camus, himself, opposed suicide on the radical libertarian ground that it attempted to resolve the inevitable conflict between the pointlessness of the universe and the "absurd" attempts by human beings to make sense of it. *See* id.

50. R. B. Brandt, "The Morality and Rationality of Suicide," in A Handbook for the Study of Suicide 72 (Seymour Perlin, ed. 1975)

51. Philip E. Devine, The Ethics of Homicide 25–26 (1978).

52. Id., at 27.

53. Margaret P. Battin, "Can Suicide Be Rational? Yes, Sometimes," in Contemporary Perspectives on Rational Suicide 14 (James L. Werth, Jr., ed. 1999).

54. *See* pp. 135–140, *supra*.

55. *See* John Keown, Euthenasia, Ethics and Public Policy: An Argument against Legalization 176–79 (2002) (summarizing the Oregon Health Division's reports on, among other data, the number of persons who received prescriptions for lethal drugs but did not use them). *See also* Sue Woodman, Last Rights: The Struggle over the Right To Die 87 (1998) (reporting that, in the Netherlands, there is evidence that assisted death is requested three times more frequently than it is actually used).

56. *See* John Keown, Euthenasia, Ethics and Public Policy: An Argument against Legalization 178 (2002) (reporting that, in interviews with family members of Oregon patients who died after using prescriptions for lethal drugs, fourteen of nineteen family members stated that the "patient was determined to control the circumstances of death").

57. *Cf.* John Keown, Euthenasia, Ethics and Public Policy: An Argument against Legalization 180 (2002) (concluding that the "stereotypical case standardly presented by campaigners for [physician-assisted suicide], [that of] the cancer patient dying in agony, is in Oregon atypical").

Index